T0330186

Putting Sustainability into Practice

Putting Sustainability into Practice

Applications and Advances in Research on Sustainable Consumption

Edited by

Emily Huddart Kennedy

Assistant Professor, Washington State University, USA

Maurie J. Cohen

Professor, New Jersey Institute of Technology, USA

Naomi T. Krogman

Professor, University of Alberta, Canada

Edward Elgar
PUBLISHING

Cheltenham, UK • Northampton, MA, USA

Published by
Edward Elgar Publishing Limited
The Lypiatts
15 Lansdown Road
Cheltenham
Glos GL50 2JA
UK

Edward Elgar Publishing, Inc.
William Pratt House
9 Dewey Court
Northampton
Massachusetts 01060
USA

A catalogue record for this book
is available from the British Library

Library of Congress Control Number: 2015945466

This book is available electronically in the **Elgar**online
Social and Political Science subject collection
DOI 10.4337/9781784710606

ISBN 978 1 78471 059 0 (cased)
ISBN 978 1 78471 060 6 (eBook)

Typeset by Servis Filmsetting Ltd, Stockport, Cheshire

Printed and bound in Great Britain by TJ International Ltd, Padstow

Contents

Figures

Tables

Contributors

Julia Backhaus is a doctoral candidate at the International Centre for Integrated Assessment and Sustainable Development at Maastricht University. Drawing on transition research, practice theories and organizational studies, her doctoral research analyses (often unacknowledged) assumptions underlying sustainability transition efforts. Further, she studies transformative social innovation and constraints for resource-efficient behaviors. Her main interests are theories of change. During previous employment at the Energy Research Centre of the Netherlands, Julia worked on energy demand-side management, behavior change, sustainable lifestyles and user involvement in the development and implementation of new energy technologies. Julia has published on the role of intermediaries in behavioral change programs and is involved in the Sustainable Consumption Research and Action Initiative. She holds an interdisciplinary BSc and an MSc in Science and Technology Studies.

Stewart Barr is a Human Geographer with interests in the policy and politics of behavioral change. Since undertaking his PhD at the University of Exeter, he has specialized in developing a range of theoretical and applied approaches for understanding behavior change and its relationship to national and local policy frameworks for promoting sustainable development. In so doing, his research explores both the ways that individuals and communities respond to environmental change and the policy instruments that drive contemporary policies for citizen engagement in issues like anthropogenic climate change. His recent research projects have focused on analyses of UK Government behavioral policies and the ways in which policy relates to social practices through the formation of specific and often narrow 'choice architectures'. Alongside this research, Stewart is exploring the role that knowledge co-production processes can play in widening choice architectures and tackling some of the knowledge controversies that surround issues like climate change. This is being undertaken at a local level, working with a range of non-academic stakeholders and focusing on issues like river and surface water flooding.

Tyler Bateman is a graduate student at the University of Toronto. Over the course of his undergraduate studies, he has been involved in a wide range of scholarship at the human–environment nexus, including research on citizen engagement in Canada, civic practices of food sustainability advocates, grizzly bear nutritional ecology, plant ecology, public attitudes toward grizzly bears in Alberta, Canada, and the social drivers of worldwide species extinction. His interests lie in using social practice theories to better understand and explicate human–environmental relations, particularly the perspectives of Pierre Bourdieu and Anthony Giddens.

Maurie J. Cohen is Professor and Director of the Program in Science, Technology, and Society at the New Jersey Institute of Technology, and Associate Fellow at the Tellus Institute. He is Editor of *Sustainability: Science, Practice, and Policy*, an academic journal founded in 2004, and co-founder and Executive Board Member of the Sustainable Consumption Research and Action Initiative. His books include *Innovations in Sustainable Consumption: New Economics, Socio-technical Transitions and Social Practices* (with Halina Brown and Philip Vergragt, Edward Elgar, 2013) and *Exploring Sustainable Consumption: Environmental Policy and the Social Sciences* (with Joseph Murphy, Emerald Group Publishing, 2001). Cohen is currently a member of the Task Force on Sustainable Consumption and Green Development created under the auspices of the China Council for International Cooperation on Environment and Development.

Francesca Forno is a tenured Researcher and Assistant Professor at Bergamo University, where she teaches Sociology and the Sociology of Consumption. Two of her ongoing research interests are political consumerism and sustainable community movements. A special focus in these areas is on the consequences of the spread of market-based forms of action for citizens' participation and mobilization. She recently co-edited a special issue of the *Journal of Consumer Culture* on 'Consumerist Culture and Social Movements'.

Mike Gismondi is a Professor of Sociology and Global Studies at Athabasca University in Alberta and a co-lead of the British Columbia–Alberta Social Economy Research Alliance. He has studied the framing of political justifications and arguments for the forest products industry and oil sands development, the place of the local in a globalizing world, and the role of the social economy at a municipal level to contribute to a sustainable future. His earlier work was on Nicaraguan social history and social justice.

Cristina Grasseni is Associate Professor of Cultural Anthropology at Utrecht University. She was also a Visiting Scholar and Department Affiliate of the Anthropology Department of Harvard University (2012–14), and the David & Roberta Logie Fellow and Harvard Film Study

Center Fellow at the Radcliffe Institute for Advanced Study (2011/12). Her most recent monograph is *Beyond Alternative Food Networks: Italy's Solidarity Purchase Groups* (Bloomsbury, 2013).

Melanie Jaeger-Erben studied Psychology and Sociology in Germany and Sweden. In her postgraduate studies at the University of Magdeburg she intensified her knowledge in qualitative methodology. Since 2004 she has worked as a Researcher in Environmental Psychology and Sociology on topics such as the introduction of renewable energies and energy efficiency measures, sustainable consumption, social practices and social innovation. In her dissertation she adopted a practice theory approach to the study of life-event-induced changes of everyday consumption. She teaches courses in qualitative research methods and applied social-scientific sustainability research. Melanie is currently working at the Environmental Psychology Section of the University of Magdeburg and is affiliated with ISInova – the Institute for Social Innovation, Berlin.

Debbie Kasper is a Sociologist and Associate Professor in the Department of Environmental Studies at Hiram College, in northeast Ohio. Her teaching and research generally aim to contribute to a better under-standing of human social processes, especially the development and socio-environmental impacts of everyday life. In particular, she teaches classes related to these themes and to aspects of societal transition, includ-ing: Environmental Activism and Policy, Human Settlements, Building Community Resilience, Sociology of Food, Permaculture, and more. Her current research focuses on the development of an integrated theoretical framework for socio-environmental studies.

René Kemp is Professor of Innovation and Sustainable Development at Maastricht University. He is one of the pioneers of sustainability transi-tion research and has a long-term interest in issues of change and stabil-ity. He has more than 100 publications in the area of eco-innovation and sustainable development, several of which are viewed as seminal. He is Advisory Editor of *Research Policy* (the world-leading innovation journal), Editor of *Sustainability Science* and Editor of the journal *Environmental Innovation and Societal Transitions*. Together with Jan Rotmans he devel-oped the model of transition management for sustainability transition, which, following many discussions with policy makers, was used by the Dutch national government as a basis for its innovation policy for sus-tainable energy. He is currently working on social innovation, urban labs, resource efficiency and the political economy of eco-innovation policy.

Emily Huddart Kennedy is Assistant Professor in the Department of Sociology at Washington State University. An Environmental Sociologist, her work focuses on individual engagement with sustainability challenges and the capacity of civic action to contribute to pro-environmental social change. Emily has published in the areas of environmental citizenship, sustainable consumption, gender, local food movements and social practice theories. Her most recent research uses local food movements as a case study to explore the motivations, contextual correlates and transformative potential of civic engagement.

Naomi T. Krogman is the Academic Director of the Office of Sustainability (2012–2015) and Professor in the Department of Resource Economics and Environmental Sociology at the University of Alberta. Naomi has conducted research on sustainable consumption; environmental policy implementation; integrated and collaborative resource management; gender, environmental change and development; and social impacts of resource development. She teaches courses on social theory about environmental change and sociology of environment and development. Her research currently addresses the future of sustainability sciences and studies in higher education, and the ways in which higher education can better prepare students to address the most pressing problems of the world today.

Juanita Marois is the Unleashing Local Capital (ULC) project coordinator at Athabasca University (AU). She has worked with the ULC project since 2011, and has played an active role in project implementation and the parallel action research. While at AU, Juanita has also participated in research projects on the social economy with the British Columbia–Alberta Research Alliance, and assisted with the development of a Traditional Ecological Knowledge database. She attained her MA degree from the University of Alberta, where she studied ethnic tourism in northern Thailand. Upon completion Juanita was fortunate to participate in a number of research and community development projects. Prior to joining AU, Juanita was Executive Director with Métis Crossing, and played a leading role in launching this Aboriginal tourism and cultural destination.

Jana Rückert-John studied social sciences in Oldenburg and Berlin. Her PhD in Social Sciences, titled 'Natural Eating: Canteens and Restaurants on the Way to Sustainable Nutrition', examined food consumption from a social practices standpoint. Her main research topics include the sociology of consumption, social innovation, environmental sociology and gender. Jana led various projects concerning the role of governance and governments in fostering sustainable consumption and social innovation. In 2000 she co-founded the Institute for Social Innovation in Berlin. She is currently working as project leader at the Center for Technology and Society in Berlin.

Marlyne Sahakian is a Research Associate in the Industrial Ecology Group at the University of Lausanne. She is currently coordinating a three-year research project on household energy consumption practices in Western Switzerland, after completing a two-year interdisciplinary project on food consumption dynamics among the middle classes in Bangalore and Metro Manila. Her research interests lie in understanding natural resource consumption patterns and practices, in relation to environmental promotion and social equity, and in identifying opportunities for transitions toward more 'sustainable' societies. She has published on issues related to energy and food consumption, housing and efficiency, the solidarity economy, social practice theories and participative methods, among other topics. Following a fellowship at Ateneo de Manila University in the Philippines, she published a book on air-conditioning consumption in Southeast Asia (Palgrave Macmillan, 2014), with a focus on urban energy consumption and changing social practices related to keeping cool. Marlyne completed a PhD in Development Studies at the Graduate Institute of International and Development Studies in Geneva (2011). She is a founding member of the Sustainable Consumption Research and Action Initiative Europe, and also works with Sustainable Project Management, a nongovernmental organization based in Metro Manila that aims to support the development of livelihood programs in a former squatter community.

Chelsea Schelly received her PhD from the Department of Sociology at the University of Wisconsin-Madison, and is an Assistant Professor of Sociology in the Department of Social Sciences and the Environmental and Energy Policy graduate program at Michigan Technological University. Her work is inspired by the belief that the technological systems used to sustain residential life structure how humans conceive of their relationship to the natural world and to one another. Her research examines the historical normalization of residential technological systems in America, how technological systems interact with social structures to shape human–nature relationships and human action, and how alternative technological systems challenge the political, economic and environmental consequences of currently dominant technological systems. She researches and writes about a diverse mix of alternative technological arrangements, including Renewable Portfolio Standards, living off-grid, intentional communities and Rainbow Gatherings.

Silvana Signori is Associate Professor at the University of Bergamo – Department of Management, Economics and Quantitative Methods. She holds a PhD in Business Administration and Strategies with a dissertation on 'Ethical Investors'. Her main areas of research are ethical investments, business ethics and corporate social responsibility, nonprofit organization accounting and accountability, ethical consumers and new forms of activism (shareholder and consumer activism). She is one of the founder members of the Italian chapter of the European Business Ethics Network, Co-director of CORES Lab (Research Group on Networks and Practices of Sustainable Economy) and member of the Board of Directors of the Centre for Young and Family Enterprise at the University of Bergamo.

Danica Straith's research and expertise are focused on change management and the role of the social economy in enabling sustainability transitions. Her graduate studies in Integrated Water Resources Management from McGill University examined the attributes, strategies and contextual knowledge of champions driving change in the Canadian water sector. She spent time working with the Institute of Ecological Economy Research in Berlin, to study the role and potential of social entrepreneurs in the water sector. Danica was particularly interested in the ways in which social entrepreneurs could scale the impact of their social missions in a sustainable manner. This involved field research in Nairobi to investigate the innovative management approaches of eco-sanitation businesses in urban informal settlements. Danica was also a part of the BALTA Scaling Innovation for Sustainability project in Western Canada – an alliance of academics, social enterprises and cooperatives driving innovation in the finance, housing, energy and food sector. Her work was dedicated to the identification of scaling strategies for niche innovations rooted in the social economy and built on social practice theories and the multilevel perspective. She is currently working with emerging citizen science initiatives involved in water stewardship across Canada.

Harald Wieser holds an interdisciplinary MSc in Socio-ecological Economics and Policy from Vienna University of Economics and Business, from which he also obtained a BSc in Economics. His current research for the Austrian Chamber of Labour is focused on the service life of durable goods and related issues of product obsolescence and slow consumption. The aim of this research is to reduce environmental pressures through the optimization of replacement cycles. Previously, Harald studied the socio-cultural values associated with ecosystem services at the European Academy of Bolzano and sustainable food consumption practices in Europe at the International Centre for Integrated Assessment and Sustainable Development, Maastricht University. His fields of interest include institutional and ecological economics, the sociology of consumption and the temporalities of consumption and divestment.

Preface and acknowledgements

A prevalent and firmly held belief is that a sustainable society will spring from a combination of inventive technological innovations and voluntary adoption of slightly more thoughtful consumer practices. By contrast, most researchers in the maturing field of sustainable consumption downplay the potential of technical inventiveness and individual behavior change and contend that a sustainable future will only emerge through complementary intertwining of lifestyle shifts and social mobilization (ultimately leading to enlightened changes in regulatory arrangements and infrastructural systems). Although we are currently witnessing various social innovations – for instance shifts toward sharing, self and communal provisioning, and localization – to supplant dominant modes of consumption, these initiatives are constrained in their capacity to transform obdurate barriers. Social movements can be effective in overcoming impediments that hamper sustainable lifestyles, yet ongoing involvement exacts steep commitments from participants and such activity is difficult to maintain over the longer term.

To both glean novel insights and inspire new opportunities, scholars have over the past decade come increasingly to apply social practice theories to the challenges of sustainable consumption. A particular strength of this approach has been in facilitating research that transcends identity politics and engages with varied and potentially supportive forms of environmental citizenship. This volume employs a global conceptual focus and a strong empirical orientation based on social practice theories to advance understanding to efficaciously enable transitions toward a more sustainable society.

Even a casual glance across the pages of a newspaper reveals that new lifestyle logics are gaining popularity in current discourse and practice, but these developments are restricted in their capacity to remove structural barriers to sustainability that actively encourage, for example, automobile dependency and reliance on extraction and consumption of fossil fuels. At the same time, social mobilization has proven an effective strategy for overturning obstacles to more sustainable lifestyles – for instance by reducing carbon emissions from food consumption through the establishment of provisioning arrangements that enable local procurement. Research on new political institutions has attracted considerable attention, but without civic engagement these new forms are unlikely to transform customary development paths. This scholarship also remains largely disconnected from changes occurring within dominant socio-technical configurations, such as transportation patterns from home to work. Further, there is a paucity of research that has the potential to effectively characterize these different forms of participation. This volume seeks to address these issues through the lens of a rich new body of theory and empirical work based on notions of social practice.

A growing number of authors are applying practice theoretical approaches to the human–environment interface. A particular strength of these investigations is their ability to inspire research that decenters the individual and instead focuses on everyday routines and their distribution across space and time. This advantage has been put to positive effect and prodigious use by social scientists in the field of sustainable consumption. Opening up new avenues for research and policy, social practice theories confront individualist conceptions of consumption by demonstrating how practices are embedded in quotidian habits, connected to socio-technical systems, influenced by emergent norms, and related to the potential for agency and conformity. In conjunction with the rise of this approach for studying sustainable consumption is expanding unease with the limits of individualistic change in the face of significant social and environmental challenges. Scholars and practitioners who argue that we must do a great deal more than change light bulbs and buy carbon offsets point to a need for civic practices that coordinate and foster community organizing and institutional reform. A small choir of voices asserts that social practice theories might be fruitfully applied to better comprehend how meaningful change is cultivated and constrained. However, most of the scholarship conducted thus far at the intersection of social practices and sustainable consumption has examined individuals in household contexts – for example, private bathing and cooking activities. Social practice researchers studying sustainable consumption have not yet started to integrate their insights into work on civic engagement and social movements. This book seeks to advance this process.

The idea for this volume was born at the inaugural conference of the Sustainable Consumption Research and Action Initiative (SCORAI) held at Clark University in Worcester, Massachusetts, USA in July 2013. Inspired by many excellent presentations that moved from theory to social change, the Editors of this book embarked on the project of assembling several of the manuscripts on which the presentations were based and supplementing the collection with contributions from other scholars working along similar lines. The end result of this process is the volume that you now hold in your hands.

It is thus not at all hyperbolic to note that this book would not exist were it not for SCORAI. Launched with modest ambitions in 2008, SCORAI has grown into a knowledge network that, as this volume goes to press, encompasses more than 800 researchers and policy practitioners around the world working at the interface of material consumption, human well-being, and technological and cultural change. A key aim of SCORAI is to foster a transition beyond the currently dominant consumer society, and its organizational activities include the coordination of conferences and workshops, the convening of colloquia on especially timely and salient topics, the facilitation of exchanges with communities of professional practice, and the preparation of reports and books that hold interest for a widening circle of interested readers.

One of SCORAI's most important achievements to date has been to bring together scholars and practitioners who were previously isolated within academic departments, government ministries, and other organizations. By operationalizing the idea of a future characterized by new lifestyle modes that transcend current consumerist commitments, achieve multifold reductions in energy and material utilization, and strive for more equitable distributions of resources, the network has created a broad interdisciplinary community, encouraged new research, and inspired novel policy interventions. Much of this success is attributable to the efforts of our SCORAI colleagues, and especially to the tireless and unwavering support of Jeffrey Barber, Halina Brown, John Stutz, and Philip Vergragt.

If SCORAI is responsible for the initial emergence of this volume, its further development and refinement is due to the generous work of the many reviewers who embraced our invitations to lend their expertise to the cause. In alphabetical order, we wish to thank Manisha Anantharaman, Mark Anielski, Stewart Barr, Ruth Doyle, Sophie Duboisson-Quellier, Bente Halkier, Rachel Macrorie, Lucie Middlemiss, Mika Pantzar, Gill Seyfang, Hal Wilhite, and Richard Wilk. In moving the book from rough idea to tangible product, we also wish to acknowledge the assistance of Bob Pickens, Erin McVicar, Victoria Nichols, and Alan Sturmer, the valuable input of two anonymous reviewers for their helpful comments on the proposal that earlier gave rise to this volume, and the careful work that Apryl Bergstrom did revising the final manuscript.

PART I

Introduction

1. Social practice theories and research on sustainable consumption

Emily Huddart Kennedy, Maurie J. Cohen, and Naomi T. Krogman

THE SOCIAL ORGANIZATION OF ENVIRONMENTAL ISSUES

Despite elaborate public awareness campaigns to motivate people to reduce their environmental impact in light of climate change threats, practices contributing to greenhouse gas emissions remain stubbornly stable. This public policy conundrum is intimately, yet perhaps surprisingly, connected to how we conceptualize and engage with processes of social change. Will households, businesses, and governments make choices that are in the best interest of environmental health and justice if provided with good information? There is great reason to doubt the likelihood of this coming to pass. In fact, as we see in the case of climate change, as well as other systemic problems such as poverty or oceanic pollution, there is very little meaningful progress occurring despite a wealth of information.

Understanding the persistence of human attitudes, beliefs, and behaviors, in the face of overwhelming evidence that significant changes are underway, brings us to the arena of social theory. In the policy community, the most popular theories of social action posit that external stimuli such as a tax or rebate can guide individuals to make decisions that are best for themselves and the common good. A particularly well-received variant of this notion is the 'nudge' approach that accepts that as decision makers we are constantly bombarded by often-contradictory information (Thaler and Sunstein 2008). As evidence of the popularity of this strategy, President Barack Obama appointed scholar Cass Sunstein to head the Office of Information and Regulatory Affairs (part of the Executive Office of the President) and Prime Minister David Cameron selected Richard Thaler to lead the Behavioural Insight Team for the United Kingdom government (Standing 2011). These initiatives made recommendations for governments to alter the social context in slight ways to encourage people to make subtle movements toward the 'right' decision. The social theory behind such logic is that we can 'nudge' people into rational decision making, leading to outcomes that would be described and expected by rational choice theory (Hands 2013).

The view of action as rationally determined behavior is not only pre-eminent in policy circles but also in theories focused on enhancing the sustainability of contemporary consumption. The dominant environmental research tradition in the social sciences is rooted in positivistic, rationalistic, and quantitative epistemologies, with psychological approaches acting as the leading expression of this research trajectory. For instance, value–belief–norm theory is one of the most cited conceptual approaches in the study of environmentally significant behavior (Stern 2000). In brief, this theory maintains that individual environmental action can be understood as dependent upon values that cohere with the environmental movement, and the belief that the environment is under threat and that one's actions can bring a measure of restoration. Social practice theories of sustainable consumption are thus forced to challenge or 'compete' with the dominant psychological tradition as well as with a fairly widespread preference for positivistic and rationalistic explanations that rely on quantitative evidence to understand societies.

Positivistic and rationalistic explanations like nudge and value–belief–norm theory overlook a salient argument from Pierre Bourdieu's theory of practice, namely that social action is highly influenced by power (i.e., by the struggle to acquire social, economic, and cultural capital) and structured by the reinforcement of class privilege (Spaargaren 2013). Bourdieu (1977; 1979) persuasively asserted that individual choices more often reflect one's position in society rather than rational calculation. Such cultural explanations of social action are markedly distinct from rational choice theories in recognizing the role of social organization, power, routine, time, and norms. In attending to the resilience of social practices, Bourdieu's theory shares much in common with Anthony Giddens' (1984) structuration theory and the related body of scholarship termed 'social practice theories' (Reckwitz 2002). Social practice theories posit that institutional, infrastructural, and cultural structures play a strong role in shaping social action, understood as a constellation of practices rather than the result of individual attitudes and values (Spaargaren 2003). It is the social practices approach that is taken up and further elaborated in this book.

Though scholars immersed in the study of education, cultural studies, and other fields have long benefitted from a practice-informed view, it has only recently entered the arena of research and policy regarding sustainable consumption (e.g., Halkier 2013; Røpke 2009; Spargaaren 2003).[1] Social practice perspectives provide a unique and powerful lens through which to examine how we collectively make decisions that undermine the common good. When applied to sustainable consumption, social practice theories make clear how earlier work on sustainability in the social sciences ignored the routine nature of everyday activities, and the relationship of daily actions to broader social contexts (Shove 2003; Warde 2005). In this light, shifting behavior is not simply a matter of deciding to do so, but an ambitious pursuit involving the acquisition of new knowledge, the alteration of other – often complementary – routines, the overturning of cultural norms, and the reconfiguration of subtle relations of power. Social practices theorists understand that well-intentioned goals for behavior change may ultimately be thwarted by each of these elements while also acknowledging that social practices are constantly evolving. As the focus of inquiry shifts from individual attitudes and values and toward social practices, scholars have the ability to widen their gaze to the institutions, routines, and norms most responsible for generating present-day problems of unsustainability.

When we face the very important question, 'why do people do what they do?' a social practice perspective asks how widely accepted societal rules affect the performances of daily life and how, in turn, these activities shape the conventions by which we live (Lemert 2012). To put this question into a more concrete example, think about how everyday car driving fits in with broader structures in society about, say, workplace conduct (positing that cycling or walking might entail arriving at work sweaty and flustered), widely accepted understandings of convenience, or assumptions about the safety of public transit. A social practices approach allows the interested researcher, practitioner, or citizen to examine a daily routine with an eye to the rules and resources in a society that make a particular mode of daily performance the default option, rather than blaming individuals for not doing what is 'right'.

Using social practice theories to analyze how routinized activity can contribute to unsustainability problems has resulted in a great deal of stimulating scholarship. In this introduction, we begin by venturing back to some of the early work on social practices and offer an account of key theoretical contributions to the contemporary study of sustainable consumption. With this literature in mind, we then summarize and synthesize the remaining chapters in the volume.

HISTORICAL PROGRESSION OF SOCIAL PRACTICE THEORIES

An exceptionally heterogeneous body of literature, the area of scholarship captured in the phrase 'social practice theories' can be difficult to identify and describe in precise terms. To grapple with this challenge, we first articulate some of the key features of a practice approach. We then place these central concepts in a historical context.

The history of social practice theories is deeply intertwined with the history of sociology and philosophy. We simplify this incredibly rich and complex terrain in this section to chart a way forward for the study and pursuit of sustainability. Shove (2010) combines rational choice and value–belief–norm theories outlined above by using the term 'ABC (atti-tude–behavior–choice) theories'. Recall that these approaches assume that social action is a product of mental structures arising out of individually held values, beliefs, and attitudes. Social practice theories formulate a decidedly different understanding of social action, and rather than main-tain that mental structures cause action, social practice theorists share an assumption that the impetus for action is found in practice (Schatzki 1997). Put simply, ABC theories offer an iteration of the dictum 'people do things because of their mental representations of what action means' whereas a social practice perspective contends that 'people do things' and proceeds to demonstrate how action is connected to historical and current social context (Martin 2011). Social practice theories attempt to remove the necessity for the dualism between mind and action, agency and struc-ture, and subject and object. Our consciousness does not cause our actions, much to the chagrin of many policy makers, as this observation under-mines the belief that with better information we can achieve certain desired outcomes. Rather, our actions reflect an ongoing dialogue between agents and structures and a historically situated relationship of people to place.

Let us examine a hypothetical example. If a group of people is going to protest a proposed trade agreement, some of the structures that might immediately come to mind include legislation (What are the rules around protesting? What will the police presence be?), the economic system (What is the ideology that promotes free trade in the first place?), and state–capital relations (How are governments and corporations linked?). But before a protest can take place, there are other structures that are built into taken-for-granted expectations. The word 'protest' likely conjures up specific images: placards with demands written on them, people shouting, and a setting, perhaps a city street or a public lawn. Thus, when a group organizes a protest, it is drawing on other practices, and in this way prac-tices structure the activity of protesting. This illustration highlights the various types of structures at play in a practice – everything from the mate-rial (a placard), to the ideal (a laissez-faire approach to economics), to the cultural (ways of communicating), to skillsets (knowing where to go, how to speak). No single individual sets out to define these structures and yet they are reproduced when people re-enact similar schemas of protests in different places and spaces, drawing on and reinforcing bodily and mental knowledge as they do so.

As previously noted, Bourdieu and Giddens are two of the most prominent theorists cited in the body of work now termed 'social practice theories' – theories that seek to explicate the relationship between agency and structure by taking everyday practices as the unit of analysis (Bourdieu 1977, 1979; Giddens 1984). The predominance of these authors can be seen in the prevalence of recent work on social practice theories that builds from concepts that they initially developed three decades ago. Of course, both theorists use earlier scholarship to inform their primary arguments; we connect the classical and contemporary contributions to social practice theories later in this introductory chapter. We selected Bourdieu's account of habitus and Giddens' notion of structuration knowing that we are excluding Bourdieu's other work (particularly on field, doxa, symbolic violence, and distinction), Michel Foucault's (1969) study of the archaeology of knowledge, Charles Taylor's (1985) theory of human agency, and Norbert Elias' (1978) concept of figurations.[2] However, as we intend to demonstrate, Giddens' ideas have had the greatest impact on social practice theories of sustainable consumption and Bourdieu's writings have had a significant effect on the study of consumption (absent an explicit sustainability orientation).[3]

Habitus

Bourdieu's concept of habitus is useful for understanding how structures are unconsciously reproduced by actors, through practices rather than by means of mental representations like beliefs or attitudes. He argues that the rules that govern a society are not necessarily strengthened by people actively enforcing those rules, but by individuals who use them to get through everyday life. In other words, people act 'strategically in a world that presumes those rules' (Swidler 2001, p. 91). The habitus is inscribed in practice, where 'practice' refers to 'socially recognized forms of activity, done on the basis of what members learn from others, and capable of being done well or badly, correctly or incorrectly' (Barnes 2001, p. 27). A practice theory is thus one that either provides an account of practices (e.g., protesting, driving) or offers an account of some social thing (e.g., international climate governance) by drawing attention to socially recognized forms of activity or practices (Reckwitz 2002; Schatzki 2001).

Habitus refers to principles that are both 'generative' of social order and 'durably installed' (Bourdieu 1977, p. 78). That is, the concept captures both the productive (practices always create a precedent for future practices) and the reproductive (practices follow a logic that is pre-determined) elements of daily life. Bourdieu argued that sociologists should challenge the notion of social reality as being either structured by macro-scale forces like the economy or micro-scale variables such as personality. Instead, social reality should be understood as a site that is constantly made and remade by everyday practices of living. Bourdieu was acutely aware of power relations, and through his theory of practice he maintained that power is reproduced by control over symbols and discourse. It is on the basis of discourse (written and verbal expressions of thought) that capital is revealed: the way we communicate reflects and reproduces differences in economic, social, and cultural capital. The habitus represents Bourdieu's efforts to overcome the agency/structure dichotomy that dogged sociology for much of the 20th century.

Structuration Theory

Like Bourdieu, Giddens was also interested in going beyond the dichotomies that long dominated sociological thinking. While his articulation of practice – 'structuration theory' – differs in several respects from Bourdieu's notion of habitus, both approaches call for a focus on practices before structure (e.g., attention to population, environment, ideology, technology) or agency (e.g., individual attitudes and behavior) and to be attentive to power relations and special interests. Structuration theory rests on an ontological concept described as the 'duality of structure' (Giddens 1984, p. 5), which denotes the idea that social systems, social rules, and economic and political resources both constrain and support everyday practices, enabling people to achieve the daunting feat of navigating daily routines but limiting their capacity to change the underlying systems, rules, and resources. For instance, while the ubiquitous layout of a university classroom may constrain peer-to-peer learning by placing students in rows rather than face-to-face, it also facilitates the process of knowledge transfer and acquisition by providing clear expectations of where students ought to sit and to where they should direct their attention during lectures.

A key difference between Bourdieu's and Giddens' theories of practice is their understanding of the basis for human action. Bourdieu understood human action as habituation of the acting body, that is, a body does a certain thing a particular way because it has always done that thing in that way. In contrast, Giddens argues that practice culminates from consciousness – that what people do and say reflects their knowledge of how and when to act and speak. This feature of Giddens' scholarship is visible in his distinction between 'practical consciousness' and 'discursive consciousness'. Practical consciousness refers to the mental states and knowledge that allow individuals to engage in routine, everyday activity.

These dimensions of consciousness are where Giddens develops his understanding of structures as being enabling: that we can perform daily routines without too much effort is a testament to the predictability of social structures. Discursive consciousness involves verbally expressing awareness of the rules, resources, and systems that shape daily life. Accordingly, everyday routines or habits can be questioned or challenged, and as they are reconsidered dismantling (and changing) a practice becomes possible. That is, in discursive consciousness lies the potential for change in practice, and therefore structure.

GENEALOGY OF SOCIAL PRACTICE THEORIES

Conceiving of social practice theories as a family tree, it is important to understand which ideas have been left out of current analyses of sustainable consumption and which have continued to shape how scholars conceive of practices. Having briefly reviewed two versions of social practice theory, we now look both backwards and forwards from these theories. In this way we briefly describe the philosophical influences on Bourdieu and Giddens (which others have done) and (more originally) comment on how certain concepts and perspectives have been included or overlooked in contemporary accounts of sustainable consumption.

Early Influences on Social Practice Theories

Scholars attribute Martin Heidegger, Ludwig Wittgenstein, John Dewey, and Charles Pierce as key influences on Bourdieu and Giddens. The impact of this work is thoroughly described elsewhere (Dreyfus 1991; Joas and Knöbl 2009; Reckwitz 2002), so we will limit our discussion here to the most relevant themes. Briefly, Heidegger was a profound influence for both sociologists, and Bourdieu described him as his 'first love' in philosophy (Dreyfus 1991).[4] This is because of Heidegger's emphasis on being: his philosophy held that people trust historically produced practices as guiding mechanisms while realizing that people do not have conscious access to all aspects of their own actions. Thus practice becomes the most valuable unit of analysis, particularly understanding how we exist and participate in daily life. To this observation, Wittgenstein added the importance of rule following as a key component of belonging in the social world. These themes are so prominent in practice theories that Reckwitz (2002, p. 250) states, 'we find everything that is original in practice theory already in the work of these authors'.[5]

In the following discussion, we attempt to demarcate two subsequent 'generations' of concepts that create a bridge between the early philosophers and contemporary researchers studying topics related to sustainability and social practice theories. We label the first generation 'early adopters of social practice theories', referring to those authors who first applied the perspective to study sustainable consumption. The second generation is labeled 'recent practice-based accounts'. We simplify the conceptual terrain in an attempt to draw out the most salient features of scholarship on sustainable consumption and social practice theories and to highlight concepts that have lost purchase in recent work. This genealogy is intended for pedagogical purposes and is not a comprehensive overview of sustainable consumption and theories of practice. Bearing this caveat in mind, we offer a small sample of these concepts in the text that follows.

Applying Social Practice Theories to Sustainable Consumption

To sustainable consumption scholars, social practice theories have a patina of novelty and innovation, as this fairly recent integration provides theoretical grounds to dismiss the formerly voluntaristic and deterministic models that dominated this field of study. The first scholars to make use of social practice theories did so to provide a theoretical framework that decentered individuals' mental intentions as a central explanatory mechanism for social action (Warde 2005). That is, scholarship on sustainable consumption at that point largely accepted the ABC models discussed earlier, presuming that if an individual or group was not consuming sustainably, this must be a function of a lack of awareness or knowledge. Instead, drawing from Bourdieusian theory, sociologists pointed out that social location is an important determinant of consumption behavior and time use (Warde 1997; Wilk 1997), and looking to structuration theory, scholars argued that consumption practices are rarely fully conscious (Hobson 2003; Spaargaren 1997, 2003).

In addition to the reintegration of culture and class into the study of sustainable consumption, the second key theoretical advance has been to draw routine, everyday actions into the foreground. In contrast, Thorstein Veblen's famed account of conspicuous consumption (consumption intended to convey status) long dominated consumer studies and resulted in a scholarly emphasis on profligate displays of wealth. From a social practice perspective, Shove and Warde (2002) introduced the idea of *inconspicuous* consumption, highlighting the possibility that quotidian consumption practices may have a more significant environmental impact and are in large part an outcome of being a competent member of society. Using Giddens' structuration theory, the authors demonstrated that everyday consumption practices such as bathing and air-conditioning cannot be explained by theories of conspicuous consumption. Perhaps the strongest theme emerging from Giddens' work is, as previously discussed, the distinction between practical and discursive consciousness. For instance, Spaargaren (1997) describes the difference between the two forms of consciousness to articulate how elements of a practice become background noise as long as they perform as expected. Using the example of water consumption, Spaargaren explains that for most individuals, the system that exists to deliver water to our homes only enters our discursive consciousness when something goes wrong, such as the water coming out brown, or leaking, or costing too much. Otherwise, much of our tangible consumption occurs in the plane of practical consciousness. Once we have established a habit, it is not easy to recall why we do what we do and even more difficult to challenge the assumptions upon which our actions are based. A large body of work builds on the same or similar premises, sharing an empirical emphasis on everyday routine practices as the key unit of analysis (Hobson 2003; Shove 2003; Shove and Pantzar 2005; Warde 1997; Warde and Martens 2000).

A third important idea influencing early social practice theories of sustainable consumption is the premise (shared by both Giddens and Bourdieu) that the relationship between habit and social context is recursive. Bourdieu's work is used to demonstrate that habits are connected not only to what we ourselves have done in recent and past history, but also to the practices of our forbearers, as they established – through practice – systems of provision, cultural norms, and ways of talking and acting.[6] In short, social practices create and are created by social context. As an example of how this concept shaped early social practice literature on sustainable consumption, we describe Spaargaren's (2003) study of the adoption of renewable energy in a Dutch neighborhood. Spaargaren relies on structuration theory to show that practices result from the interaction of agency (e.g., norms) and structure (e.g., infrastructure). For Spaargaren (2003), Giddens' description of lifestyle is central – where lifestyle is 'the set of social practices that an individual embraces, together with the storytelling that goes along with it' (p. 689). Thus, if we are to understand the impact of daily life on the biophysical environment, it is necessary to look at what people do and how their actions are implicated in a recursive dialogue between self and place. Practices, agency, and structure are reciprocally intertwined, a viewpoint that is ubiquitous in subsequent literature on sustainable consumption and social practice theories.

Looking at the broad ideas discussed above as a whole, three themes emerge. First, in the process of applying social practice theories to understand sustainable consumption, scholars used perspectives from the work of both Bourdieu and Giddens (and others) to inform accounts of household consumption practices. Secondly, this era of scholarship established the idea that material objects are implicated in the practice of everyday life and should thus be given scholarly attention (Shove 2003; Spaargaren 2003; Warde 2005). Finally, notable is the emphasis on consumption that takes place in the private sphere, or household. As we discuss next, these themes persist in current social practice scholarship on sustainable consumption.

Recent Practice-based Accounts of Sustainable Consumption

Between 2007 and 2015 social practice theoretical accounts of sustainable consumption proliferated. Numerous theses have been written at this nexus of scholarship, suggesting that emerging scholars will continue to apply and shape this area of research (e.g., Doyle 2013; Glover 2012; Jensen 2014; Kennedy 2011; Sahakian 2011). Groups have formed to support further study in the area (e.g., Sustainable Practices Research Group at the University of Lancaster and an early career researcher network called Practices, the Built Environment and Sustainability based at Aalborg University) and courses and edited volumes such as this one are now emerging (e.g., Cohen, Brown, and Vergragt 2013; Shove and Spurling 2013). In the discussion below, we briefly demonstrate how the themes from the early adopters of social practice theories continue to influence current scholarship and draw attention to ideas that have lost purchase in the field of sustainable consumption.

Recent scholarship is more closely tied to the issue of climate change (Shove and Spurling 2013) and has broadened the emphasis on household practices to include the workplace (Hargreaves 2011) and commercial settings (Seyfang 2009). These accounts emphasize primarily their rejection of individualist accounts; the theoretical move of decentering the individual plays a strong role shaping contemporary research. For example, in his study of sustainable consumption practices in the workplace, Hargreaves (2011) draws from the work of Elizabeth Shove and Alan Warde to illustrate the inadequacy of ABC models of behavior. The resultant theoretical framework is much more akin to Shove's (2003) work than to that of Bourdieu, Giddens or other early social practice theorists. For instance, Hargreaves raises the same contrast highlighted by the initial adopters of social practice theories in sustainable consumption (regarding the inadequacy of voluntaristic models of behavior) in the following excerpt:

> The focus is no longer on individuals' attitudes, behaviours and choices, but instead on how practices form, how they are reproduced, maintained, stabilized, challenged and ultimately killed-off; on how practices recruit practitioners to

maintain and strengthen them through continued performance, and on how such practitioners may be encouraged to defect to more sustainable practices. (Hargreaves 2011, p. 84)

The above quotation also describes what has become a clear research agenda among social-practice-oriented sustainable consumption scholars. This agenda certainly builds from the ontological perspectives of Bourdieu and Giddens by emphasizing practices as the building blocks of social life, but it is also highly unique and much more characteristic of theory construction from the early adopters in its aim to understand the making and breaking of social practices. This interest in shaping social practices suggests that there is agency involved in practice (a view that reflects Giddens' concept of discursive consciousness). The increased role of agency is a departure from a Bourdieusian perspective.

Theory constructed on the basis of a belief in recursivity between agency and structure continues to influence the field. For example, focusing on eating practices, Halkier and Jensen (2011) emphasize that eating is collectively structured – that is, what we eat and how we eat is shaped by where we eat, what norms exist, what foods are available to us, and the eating norms of our reference group. A voluntaristic ABC model would not create the opportunity to consider the influence of such a broad range of variables. Like Hargreaves' scholarship, Halkier and Jensen's focus is more akin to the early adopters of social practice theories in sustainable consumption than to Bourdieu or Giddens.

We discuss the current state of social practice scholarship in the study of sustainable consumption in greater detail in the concluding chapter of this volume. For now, we draw our readers' attention to two points. First, the adoption of social practice perspectives into the field of sustainable consumption has led to an array of questions and perspectives that is different from early scholarship. Secondly, in the hands of contemporary social practice theorists, the influence of earlier authors has largely fallen away. This means that the work of the early adopters is actively shaping the research questions, analytic frameworks, and research agendas of contemporary scholars. On one hand, this observation suggests that social practice perspectives on sustainable consumption have drawn some definite disciplinary boundaries and a field has been constituted that is now generating new insights on theory and practice. On the other hand, severing ties with the foundational literature has resulted in a plethora of middle-range theories that seldom engage in ontological and epistemological debates. That is, Bourdieu and Giddens were involved in explaining social order and social action. The debates in which they were engaged necessarily invoked themes such as power and conflict, class, and agency.

For the most part, these issues are absent among those who study sustainable consumption from a social practice perspective.[7] However, as we point out in the discussion of the chapters in this volume, there is some evidence of a re-emergence of these themes and other indications of advances in the study of sustainable consumption.

OVERVIEW OF THE BOOK

The remainder of this book is divided into three main Parts (II through IV) and a concluding chapter (Part V). Part II, 'Social Mobilization and Sustainable Consumption', explores how the study of sustainable consumption must move beyond the household and into the public sphere. The third Part, 'Collective Dimensions of Household Practices', illustrates how the routines in a household such as driving and eating are shaped by societal variables and thus not a reflection of individual agency. Part IV, 'Sustainable Consumption and Social Innovation', examines shifts in systems of provision that shape daily routines that have environmental consequences.

We survey first the three chapters within Part II, which as a whole look at social practice theories and sustainable engagement outside the boundaries defined by recent scholarship in the field. In Chapter 2, Debbie Kasper makes a strong case that the social sciences need a grand theory with more explanatory power than current middle-range social practice theories, and she begins the work of defining such an understanding. Using figurational theory and the concept of habitus in tandem, Kasper develops a theoretical model that 'is intended to sensitize us to, and help us envision, relationships among fundamental processes at the social level'. Her model integrates the biophysical environment with the social and offers researchers in socio-ecological fields the refreshing advantage of studying social practices without leaving behind analyses of power relations. This chapter integrates power, biophysical environments, history, and daily practice in a way that few, if any, existing theoretical treatments to date have done.

The next two chapters explain the connection between private practices and civic engagement in ways that extend and normalize sustainable consumption. Kennedy and Bateman (Chapter 3) define and illustrate 'environmental civic practices' in relation to social change agents involved in reimagining the production, preservation, and consumption of food in urban areas. The authors discuss qualitative data collected from individuals working with others to reduce the negative environmental and social costs of the food system. A key element of these practices – termed environmental civic practices – that contributes to their capacity to incite social change lies in creating contexts for citizen engagement. Environmental civic practices involve speech acts and activities that precede strategic relationships, community organizing, and institutional reform, and in this way make mainstream the logic and possibility of alternative food systems. Notable is that the participants in this study rarely used environmental civic practices as a form of resistance to the current food system or as a challenge to the cultural meanings that oppose urban agriculture. Nonetheless, the authors contend that environmental civic practices have the potential to catalyze collective action that links households to communities and communities to institutions, and that this is integral to social change toward sustainable consumption.

In the final chapter of Part II, Francesca Forno, Cristina Grasseni, and Silvana Signori distinguish between the competing roles of citizens and consumers in a study of Italy's Solidarity Purchase Groups (Gruppi di Acquisto Solidal). These organizations provide a particularly interesting case study because they reveal collective processes on the part of consumers. They aim not only to practice ethical or critical consumption but also to co-produce common benefits, to intervene in local food-provisioning chains, and to reintroduce issues of social and environmental sustainability in regional economies. In addition, the purchase groups occasionally express their intention to engage with issues related to the common good such as water privatization and alternative energy. On the basis of detailed quantitative and qualitative research, this chapter contextualizes these dynamics within a theoretical framework of sustainable citizenship as social practice. We learn from this study that political consumerism may be not only the objective, but also frequently the result, of engaged practices, particularly solidarity purchasing.

Part III begins with Stewart Barr's illustration of how to effectively apply a social practice lens to understand the collective nature of daily consumption practices. This chapter takes up a critique of the 'nudge' concept popularized by Thaler and Sunstein (2008) that was mentioned earlier. Using a social practice perspective, he describes how the deployment of nudges to influence private car use would be lost in a sea of guidelines and recommendations for how we should drive, from speed limits to appeals for carpooling. Much more influential, he argues, is our essential relationship to the places in which we reside, and how such connections are reproduced and changed over the course of history. In closing, Barr outlines, 'three pathways for the use of practice theory to dislodge the dominance of short-term, incrementalist and individualistic thinking on sustainable mobility'. He calls on policy makers to focus their attention on what impels people's need or want to move in the first place. Barr furthermore highlights how a social practices approach to studying sustainability reveals how practices are learned over time. Finally, the chapter discusses how an emphasis on practices rather than behaviors can call attention to the interconnections between people and the places in which they live.

Barr's call to apply the practice perspective to enable a more robust environmental politics is taken up by Julia Backhaus, Harald Wieser, and René Kemp in Chapter 6. In doing so, they also make a number of methodological observations that future scholars should consider: the authors argue that practice theories are valuable because they overcome conceptual individualism but are empirically difficult to operationalize because of the sheer diversity and variability of practices. Backhaus and her colleagues formulate a framework based on the idea of 'webs of entangled elements' that extend across practices, their carriers, and production–consumption systems. They seek in their chapter to unravel these webs by applying both qualitative and quantitative research methods to a large-scale survey involving more than 1200 respondents in Austria, Hungary, and the Netherlands, and include a few in-depth interviews with consumers in each country. This approach enables the authors to identify country-specific food cultures and production–consumption systems, and to explore varying levels of trust in production chains, and subjectively understood time constraints, life circumstances, values, and expectations.

The final chapter in Part III is Marlyne Sahakian's discussion of how emotions and discourse – two collectively structured entities – can shape food-related practices. Sahakian draws on the notion of emotional energy described by Gert Spaargaren (as extrapolated from the work of Randall Collins) and applies this concept to two case studies. The first case study is historical and uses archival marketing and sales materials to demonstrate how appliance manufacturers in Europe during the 20th century went about the process of purposefully instilling their products with emotional energy. Using conventional approaches like trade fairs had the effect of infusing in the equipment ideals of modernity, freedom, and stylized comfort that contributed heavily to its successful diffusion. Sahakian's second case study focuses on the discursive construction of community-supported agriculture (CSA), a contemporary food-provisioning practice whereby local farms deliver a weekly basket of produce to urban consumers. With a specific focus on a contemporary CSA in Geneva, she demonstrates how proponents of this arrangement also seek to infuse emotional energy. In this instance, nostalgia, trustworthiness, community belonging, and spontaneous wonderment come to be infused into the vegetables and other farm products. The two case studies raise interesting questions for social practice theorists about how emotional energy is created and transferred and how it could be imparted to stimulate interest in more sustainable lifestyles.

Part IV extends the corpus of social practice theories and sustainable consumption advanced in Part III. In Chapter 8, Melanie Jaeger-Erben and Jana Rückert-John shift social practice theories toward the study of innovative sustainable consumption practices. They develop a framework of sustainable social innovations that draws from social practice theories and innovation theories. Innovation theories, they assert, are dominated by a technophilic orientation that downplays the importance of social change. Social practice theories can more effectively inform the study of social innovation through a unique emphasis on the interplay among skills, meanings, materials, and social settings. The resulting model allows researchers and practitioners to distinguish sustainable social innovations by highlighting unique modes of alternative consumption patterns. Each type of sustainable social innovation has distinct opportunities to remake the elements of a practice.

In Chapter 9, Chelsea Schelly demonstrates how the practice of housing can be shaped by policy. Schelly employs a social practices perspective to focus attention on the routines and habits of social groups, moving away from individualistic and value-oriented explanations for behavior. Specifically, a social practices perspective illustrates how action takes place within material, structural, and cultural frameworks that nudge, constrain, and shape human behaviors. This chapter explores how policies shape practice through an empirical examination of three cases of alternative residential dwelling: 1) solar electric technology adoption, 2) radically sustainable off-the-grid homes called Earthships, and 3) an intentional community. These three case studies demonstrate how particular policies work to shape collective routines as well as the understandings symbolically assigned to practices. The policies addressed are at multiple scales, including local, state, federal, and global, and by showing their influence, Schelly argues that policies are actually systems of provision that influence, shape, and give meaning to social practices.

In the final chapter of Part IV, Mike Gismondi, Juanita Marois, and Danica Straith examine a case study of sustainable finance. The 'Unleashing Local Capital' (ULC) project is a social innovation through which people invest in local business opportunities using a cooperative business structure. Deploying a combined theoretical model that integrates the multilevel perspective and social practice theories, the case study focuses on how regime, landscape, and niche practices were confronted and highlights particular social practices that impeded the success of the ULC project. Their analysis reveals how tightly woven social practices are with each level. For instance, though the program undertook key regime changes such as revising regulatory systems to allow local investments in cooperatives, the spread of the innovation was hampered by the resilience of investing and borrowing practices. Some key elements of these practices that were not present in the social finance approach include privacy (in how one invests one's money and operates one's business) and speed (expecting a quick return on investment). The authors point out that shifting to social finance practices requires new meanings and a new vocabulary, where the patient goals of community development become a normal part of an investment portfolio, and the blind trust in faceless bank managers is questioned. This chapter shows that investment and borrowing practices are an especially challenging area to change: regime and landscape changes may well be conducive to local investing but common practices are more difficult to change.

Finally, the concluding chapter summarizes the key ways in which social practice approaches to sustainable consumption have become increasingly appealing to policy makers, program developers, and applied academics. This chapter also links social practice theories to a sense – illustrated in texts beyond academia – that changing behaviors must necessarily invoke altering social contexts if we wish to foster desirable behavior change. We conclude by arguing that social practice research on the household needs to continue to broaden to communities, schools, workplaces, governments, and large organizations to break down patterns of human thought and action, and identify new patterns that lead to more systematic and lasting change.

NOTES

1. Development of the field of sustainable consumption research began during the aftermath of the United Nations Conference on Environment and Development held in Rio de Janeiro in 1992. *Agenda 21*, the keystone document of this event, devoted an entire chapter to the issue of sustainable consumption and noted that 'all countries should strive to promote sustainable consumption patterns'. Refer to Cohen and Murphy (2001) for further discussion of this policy history. Over the past two decades, sustainable consumption has become a robust area of research and policy practice that draws together various interdisciplinary areas including ecological economics, environmental sociology, science and technology studies, and social psychology. The recent compendium by Reisch and Thøgersen (2015) provides a comprehensive overview.
2. Refer to Reckwitz (2002) for an excellent overview of social practice theories. We exclude these other authors in the interest of brevity and on the basis of limited integration of their work into the study of sustainable consumption to date. This is not to say such integration is not possible; indeed in Chapter 2 Kasper uses figurational theory to inform her efforts to develop a foundational theory in the social sciences.
3. A notable absence in the genealogy is Schatzki's Wittgensteinian approach to social practice theories. Schatzki (1997) takes issue with both Bourdieu's and Giddens' social practice theories as over-intellectualizing social practices and argues that Wittgenstein's approach more satisfactorily resolves agency–structure dualisms. Readers should note that Schatzki's work is also a considerable influence to scholars adopting a practice perspective on sustainable consumption (i.e., Halkier and Jensen 2011).

4. Tyler Bateman drew our attention to this point.
5. The same focus on everyday life exists in the work of the American pragmatists as well but here we narrow our focus to Heidegger and Wittgenstein, who Reckwitz (2002) argues are central influences on social practice theories.
6. Systems of provision include supportive policies and regulations, cultural norms, and built infrastructure.
7. For two notable exceptions, see Carfagna et al. (2014) and Dubuisson-Quellier (2013).

REFERENCES

Barnes, Barry (2001), 'Practice as collective action', in T.R. Schatzki, K. Knorr Cetina, and E. von Savigny (eds), *The Practice Turn in Contemporary Theory*, London: Routledge, pp. 17–28.

Bourdieu, Pierre (1977), *Outline of a Theory of Practice* (R. Nice, trans.), Cambridge: Cambridge University Press.

Bourdieu, Pierre (1979), *Distinction: A Social Critique of the Judgment of Taste*, New York: Routledge.

Carfagna, Lindsay B., Emilie A. Dubois, Connor Fitzmaurice, Monique Y. Ouimette, Juliet B. Schor, Margaret M. Willis, and Thomas Laidley (2014), 'An emerging eco-habitus: the reconfiguration of high cultural capital practices among ethical consumers', *Journal of Consumer Culture*, **14** (2), 158–178.

Cohen, Maurie J. and Joseph Murphy (eds) (2001), *Exploring Sustainable Consumption: Environmental Policy and the Social Sciences*, Amsterdam: Pergamon.

Cohen, Maurie J., Halina S. Brown, and Philip J. Vergragt (eds) (2013), *Innovations in Sustainable Consumption: New Economics, Socio-technical Transitions and Social Practices*, Cheltenham and Northampton, MA: Edward Elgar Publishing.

Doyle, Ruth (2013), Towards a future of sustainable consumption: a practice oriented, participatory backcasting approach for sustainable washing and heating practices in Irish households. *University of Dublin, Trinity College*. Unpublished PhD thesis.

Dreyfus, Hubert L. (1991), *Being-in-the-World: A Commentary on Heidegger's Being and Time, Division I*, Cambridge, MA and London: The MIT Press.

Dubuisson-Quellier, Sophie (2013), *Ethical Consumption*, Halifax, NS: Fernwood Publishing.

Elias, Norbert (1978), *What is Sociology?*, London: Hutchinson.

Foucault, Michel (1969), *The Archaeology of Knowledge*, New York: Pantheon Books.

Giddens, Anthony (1984), *The Constitution of Society: Outline of the Theory of Structuration*, Cambridge: Polity Press.

Glover, Andrew (2012), Should it stay or should it go? Negotiation value and waste in the divestment of household objects. *University of Sydney*. Unpublished PhD thesis.

Halkier, Bente (2013), 'Sustainable lifestyles in a new economy: a practice theoretical perspective on change behavior campaigns and sustainability issues', in M.J. Cohen, H.S. Brown, and P.J. Vergragt (eds), *Innovations in Sustainable Consumption: New Economics, Socio-technical Transitions and Social Practices*, Cheltenham and Northampton, MA: Edward Elgar Publishing, pp. 209–228.

Halkier, Bente and Iben Jensen (2011), 'Methodological challenges in using practice theory in consumption research. Examples from a study of handling nutritional contestations of food consumption', *Journal of Consumer Culture*, **11** (1), 101–123.

Hands, D. Wade (2013), 'Normative rational choice theory: past, present, and future', working paper, available at http://papers.ssrn.com/sol3/papers.cfm?abstract_id=1738671 (accessed 27 February 2015).

Hargreaves, Tom (2011), 'Practice-ing behavior change: applying social practice theory to pro-environmental behaviour change', *Journal of Consumer Culture*, **11** (1), 79–99.

Hobson, Kersty (2003), 'Thinking habits into action: the role of knowledge and process in questioning household consumption practices', *Local Environment*, **8** (1), 95–112.

Jensen, Charlotte L. (2014), What is energy efficient light? A socio-technical analysis of lighting in transition. Institut for Planlægning, *Aalborg Universitet*. Unpublished PhD thesis.

Joas, Hans and Wolfgang Knöbl (2009), *Social Theory: Twenty Introductory Lectures*, Cambridge: Cambridge University Press.

Kennedy, Emily H. (2011), Reclaiming consumption: sustainability, social networks, and urban context. Department of Rural Economy, *University of Alberta*. Unpublished PhD thesis.

Lemert, Charles (2012), *Social Things: An Introduction to the Sociological Life*, New York: Rowman & Littlefield Publishers.

Martin, John L. (2011), *The Explanation of Social Action*, New York: Oxford University Press.

Reckwitz, Andreas (2002), 'Toward a theory of social practices: a development in culturalist theorizing', *European Journal of Social Theory*, **5** (2), 243–263.

Reisch, Lucia A. and John Thøgersen (2015), 'Research on sustainable consumption: introduction and overview', in L.A. Reisch and J. Thøgersen, *Handbook of Research on Sustainable Consumption*, Cheltenham and Northampton, MA: Edward Elgar Publishing, pp. 1–17.

Røpke, Inge (2009), 'Theories of practice – new inspiration for ecological economic studies on consumption', *Ecological Economics*, **68** (10), 2490–2497.

Sahakian, Marlyne (2011), Staying cool: towards a deeper understanding of household energy consumption in Metro Manila, the Philippines. Development Studies, *The Graduate Institute of International and Development Studies*. Unpublished PhD thesis.

Schatzki, Theodore R. (1997), 'Practices and actions: a Wittgensteinian critique of Bourdieu and Giddens', *Philosophy of the Social Sciences*, **27** (3), 283–308.

Schatzki, Theodore R. (2001), *The Practice Turn in Contemporary Theory*, London: Routledge.

Seyfang, Gill (2009), *The New Economics of Sustainable Consumption: Seeds of Change*, New York: Palgrave Macmillan.

Shove, Elizabeth (2003), *Comfort, Cleanliness and Convenience: The Social Organization of Normality*, Oxford and New York: Berg.

Shove, Elizabeth (2010), 'Beyond the *ABC*: climate change policy and theories of social change', *Environment and Planning A*, **42** (6), 1273–1285.

Shove, Elizabeth and Mika Pantzar (2005), 'Consumers, producers and practices: understanding the invention and reinvention of Nordic walking', *Journal of Consumer Culture*, **5** (1), 43–64.

Shove, Elizabeth and Nicola Spurling (eds) (2013), *Sustainable Practices: Social Theory and Climate Change*, Abingdon, UK and New York: Routledge.

Shove, Elizabeth and Alan Warde (2002), 'Inconspicuous consumption: the sociology of consumption, lifestyles, and the environment', in R.E. Dunlap, F.H. Buttel, P. Dickens, and A. Gijswijt (eds), *Sociological Theory and the Environment*, Lanham, MD: Rowman & Littlefield, pp. 230–251.

Spaargaren, Gert (1997), The ecological modernization of production and consumption: essays in environmental sociology. *Wageningen University*. Unpublished PhD thesis.

Spaargaren, Gert (2003), 'Sustainable consumption: a theoretical and environmental policy', *Society and Natural Resources*, **16** (8), 687–701.

Spaargaren, Gert (2013), 'The cultural dimension of sustainable consumption practices: an exploration in theory and policy', in M.J. Cohen, H.S. Brown, and P.J. Vergragt (eds), *Innovations in Sustainable Consumption: New Economics, Socio-technical Transitions and Social Practices*, Cheltenham and Northampton, MA: Edward Elgar Publishing, pp. 229–251.

Standing, Guy (2011), *The Precariat: The New Dangerous Class*, London and New York: Bloomsbury Academic.

Stern, Paul C. (2000), 'Toward a theory of environmentally significant consumption', *Journal of Social Issues*, **56** (3), 407–424.

Swidler, Ann (2001), 'What anchors social practices?', in T.R. Schatzki, K. Knorr Cetina, and E. von Savigny (eds), *The Practice Turn in Contemporary Theory*, London: Routledge, pp. 83–101.

Taylor, Charles (1985), 'What is human agency?', in *Philosophical Papers. Vol. 1, Human Agency and Language*, Cambridge: Cambridge University Press, pp. 15–44.

Thaler, Richard and Cass Sunstein (2008), *Nudge: Improving Decisions about Health, Wealth, and Happiness*, New Haven: Yale University Press.

Warde, Alan (1997), *Consumption, Food and Taste: Culinary Antinomies and Commodity Culture*, London: Sage.

Warde, Alan (2005), 'Consumption and theories of practice', *Journal of Consumer Culture*, **5** (2), 131–153.

Warde, Alan and Lydia Martens (2000), *Eating Out: Social Differentiation, Consumption and Pleasure*, Cambridge: Cambridge University Press.

Wilk, Richard (1997), 'A critique of desire: distaste and dislike in consumer behavior', *Consumption, Markets & Culture*, **1** (2), 175–196.

PART II

Social mobilization and sustainable consumption

2. Contextualizing social practices: insights into social change

Debbie Kasper

INTRODUCTION

There is increasing evidence that continuing on our current trajectory – what many environmental analysts refer to as 'business as usual' – will lead to ongoing increases in global average temperatures which, the Intergovernmental Panel on Climate Change (2014) anticipates, will lead to 'severe, pervasive, and irreversible impacts' (p. 2). In response to conclusions such as this, a growing number of socio-ecological researchers are calling for immediate and sweeping changes in our economic, political, and energy systems, especially those aimed at reducing carbon dioxide emissions. With or without such efforts, analysts agree, we will end up with massive social change. Without them, however, they expect such changes will be shaped by a series of reactions to unfolding crises. Advocates of proactive societal transition argue that it is preferable for social change to be made, in the words of Peter Victor's 2008 book title, 'by design, not disaster'.

Among socio-ecological researchers, the goal of thoughtful and pre-emptive transition efforts toward sustainability is widely shared. Missing, however, is a clear sense of how to make it happen and where to begin. Numerous scholars have perceived a crisis in the available paradigms for understanding socio-ecological problems and for thinking about possible means of effecting change. There are two major problems.

One is the flawed but dominant paradigm that prioritizes individual behavior and the role of consumerism in addressing urgent environmental problems (Harrison and Davies 1998; Shove 2010a) (see Chapter 1). The other is the absence of a widely accepted general theory of how social life, and thus social change, works (Brulle 2012; Kasper 2011). Without greater convergence, there is little hope for thoughtfully planning and effectively implementing the changes deemed necessary to avoid catastrophe.

In response to the predominance of consumption-based responses, there is a growing body of work intended to develop alternatives to the dominant individualistic approach in socio-ecological research and policy. As noted elsewhere in this volume, one particularly encouraging development is the study of social practices. Social practice theories take a broader view than the conventional approach to studying behavior, situating human action in larger social contexts that underlie the ongoing development of routine practices over time. Despite great promise, however, social practice theories have not been comprehensively integrated into the study of collective environmental action and other areas of socio-ecological research and policy.

Regarding the second and more fundamental issue (because it is, in large part, the source of difficulties in studying and understanding social processes), there is increasing recognition of the absence of reliable theory to guide our understanding of social change. While lamentable, this lack is hardly surprising given the long recognized absence of a widely accepted and empirically useful general theory of human social life, a theme that is especially prominent in sociology (Cole 1994; Davis 1994; Kasper 2011). The gravity of the situation is compounded within a context of calls for even more broadly integrated theories of *socio-ecological* relations and processes (Moran 2010; Stafford et al. 2010; Waring and Richerson 2011).

In this chapter, I seek to provide an overview of these problems and to discuss figurational theory as a means to address both of them. I draw heavily from the valuable but underutilized concept of figurations (see Elias 1978; Gabriel and Mennell 2011; Morrow 2009) and the more familiar, but still not mainstream or consistently applied, concept of habitus. Making dynamic interdependence implicit, these concepts provide a more adequate means for thinking and talking about and understanding social – and thus necessarily socio-ecological – phenomena than do conventional concepts.[1]

The resulting framework, I argue, can contribute to the advancement of alternative approaches to understanding human behavior and implementing transitions to sustainability, thus helping to de-legitimate the dominant paradigm of consumer-based change. I focus here on social practice theories and how contextualizing these approaches in a larger theoretical framework – including mechanisms of long-term social change – can make such theories more practice-able and create new possibilities to implement the findings of social practice research to inform transition efforts.

THE NEED FOR TRANSITION

Discussions of socio-ecological problems tend to be accompanied by calls for change. Lower pollutant emissions, novel conservation and efficiency strategies, new legislation, and greater awareness, for example, have long been common goals for targeted changes to mitigate harm and/or to promote particular kinds of social and environmental improvements. Of more recent origin are increasingly standard pronouncements of the need for, and the inevitability of, radical and sweeping societal transitions, especially in the systems that govern economics, politics, and energy.

One representative report summarizes the primary reasons for imminent social changes: 'The era of cheap and easy fossil fuels is over . . . climate stability is now a thing of the past . . . [and] we've reached the end of economic growth as we've known it in the U.S.' (Miller and Hopkins 2013, p. i). Given that the long-term decline of cheap abundant oil (episodic countertrends notwithstanding) will have unavoidable impacts on economic systems which depend on massive amounts of energy, sociologist John Urry expresses the conclusion of many climate and social scientists when he points out that 'to slow down, let alone reverse, increasing carbon emissions and temperatures requires the total reorganization of social life, nothing more and nothing less' (2010, p. 198). Overall, researchers seem to agree that major changes are necessary and that a transition to sustainability 'requires a social avalanche of unprecedented proportions' (Fischer et al. 2012, p. 158).

The increasingly dire conclusions of climate scientists – for example that 'a planned economic contraction to bring about the almost immediate and radical reductions [is] necessary to avoid the 2°C characterization of dangerous climate change' (Anderson and Bows 2011, p. 41) – elicit spirited discussion among social scientists. In one such exchange, sociologist John Bellamy Foster (2012) affirms that it would take a 'revolution in the sense of massive social movements and alterations in how we run our economy and use energy and resources'. Based on what the science tells us, sociologist Robert Brulle (2012) affirms, we know that 'business as usual, or incremental changes are a path to catastrophe'.

Generic prescriptions for change abound. We are told, for instance, that 'sustainability demands changes in human behavior' (Fischer et al. 2012, p. 153), 'consumer cultures will have to be re-engineered' (Assadourian 2013, p. 113), and that it will take 'massive political will to counter the momentum of dangerous trends' (Raskin 2014, p. 1). The trouble is that there is almost no agreement on how such changes can be effectively brought about, who will make them, or where to begin.

Fischer et al. conclude with the question: 'who or what might start this avalanche?' (2012, p. 159). More than a decade after an initial visionary report (Raskin et al. 2002), and despite great hope in the potential of a global citizens' movement, we are left wondering, as Raskin (2014) does, 'who will change the world?' With regard to the changes needed, Brulle (2012) states that he has 'seen no viable theory of just exactly [how] this miraculous social transformation is supposed to come about ... [and thinks] that ... we really don't have one'. In response, Damian White (2012) observes that, in addition to ecological and social crises, we have a profound crisis in the dominant paradigms of environmental social science, which 'can merely define a problem but offer no coherent and politically plausible program of action ... to address the problems'.

THE REIGNING PARADIGM AND CRITIQUES

The dominant paradigm in socio-ecological research has given rise to a prioritization of individual consumer action. Tim Jackson encapsulates this view, explaining that 'consumer behaviour is key to the impact that society has on the environment' (2005, p.iii). As such, he adds, it has become a central focus for national and international policy and the basis for believing that strategies which make it easy to behave more sustainably are needed. Its appeal is due, in part, to the fact that such ideas resonate (especially in the United States) with an individual-oriented culture and are well aligned with the aims of economic systems dependent on growth, but there has been increasing recognition of a paradigmatic crisis.

Jackson acknowledges that individual behavior is embedded in social and institutional contexts, yet relevant studies, reports, and policy initiatives in the United States and Europe are predominantly individualistic in focus. To illustrate the point, Shove (2010a) cites a long series of such efforts framed in terms of individual behavior and personal responsibility. To her list of examples, one could add a recent string of reports – including the OECD's *Greening Household Behaviour*, S.C. Johnson's *The Environment: Public Attitudes and Individual Behavior, A Twenty-Year Evolution*, The European Commission's *Future Brief: Green Behaviour*, and National Geographic's *Greendex: Consumer Choice and the Environment* – as reflecting this general perspective in which 'social change is thought to depend upon values and attitudes (the A), which are believed to drive the kinds of behaviour (the B) that individuals choose (the C) to adopt' (Shove 2010a, p.1274). Referring to this as the ABC approach, Shove highlights its roots in psychology and economics and prevailing assumptions of rationality and individual choice.

This individualistic paradigm has come under increasing criticism as evidence undermining these assumptions accumulates. Most fundamentally, it fails to accurately portray human social processes in the world, assuming behavior as 'the outcome of a linear and ultimately rational process' (Harrison and Davies 1998, p.2). A disproportionate focus on the individual poses challenges for incorporating contextual factors. But even

efforts to redress this problem have merely 'led to the gradual incorporation of various proxies for context . . . as yet more variables in individual
decision-making processes' (Hargreaves 2011, p. 1). While the increasing
inclusion of 'situational', 'social,' and 'contextual' factors is encouraging,
there is no limit to the possible causal factors one might identify, and so
efforts to find the 'right' combination of factors have proliferated, as has
confusion about which model to employ (Bamberg and Schmidt 2003;
Kollmuss and Agyeman 2002).

An additional problem involves the explicit division in dominant models
of 'internal' (for example, attitudes, values, personal norms) and 'external'
(for example, incentives, institutional constraints, social norms) factors.
Jackson endorses this divide, attributing unresolved tensions to the old
'structure–agency' debate and accepting the validity of this dualism as a
matter of course (2005, p. 24). Rather than being inevitable, though, this
so-called debate is merely the manifestation of inadequacies in the concepts used to think and talk about human social phenomena which, being
relational in nature, cannot be contained in neat 'inner' and 'outer' boxes.
The difficulties encountered in efforts to model behavior reflect a basic
need for more satisfactory concepts at more appropriate levels of analysis.

Critiques of the fruits of the ABC approach provide additional evidence
of its deficiencies. In general, Shove (2010a) argues, it is incapable of
meaningfully addressing socio-ecological crises. First, the view that environmental problems and their solutions stem from individual behavioral
choices deflects attention from the role of social systems in structuring
unsustainable ways of life. Secondly, the prevailing approach is not useful
for comprehending or intervening in dynamic processes of social change
on the massive scale demanded by contemporary global problems. Even
with recognition of the imperative to change how we satisfy our needs
and wants, an ABC approach offers 'no scope at all for wondering about
how needs and aspirations come to be as they are' (Shove 2010a, p. 1277).
Finally, the widespread acceptance of this paradigm has shaped perceptions of what counts as valid research, marginalizing approaches that do
not fit the mold, thus hindering advancements in scholarship. Establishing
a place for social theory beyond that defined as legitimate within the ABC
paradigm 'means building new audiences and . . . new agendas' (Shove
2010b, p. 285).

There have, despite these circumstances, been some encouraging developments in research aimed at understanding socio-ecological problems
and the means for transitioning to more resilient and sustainable systems.
Among them, the more comprehensive analysis of lifestyle, social mobilization studies, transition management, and social practice theories
all seek to de-center the individual and more explicitly account for the

co-evolutionary nature of social and environmental change. I focus here on social practice theories and how grounding these perspectives in a broader theoretical framework can render them more effective for understanding how environmentally significant social practices come about and change.

SOCIAL PRACTICE THEORIES: A PROMISING ALTERNATIVE

In shifting attention from individual behaviors to dynamic social practices within their larger cultural and infrastructural milieus, social practice theories represent an effort to correct the 'undersocialized methodological individualism of the behavioural models' (Hargreaves 2011, p. 83). The practice approach views environmentally significant actions as routine accomplishments embedded within 'normal' ways of life and, in general, seeks to account for the fact that individual agency and social structures are mutually constitutive of one another, and not opposites as is often supposed. Accounting for relations among the various components of social practices and including the material dimension of them are especially important innovations.

In one version of social practice theory, practices are portrayed as consisting of interdependencies among diverse elements including 'forms of bodily activities, forms of mental activities, "things" and their use, a background knowledge in the form of understanding, know-how, states of emotion and motivational knowledge' (Reckwitz 2002, p. 249). These are not viewed as qualities of an individual, but as elements of a practice in which an individual participates. Schatzki et al. offer an even stronger emphasis on the fact that practices always involve 'apprehending material configurations', making explicit that one cannot understand specific practices without examining the particular configurations of the things, technologies, and resources involved in them (2001, p. 3). More recently, the account by Shove and colleagues (2012) employs the concepts of meanings, materials, and competencies to represent elements of practice; in it they point out the diversity of the dynamic configurations of the elements implicated in social practices.

In general, a social practices approach 'raises a series of radically different questions about how to create more sustainable patterns of consumption' related to how practices form, spread, endure, change, and disappear (Hargreaves 2011, p. 84). With reference to food-related practices, for example, rather than asking which variables predict discrete eating behaviors, social practice theories encourage inquiry into how the eating practices of interest emerged and are maintained, what other bundles of practices they are related to, and how the elements underlying practices and the links between them are generated, reinforced, reproduced, or de-activated.

Social practice theories align well with the increasing recognition and evidence in socio-ecological research that modifications in consumer behaviors are insufficient for addressing the problems we face. What we need, rather, are new *ways of being* in transformed cultural, social, and biophysical contexts. With an orientation toward dynamic relations, rather than discrete static factors, social practice theories represent a significant improvement relative to the dominant approach. At present, however, champions of social practice theories acknowledge some weaknesses holding back progress on this front.

First, there is no clear, authoritative, or synthetic theory of social practice (Hargreaves 2011; Reckwitz 2002; Warde 2005). The absence of a commonly accepted set of concepts and propositions has hindered the spread and wider adoption of a social practice approach. Secondly, social practice theorists recognize particular gaps in the research, especially regarding relations among practices and communities of practice, the power relations that produce and are produced by certain practices, and the experiences and identities of practitioners (Hargreaves 2011; Sahakian and Wilhite 2014). Understanding these aspects of practice better would helpfully inform more comprehensive efforts toward broad goals like sustainable consumption. Finally, there is the sense that, although promising, social practice theories 'could benefit from becoming more "practicable"' (Sahakian and Wilhite 2014, p. 27). In other words, this work needs to be developed in ways that promote the generation of useable insights to be able to influence policy and inform actions intended to promote sustainability. While researchers usefully highlight the need to target linkages among 'elements' rather than behaviors (Hargreaves 2011; Shove et al. 2012), there is little guidance about *how* to do that – how to operationalize concepts like meanings, materials, and competencies.

An especially prominent obstacle to advancements in social practice theories, I maintain, is the longstanding absence of a widely accepted foundational sociological theory, with reference to which social practice theories might usefully be connected to other relevant areas of inquiry. Decades of assessments agree that sociological theory is incoherent and lacks a core of organizing principles as well as anything resembling a foundational theory (Abrutyn 2013; Becker and Rau 1992; Cole 1994; Davis 1994; Kalberg 2007; Kasper 2011; Keith 2000; Phillips 1999; Rule 1994; Sanderson 2005; Stinchcombe 1994; Turner 2004; Turner and Turner 1990).[2] In short, a basic framework for understanding how human social life works – inherent to which is a theory of social change – is missing. This deficiency is particularly problematic, Hargreaves argues, when the enormous socio-ecological challenges 'and the extensive transformations they appear to require across whole domains of society demand, in turn, a broad and sophisticated understanding of social life and change' (2011, p. 96).

The opening contention advanced by Shove and colleagues in *The Dynamics of Social Practice* is that 'theories of practice have as yet untapped potential for understanding change' (2012, p. 1). This unrealized promise, I contend, is largely due to a mismatch between theoretical goals and the guidance available for more systemically pursuing them. For example, while nearly every author who discusses social practice theories is quick to cite Giddens' declarations that the basic domain of study of the social sciences is 'social practices ordered across space and time' (1984, p. 2) and that individual agency and social structures are mutually constitutive of one another, missing still is a clear and accessible theoretical framework which takes these ideas seriously and can systematically guide empirical research. Especially acute is the need for theories and methods 'based on the fundamental interactions between people and the biophysical environment' (Moran 2010, p. 143). Such a 'unified science is needed soon, and we have not even a common framework to unite these approaches' (Waring and Richerson 2011, p. 302).

I believe this particular combination of gaps (in social practice theories, sociological theory, and the consequent lack of a theory of social change) presents tremendous opportunity. The elucidation of an overarching and scientifically accurate sociological theory could redress these problems and achieve several gains at once. First, a theoretical framework in which social practice theories could be contextualized would help to clarify and unify the approach while guiding more systematic empirical inquiry, thus rendering it more practicable. Secondly, the 'bigger picture' provided would afford the capacity to meet the new needs posed by combined interests in social practices and societal transformation – 'an agenda that is positively fizzing with potential' (Shove 2010b, p. 283) – namely to integrate multiple levels of inquiry and handle the many new lines of questions which emerge. Finally, we would gain the basis for a rigorous theory of social change. In describing and naming the mechanisms of human social processes (which inherently involve stability and change simultaneously happening at different levels at different times) more systematic means of inquiring about, studying, and guiding particular kinds of social change emerge.

A CENTRAL THEORY FOR SOCIOLOGY . . . AND SOCIO-ECOLOGICAL STUDIES

A set of core principles, it has been argued, rather than an infinite set of variables, is essential if the social sciences are to make meaningful progress in contributing to explanations of how the social world works (Keith 2000; Lieberson and Lynn 2002; Turner 2008; York and Clark 2007). Crucial to achieving this is a grounding in basic facts about the human species and human social life. Absent such premises we are 'without anchorage in the observable world . . . left hanging in the air' (Elias 1991b, p. 43), an impossible starting point for understanding human social processes in the biophysical world, much less how to deliberately shift their course. Norbert Elias' attention to the biological bases of the human condition and, in particular, how they can inform theories of long-term social processes are at the heart of the figurational theory that I advance here. The overall framework itself, its concepts and shape, derives primarily from a synthesis of key contributions from Elias (especially the concept of figurations), Bourdieu (in particular his explication of habitus), and relevant scientific knowledge that extends and deepens our understanding of both of these conceptual approaches. I am not alone in recognizing their worth.

There has been, in recent years, increasing attention devoted to the great value of Elias' work (Gabriel and Mennell 2011; Morrow 2009; Kilminster 2007), with some scholars arguing that it 'provides a compelling framework for a "central theory" in sociology, [one that] is itself potentially well placed to play an orchestrating role in a broader *human science*, encompassing phenomena . . . engendered by distinct but intertwined biological and social planes of integration' (Quilley and Loyal 2005, p. 810). And Bourdieu is credited with 'bringing concepts of practice into the social theoretical debates of the 1980s' (Shove et al. 2012, pp. 5–6) and for providing 'the contours of social practice theory today' (Sahakian and Wilhite 2014, p. 26).

There are any number of theoretical works which share similar insights and align well with the proposed theory, and my intent in highlighting the contributions of Elias and Bourdieu is not to exclude those works. The inspiration and development of figurational theory as I have codified it, however, have been influenced primarily by these particular scholars. In what follows, I review the underlying premises, the theory, and its core concepts and then focus on how to advance social practice theories by contextualizing them within this broader framework.

Overview of Figurational Theory

An appreciation of relations among levels of physical, biological, and social phenomena suggests key sociological premises, often overlooked in the social sciences. These include the facts that humans are social organisms whose survival and development rely heavily on social learning – facilitated by a high degree of brain plasticity – and who, as a result, are necessarily embedded in functional relations of interdependence with others (see Kasper 2014). These premises underlie a central theory which, viewing human social life from a high level of synthesis (see Figure 2.1[3]), outlines the basic pattern of human social processes and thus of social change. Its core concepts offer the means to more adequately think and communicate about both.

To understand Figure 2.1, one must first grasp its representation of time. It is helpful to begin by visualizing (space) time's arrow and then 'zooming in' to see it as a spiral in which each layer represents an undefined 'moment' in time in which the processes depicted are continuously happening and feeding into one another. Turning this spiral on its end, we can more closely examine the model's basic components, described briefly below.

Biophysical conditions (reflected by the spiraling line) underlie all social

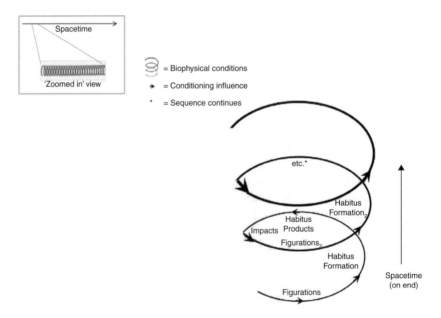

Figure 2.1   Model of human social processes

activity. These include a wide range of interrelated conditions, including those that are: fixed (for example, the laws of physics, chemical processes), relatively fixed over time periods meaningful to humans (for example, atmospheric composition, species characteristics), and more open to change, to varying degrees (for example, population characteristics, the built environment, resources, tools, and material technologies). Biophysical conditions influence and (many of them) are, in turn, influenced by human activities, though at varying scales of space and time. Some of these effects occur locally and/or are manifest in the short term, while others do not become apparent in immediate locales and/or for longer periods of time. Writ large, these are the conditions within which humans form, exercise, and re-form particular patterns of interdependence.

The concept of figurations refers to the overall patterns of bonds of functional interdependence that people form with each other. As social organisms who meet certain needs through relations with others, humans naturally have valencies – points of openness for connecting with others. These connections can be direct or, at varying spatial and temporal distances, indirect, and they include linkages via common attachment to symbols. Acknowledging humans' capacity and need to connect with other individuals and groups, the concept of figuration conveys our inherent sociality, a significant advancement from conventional concepts to which relations must be 'added'. Figurations, then, are natural results of human social processes. The concept conveys the inherent relationality of human life and provides a more empirical understanding of 'society' as a figuration formed by interdependent people. Thinking figurationally is especially helpful for orienting oneself in complex social contexts which, though difficult to discern, exert enormous influence over our lives and how we develop.

Developing within particular kinds of figurations, people form a socially conditioned way of being in the world, or habitus, which is recognizably similar to those developing in like conditions, at varying levels of generality. Because human sociality is inherent in the concept of habitus, it negates the need for continued puzzlement over the relationship between 'the individual' and 'society' and the supposed 'internal' and 'external' factors which 'cause' behavior. Understanding habitus entails investigations of the mechanisms of its formation and, to use Bourdieu's term, the *products* which habitus engenders, that is, the particular thoughts, perceptions, expressions, actions, dispositions, and practices produced via basic human activity. The concept, then, is a convenient referent for a natural, albeit complex, phenomenon through which social learning orients the products of human activity (via interacting chemical, biological, neurological, and other underlying processes). The result is a kind of 'second nature', operating in addition to and in conjunction with the 'first nature' derived from humans' common evolutionary heritage.

Importantly, the products of our 'second nature' have consequences for other people and the world. These social and environmental impacts occur at a wide range of distances and time scales. Wherever and whenever socio-ecological impacts manifest, they shape the conditions within which humans continue to form and exercise figurational patterns – ultimately contributing to their reinforcement and modification, and to the social changes which follow.

The model is intended to sensitize us to, and help us envision, relationships among fundamental processes at the social level. Its components are arrayed in a certain sequence according to the contingencies of the conditions that necessarily precede them, but there is a great deal going on simultaneously, as perceived within increments of time meaningful to humans. In its simplicity, this framework encompasses the enormous complexity of human social life. It focuses our attention on the basic pattern of social processes at a high level, while containing and integrating the many parts and processes at underlying levels.

In particular, this framework highlights the role of figurational patterns in shaping the development of people's normal everyday life, or 'second nature', the expression of which exerts corresponding socio-ecological impacts. In terms of providing an integrated framework for socio-ecological research, it also highlights the general categories of inquiry within which we can more easily place and discern meaningful connections among seemingly disparate works. The model suggests the following fundamental categories of inquiry, within which fit countless possible specific questions and theories:

- characteristics of the figurational patterns in question;
- habitus formation within different kinds of figurations;
- the products which certain types of habitus generate;
- the impacts those products have on people and the world;
- the ways those impacts could or do affect subsequent development of the figurations in question;
- the biophysical conditions with which each of the above necessarily engages.

I have begun to suggest how this framework can help us locate different kinds of inquiry into the kind of integrated socio-ecological framework researchers are calling for (see Kasper 2014). I focus here on social practice theories, where they fit in the framework, and how contextualizing these approaches within this general theory can enhance their utility and progress.

SITUATING SOCIAL PRACTICE THEORIES

Shifting the focus from individual behaviors to dynamic social practices within their cultural and infrastructural milieus, social practice theories view environmentally significant behaviors as routine accomplishments embedded in normal ways of life. The appreciation of the importance of 'normal' is one of the greatest merits of this approach and points to the need to focus change efforts at the cultural and infrastructural contexts of 'normal' practices, rather than the behaviors of individuals. Contextualizing social practices, and the theories that study them, within the broader pattern of socio-ecological processes depicted in the model above creates multiple opportunities for advancement. It enables us to redress some of the shortcomings identified in social practice theories, better tap their full potential, and avail ourselves of the resulting practical applications for societal transition efforts, in particular attempts to decommission unsustainable ways of life and to establish new modes of operating.

Placing key concepts of social practice theories within those of figurational theory reveals routinized practices as 'products' of habitus. To understand the theoretical and practical implications of this point, we must take a closer look at habitus, a concept favored by Bourdieu and Elias for its capacity to represent an individual's inherent sociality and to demystify the supposed puzzle of individual–society relations so difficult to solve without acknowledgment of the characteristics of the human organism.

Social Practices: Products of Habitus

With basic sociological premises in mind, we can grasp, for example, that, although one's distinctive makeup (via genetics, conditions of development, and a particular sequence of experiences) has an indelible influence on one's entire fate, the way children's malleable features gradually take shape as they grow '*never* depends solely on [their] constitution and always on the nature of the relations between [them] and other people' (Elias 1991a, p. 22). In short, one's character, however unique, is necessarily 'a network product formed in a continuous interplay of relationships to other people, and that the individual form of the adult is a society-specific form' (Elias 1991b, p. 27). Habitus *is* that society-specific form.

Although not reducible to the chemical, biological, neurological, psychological, and other processes (interacting at multiple levels) which underlie it, a basic understanding and acknowledgment of these underlying systems and processes enhances our ability to grasp the meaning of habitus as the group-specific system of schemas that generate and orient the products of natural human activities (for example, thoughts, perceptions, expressions, actions, dispositions, practices) on a dynamic and ongoing basis. As 'an open system of dispositions that is constantly subjected to experiences, and therefore constantly affected by them' (Bourdieu and Wacquant 1992, pp. 132–133), the concept of habitus provides a way to understand the stability and perpetual changeability that characterizes the human condition. Schemas and systems of dispositions cannot themselves be directly observed, but habitus can be operationalized through the study of its 'products'.

In examining practices (the routine accomplishments embedded within 'normal' ways of life), competencies (the understandings, skills, and knowledge necessary for performing them), and meanings (ways of perceiving and interpreting all of those), work from the perspective of social practice theories within the study of sustainable consumption is already engaged in studying the products of habitus. Situating those interests and concerns with materials in a broader framework provides the theoretical coherence social practice theorists seek and guides empirical inquiry in important ways.

The accompanying premises, core concepts, and visual model usefully connect practices with other phenomena at different scales. Doing so fosters sustained awareness, for example, that particular social and environmental impacts are rooted in specific social practices and other aspects of the habitus (at varying levels of generality) in operation.[4]

Take food, for instance. Thanks to research on the impacts of practices related to food production and consumption (from the fourth item in the list above), we know much about the negative social and environmental impacts of the current industrial food system – such as high fossil fuel consumption and greenhouse gas emissions, soil degradation, water pollution, habitat destruction, and more.[5] Assuming that one goal of socio-ecological research is to inform efforts to mitigate some of those impacts, it is necessary to first understand their origins.

Within this framework, tracing those impacts back to the offending practices that are manifest through the expression of habitus prompts recognition that they fit within a larger system of perceptions, thoughts, dispositions, tastes, and skills. Accompanying specific practices, for example, we might find that contemporary Americans' food-relevant aspects of habitus (at a high level of generality) can be characterized by, among other things: the expectation of year-round availability of most foods, the perceived normalcy of food to-go, the anticipation of standardized fare at fast-food restaurants regardless of location, and the skills (or lack thereof) associated with living in residences equipped with refrigerators, microwaves, and other food-related appliances. These attributes matter for what people do and the impacts of what they do. Examining narrower varieties of habitus (associated, for example, with a particular region, ethnicity, occupation, and the like) would allow us to characterize traits with greater specificity.

The important point is that the concept of habitus helps guide the study of social practices beyond the practices themselves to more holistically explore the *ways of being* of which practices are part. A second key point is that in the framework we are reminded that the types of habitus we observe necessarily develop within certain figurational conditions, representing the kind of continual mutual constitution of 'agency' and 'structure' which social theorists have long struggled to articulate. It is to these relational contexts that I now turn.

Social Practices: Developing within Figurations

Thinking figurationally prompts us to consider the networks of relations in which people and their ways of life are necessarily embedded, and made possible in the first place. In a contemporary globalized context those networks have become too vast and complex for one to see directly. A means for systematically analyzing them, then, is invaluable for facilitating both a greater sense of general orientation in the world, as well as rigorous study of the conditions within which practices emerge, are maintained, and change.

Again, beginning with basic sociological premises, figurational thinking acknowledges the human needs that necessitate certain bonds of functional interdependence. Elias (1978) identifies three universal categories of bonds: survival and development (involving functions related to resource procurement, protection, learning, and communication), sex and reproduction (involving the organization of sexual and reproductive activities), and emotional (involving the fulfillment of needs related to the other-directedness of the human species which, incidentally, occurs through attachments to larger social units and the people who comprise them via symbols as well as direct interpersonal bonds). These and other needs are met via human relations in any number of ways.

Despite great variation in size and shape, figurations lend themselves to empirical observation. In smaller social units, relations of functional interdependence are directly comprehensible. In small foraging societies, for instance, the links themselves and the overall pattern of bonds are readily apparent. As chains of interdependence become longer and more complex, however, figurations must be perceived more indirectly from available data about four particularly important traits of the relevant figurations (Elias 1978, pp. 128–145).

One such trait is *degrees of differentiation*, or the quantity of functions represented in a figuration. A possible indicator of this is the number of occupational titles. These functions are coordinated and implemented on the basis of the second trait, entailing certain *levels of integration*. It is conceivable that in a small band of hunter/gatherers, most or all functions could be integrated through one or just a few levels. In a modern globalized setting, however, there are many possible levels through which various functions are organized and carried out. There is in the United States, for example, a hierarchy of levels through which political activity is orchestrated, including community organizations, local municipalities, and governance structures at county, state, regional, national, and international levels. The third characteristic to note in figurations is the general *balance of power* among bonds, or categories of bonds. The proposed framework promotes a more accurate view of power as relational, a structural characteristic of the flow of every figuration, and not as a thing or substance one *has*. The recommendation of specific methodologies or means of quantifying power ratios is beyond the scope of this chapter, but suffice to say the proposed understanding of figurations, importantly, draws attention to the ways that certain parties may have greater or lesser abilities to achieve their ends and/or exercise constraint over each other (often by withholding that which others need or want). The last feature is *rates of change* in the other three. In short, over what period of time and to what degree has differentiation, the number of levels of integration, and power ratios among certain bonds increased or decreased?

A crucial task for this type of research will be the creation and use of figurational maps (which will almost certainly benefit from existing strategies in network analysis, supply chain studies, and other techniques for representing relational data). For the moment, I return to the topic of food to sketch a rough figurational picture depicting the many people and processes to which a typical American is linked through the seemingly simple act of eating and to shed some light on the conceptual value of figurations for imagining how habitus develops differently within different patterns of interdependent relations.

Examining the bonds of interdependence connecting eaters to their food in a globalized industrial society reveals a web of astonishing complexity, with threads stretching across vast distances of space and time. Only with great effort can one come to know that the act of procuring and eating food links one to untold numbers of researchers, developers, manufacturers, and providers of seeds, chemicals, and farm equipment; growers, processors, corporations, and their shareholders, lobbyists, policy makers, advertisers and those who work with the media they employ; flavor and nutrition scientists; market researchers; other brand-loyal consumers;

shippers, sellers, and the coordinators and regulators of all these; the many employees involved in these various activities, and more. Mapping such relations of interdependence over time would reveal the ways in which, and how rapidly, the chains of social bonds underlying food production and consumption have grown longer and more complex and would provide a means for identifying significant imbalances of power and highlighting when (and perhaps how) they emerged.

Observing and tracking changes in figurations provide insights into larger processes of social stability and change. Because social and environmental conditions at any given moment are chronologically and otherwise dependent on the accumulated circumstances of past moments, change *does* exhibit a kind of order discernible in long-term trends. It is the overall direction of these trends – comprising pockets of activity both in and counter to that direction – which is important to perceive and which a figurational analysis can help explain.

As these figurational conditions vary, so, too, do the habituses developing within them and the impacts that stem from their expression.[6] To demonstrate with a stark contrast, people in foraging societies are more directly linked to the origins of their food. Food is either procured by eaters themselves or by someone closely connected to them. A figurational map of these would show the number of food-relevant bonds of interdependence to be much smaller, less functionally differentiated, and involve fewer levels of integration. One can easily imagine how different the habitus developing within this figurational pattern would be from our own, with radically dissimilar sensibilities regarding where and how to procure food, what foods are consumed, when, in what quantities, how, and with whom.

Importantly, as aspects of habitus and its products differ, so do the nature and degree of the impacts that it generates. The lens that this theory provides reveals that when we choose to 'buy local' or eat a low-carbon diet – or when we try to get consumers to make those choices – what we are really doing is altering the *pattern of relations* through which we get our food. And changes in those relations give rise to changes in habitus and ultimately to its impacts (some of which may be immediate and others long term). Tracing the development of habitus products back to particular figurational patterns, this theory leads us to valuable insights into the formation, duration, and transformation of social practices. We see that to modify impacts we need to change practices and likely the habitus orienting them. To do that, over the long term, we need to strategically alter the figurations within which habitus develops. This is the most powerful insight that the wider perspective of figurational theory affords, and it expands the capacity of approaches like social practice research to inform the development of social change strategies and of efforts to implement them.

CONCLUSION

No one can predict exactly how the future will unfold, but certain facts about energy, economics, carbon emissions, and climate change give some indication as to what are most probable imminent changes in the conditions in which people make a life *and* develop a way of life. Even without intentional transition efforts on our parts, reduced availability of inexpensive fossil fuel alone would force changes in the patterns of relations through which people currently meet certain needs (and wants) and would bring accompanying changes in lifestyles.

This is the point that dystopian fiction (especially the peak oil and 'cli-fi' varieties) illustrates so well. New ways of life emerge – often after painful periods of transition – in new configurations of human interdependence. Social practice theories are especially well poised to make use of this insight to strengthen and systematize the study of the practices in which people engage, that are shaped within figurations, and affect the world in significant ways. This is important work, and I maintain that putting the study of social practices on solid theoretical ground will enhance its capacity to effectively engage in it.

Admittedly, the theoretical framework proposed and its concepts demand an historical perspective and a wider view of a topic than is typical in contemporary socio-ecological research. In Bourdieu's words, it requires the 'combination of broad ambition and long patience that is needed to produce a work of science' discouraged by the current system that rewards a 'safe thesis and a flash in the pan' (Bourdieu 1984, p. 512). And while much work remains to be done to develop and test the ideas suggested here, I contend that the proposed framework offers a significant step forward in synthesizing a basic map of social change – including a sense of how it works and a means for identifying entry points for change – where there was none before.

Such a framework, of course, will not enable us to predict or control the future. Humans are emergent and contingent processes, embedded in contexts of interacting emergent and contingent processes. As such, prediction and control are impossible. But with a reliable means for thinking about the big picture and long-term social change more systematically, we can more intentionally steer the directions of social change in ways previously not conceived. Figurational bonds are key points of intervention for making deliberate and lasting changes in the nature and degree of the impacts being exerted on people and the environment. Careful attention to the various functions being met and by whom within a figuration, levels of integration coordinating that activity, power balances among the parties involved, and a sense of when these all came about (which importantly underscores their changeability) provides crucial information for identifying optimal places to cut, add, and rearrange figurational bonds to begin to effect desired changes.

Put simply, to avoid disaster and create social transition by more deliberate design, the focus of socio-ecological policy and action should be on the strategic reconfiguration of relevant relations of interdependence, rather than on individual consumer attitudes, behaviors, and choices. No matter what we do, social change is inevitable. Equipped with a better sense of how transformation works and a longer-term perspective, it becomes at least possible to more consciously direct change, rather than being mindlessly swept along in its current.

NOTES

1. For example, as useful as concepts like structure, institution, and society are, relationality and dynamism must be 'added'. In contrast, these qualities are inherent in the concepts of figurations and habitus.
2. There has long been controversy over the notion of a general sociological theory, with the debate portrayed in terms of empiricists seeking a theory that emulates the natural sciences versus post-structuralists who advocate more relativistic theories (Alexander 1991; Gross 2009; Turner 2008). On one hand are arguments that sociology's search for foundations and a correct grounded set of premises should be renounced (Seidman 1991, p. 131), and, on the other hand, is the contention that, like any science, sociological theory should be about developing abstract testable theories, laws, and models to explain the operation of relevant forces (Turner 2008, p. 282). I take the latter view.
3. This model was originally inspired by Bourdieu's model of habitus that appears in his book *Distinction* (1984, p. 171), but has been substantially modified over time in response to developments in the author's understanding of figurations, habitus, and the scientific evidence that elucidates them, as well as the desire for clarity and parsimony.
4. Degrees of generality refer to the multiple 'layers' of habitus people acquire as they develop within multiple sets of interrelated figurations. The larger and more complex figurational patterns become, I hypothesize, the more layers of group-specific sociality people developing within them acquire. This approach offers an alternative way of thinking about the significance of what are commonly considered key 'variables' (for example, sex, age, ethnicity, socioeconomic status). Rather than taking their significance for granted, figurational theory suggests that they matter in as much as functional bonds of interdependence, in a given setting, differ along those lines.
5. See http://www.ucsusa.org/our-work/food-agriculture/our-failing-food-system/industrial-agriculture#.VNtzpiy8p2A (accessed 11 February 2015) and the reports, analyses, and research on which overviews like this are based.
6. The correct plural form would be '*habitūs*', as a 'fourth declension' plural noun. Some erroneously construct an 'i' ending, but I choose here to use the commonly anglicized version, *habituses*, to avoid confusion and clearly indicate the plural.

REFERENCES

Abrutyn, Seth (2013), 'Teaching sociological theory for a new century: contending with the time crunch', *American Sociologist*, **44** (2), 132–154.

Alexander, Jeffrey C. (1991), 'Sociological theory and the claim to reason: why the end is not in sight', *Sociological Theory*, **9** (2), 147–153.

Anderson, Kevin and Alice Bows (2011), 'A new paradigm for climate change', *Nature Climate Change*, **2**, 639–640.

Assadourian, Erik (2013), 'Re-engineering cultures to create a sustainable civiliza- tion', in Worldwatch Institute (ed.), *Is Sustainability Still Possible? State of the World 2013*, Washington, DC: Island Press, pp. 113–125.

Bamberg, Sebastian and Peter Schmidt (2003), 'Incentives, morality, or habit? Predicting students' car use for university routes with the models of Ajzen, Schwartz, and Triandis', *Environment and Behavior*, **35** (2), 264–285.

Becker, Howard S. and William C. Rau (1992), 'Sociology in the 1990s', *Society*, **30** (1), 70–74.

Bourdieu, Pierre (1984), *Distinction: A Social Critique of the Judgment of Taste*, Cambridge, MA: Harvard University Press.

Bourdieu, Pierre and Loïc J.D. Wacquant (1992), *An Invitation to Reflexive Sociology*, Chicago: University of Chicago Press.

Brulle, Robert (2012), Listserv of the Environment, Technology, and Society Section of the American Sociological Association, 17 November.

Cole, Stephen (1994), 'Why sociology doesn't make progress like the natural sciences', *Sociological Forum*, **9** (2), 133–154.

Davis, James A. (1994), 'What's wrong with sociology?', *Sociological Forum*, **9** (2), 179–197.

Elias, Norbert (1978), *What is Sociology?*, New York: Columbia University Press.

Elias, Norbert (1991a), *The Society of Individuals*, M. Schröter (ed.) translated by E. Jephcott, Oxford and Cambridge, MA: Basil Blackwell.

Elias, Norbert (1991b), *The Symbol Theory*, Richard Kilminster (ed.), London and Newbury Park, CA: Sage.

European Commission (2012), *Future Brief: Green Behaviour*, Science for Environment Policy Report 6, European Commission.

Fischer, Joern, Robert Dyball, Ioan Fazey, Catherine Gross, Stephen Dovers, Paul R. Ehrlich, Robert J. Brulle, Carleton Christensen, and Richard J. Borden (2012), 'Human behavior and sustainability', *Frontiers in Ecology and Environment*, **10** (3), 153–160.

Foster, John B. (2012), Listserv of the Environment, Technology, and Society Section of the American Sociological Association, 17 November.

Gabriel, Norman and Stephen Mennell (eds) (2011), *Norbert Elias and Figurational Research: Processual Thinking in Sociology*, Hoboken, NJ: Wiley-Blackwell.

Giddens, Anthony (1984), *The Constitution of Society: Outline of the Theory of Structuration*, Berkeley: University of California Press.

Gross, Neil (2009), 'A pragmatist theory of social mechanisms', *American Sociological Review*, **74** (3), 358–379.

Hargreaves, Tom (2011), 'Practice-ing behaviour change: applying social practice theory to pro-environmental behaviour change', *Journal of Consumer Culture*, **11** (1), 79–99.

Harrison, Carolyn and Gail Davies (1998), *Lifestyles and the Environment:*

Environment and Sustainability Desk Study Prepared for the ESRC's Environment and Sustainability Programme, London: ESRC.

Intergovernmental Panel on Climate Change (2014), *Fifth Assessment Report (Summary for Policy Makers)*, Geneva: IPCC.

Jackson, Tim (2005), *Motivating Sustainable Consumption: A Review of Evidence on Consumer Behaviour and Behavioural Change*, London: Sustainable Development Research Network and ESRC Sustainable Technologies Research Programme.

Kalberg, Stephen (2007), 'A cross-national consensus on a unified sociological theory? Some inter-cultural obstacles', *European Journal of Social Theory*, **10** (2), 206–219.

Kasper, Debbie (2011), 'Finding coherence in sociology: (finally!) a foundational theory', in I. Zake and M. DeCesare (eds), *New Directions in Sociology: Essays on Theory and Methodology in the 21st Century*, Jefferson, NC: McFarland, pp. 121–144.

Kasper, Debbie (2014), 'Codifying figurational theory and mapping common ground in sociology . . . and beyond', *Human Figurations*, **3** (1), available at http://hdl.handle.net/2027/spo.11217607.0003.104 (accessed 26 January 2015).

Keith, Bruce (2000), 'Taking stock of the discipline: some reflections on the state of American sociology', *The American Sociologist*, **31** (1), 5–14.

Kilminster, Richard (2007), *Norbert Elias: Post-Philosophical Sociology*, New York: Routledge.

Kollmuss, Anja and Julian Agyeman (2002), 'Mind the gap: why do people act environmentally and what are the barriers to pro-environmental behavior?', *Environmental Education Research*, **8** (2), 239–260.

Lieberson, Stanley and Freda B. Lynn (2002), 'Barking up the wrong branch: scientific alternatives to the current model of sociological science', *Annual Review of Sociology*, **28** (1), 1–19.

Miller, Asher and Rob Hopkins (2013), *Climate After Growth: Why Environmentalists Must Embrace Post-Growth Economics and Community Resilience*, Santa Rosa, CA: Post-Carbon Institute (available at http://www.postcarbon.org/reports/Climate-After-Growth.pdf).

Moran, Emilio (2010), *Environmental Social Science: Human–Environment Interactions and Sustainability*, Hoboken, NJ: Wiley-Blackwell.

Morrow, Raymond (2009), 'Norbert Elias and figurational sociology: the comeback of the century', *Contemporary Sociology*, **38** (3), 215–219.

National Geographic (2012), *Greendex 2012: Consumer Choice and the Environment. A Worldwide Tracking Survey*, National Geographic, July.

Organisation for Economic Cooperation and Development (2011), *Greening Household Behaviour: The Role of Public Policy*, Paris: OECD Rights and Translation Unit.

Phillips, Bernard (1999), 'Confronting our Tower of Babel', *Perspectives*, **21** (4), 2–6.

Quilley, Stephen and Steven Loyal (2005), 'Eliasian sociology as a "central theory" for the human sciences', *Current Sociology*, **53** (5), 809–830.

Raskin, Paul (2014), 'A great transition? Where we stand', keynote address at the Conference of the International Society for Ecological Economics, Reykjavik, Iceland, 13–15 August.

Raskin, Paul, Tariq Banuri, Gilberto Gallopín, Pablo Gutman, Al Hammond, Robert Kates, and Rob Swart (2002), *Great Transition: The Promise and Lure of the Times Ahead*, Boston: Stockholm Environment Institute.

Reckwitz, Andreas (2002), 'Toward a theory of social practices: a development in culturalist theorizing', *European Journal of Social Theory*, **5** (2), 243–263.

Rule, James B. (1994), 'Dilemmas of theoretical progress', *Sociological Forum*, **9** (2), 241–257.

Sahakian, Marlyne and Harold Wilhite (2014), 'Making practice theory practicable: towards more sustainable forms of consumption', *Journal of Consumer Culture*, **14** (1), 25–44.

Sanderson, Stephen K. (2005), 'Reforming theoretical work in sociology: a modest proposal', *Perspectives*, **28** (2), 1–4.

SC Johnson and GFK Roper (2011), *The Environment: Public Attitudes and Individual Behavior – A Twenty-Year Evolution*, SC Johnson.

Schatzki, Theodore, Karin Knorr-Cetina, and Eike von Savigny (2001), *The Practice Turn in Contemporary Theory*, New York: Routledge.

Seidman, Steven (1991), 'The end of sociological theory: the postmodern hope', *Sociological Theory*, **9** (2), 131–146.

Shove, Elizabeth (2010a), 'Beyond the ABC: climate change policy and theories of social change', *Environment and Planning A*, **42** (6), 1273–1285.

Shove, Elizabeth (2010b), 'Social theory and climate change', *Theory, Culture & Society*, **27** (2–3), 277–288.

Shove, Elizabeth, Mike Pantzar, and Matt Watson (2012), *The Dynamics of Social Practice*, Thousand Oaks, CA: Sage.

Stafford, Susan G. et al. (2010), 'Now is the time for action: transitions and tipping points in complex environmental systems', *Environment*, **52** (1), 38–45.

Stinchcombe, Arthur (1994), 'Disintegrated disciplines and the future of sociology', *Sociological Forum*, **9** (2), 279–291.

Turner, Jonathan H. (2004), 'Is grand theory dead and should sociology care? A reply to Lamont', *Perspectives*, **27** (2), 2–12.

Turner, Jonathan H. (2008), 'The practice of scientific theorizing in sociology and the use of scientific theory in sociological practice', *Sociological Focus*, **41** (4), 281–299.

Turner, Stephen P. and Jonathan H. Turner (1990), *The Impossible Science: An Institutional Analysis of American Sociology*, Newbury Park, CA: Sage.

Urry, John (2010), 'Consuming the planet to excess', *Theory, Culture & Society*, **27** (2–3), 191–213.

Victor, Peter (2008), *Managing Without Growth: Slower by Design, Not Disaster*, Cheltenham and Northampton, MA: Edward Elgar Publishing.

Warde, Alan (2005), 'Consumption and theories of practice', *Journal of Consumer Culture*, **5** (2), 131–153.

Waring, Timothy M. and Peter J. Richerson (2011), 'Towards unification of the socio-ecological sciences: the value of coupled models', *Geografiska Annaler: Series B, Human Geography*, **93** (4), 301–314.

White, Damian (2012), Listserv of the Environment, Technology, and Society Section of the American Environmental Association, 17 November.

York, Richard and Brett Clark (2007), 'The problem with prediction: contingency, emergence, and the reification of projections', *The Sociological Quarterly*, **48** (4), 713–743.

3. Environmental civic practices: synthesizing individual and collective sustainable consumption

Emily Huddart Kennedy and Tyler Bateman

CIVIC ENGAGEMENT IN EVERYDAY LIFE

A cursory Internet search on 'how to save the planet' will unearth thousands of lists, most of which include acts like recycling and turning down the thermostat to save energy. Taking these compilations at face value might give the impression that consuming sustainably is a simple matter of individual choice. Individual choice, which undergirds the notion of individual actions, is one-third of what Mark Dowie (1996) calls 'the environmental imagination' (p. 27). The environmental imagination refers to three interconnected forms of civic engagement that are necessary for socio-ecological change: individual actions, community organizing, and institutional reform. Distinguishing among these individual, civic, and political activities is useful for drawing attention to contemporary over-reliance on household behaviors to 'save the planet'. However, this conceptualization also overlooks the civic and political practices that are a necessary foundation for widespread individual actions.

In North America and beyond, 'individual' actions that embody sustainable consumption, while not widespread, are certainly more prevalent than either community organizing or institutional reform (Shah et al. 2007). For example, an individual concerned with the environmental impact of her eating, transportation, and bathing practices is more inclined to buy local food, drive a hybrid vehicle, and take shorter showers (Stern 2000) than seek to influence public debate and state regulation, or engage in civic protest (Maniates 2001). In this way, the example of the environmental imagination foregrounds the discussion that follows. First, a review of literature in social practice theories and sustainable consumption shows the limits of individual choice. Secondly, it draws attention to the fact that when it comes to 'saving the planet', civic and political engagement are highly relevant topics for sustainable consumption research. The discussion below prefaces the analytic component of the chapter, which draws on qualitative data collected in a comparative ethnographic study of environmental civic practices in local food movements.

SOCIAL PRACTICES: BEYOND BEHAVIOR AND INDIVIDUAL ACTION

Social scientists have long demonstrated reasons to be wary of the notion of 'individualized' behaviors. One prominent theme in the sociology of sustainable consumption is that labeling these practices as individualized is flawed. For instance, Dubuisson-Quellier (2013) describes the collective dimension of consumption practices, building on the work of Pierre Bourdieu and Mary Douglas to show that consumption choices are deeply embedded in notions of status and reciprocity and projects of identity building. This work highlights how seemingly 'private' decisions are made with reference to cultural norms and other institutions, while reminding us of the socially constructed nature of all institutions. In another example, Willis and Schor (2012) argue that viewing sustainable consumption as a strictly private activity is too simplistic. The authors use several examples to unpack the association between 'individualized' acts and self-interested acts and point out that private sphere actions (such as buying local food) are often judged to be egoistic whereas public sphere acts are cast in an altruistic light. They argue that a consumer paying a premium for a product she believes to be socially and ecologically just is more altruistic than a business owner donating money to a political candidate in the hopes of advancing his own interests. Willis and Schor support these hypothetical examples with survey data from the United States that show that sustainable consumption and political engagement are correlated – political consumption does not displace political activism.

Scholarship like the examples above reminds us that sustainable practices do not exist simply because a website inspires citizens to lower their thermostat, and that 'private' decisions like turning down the heat to save energy are more accurately viewed as the outcome of collective mobilization. What these studies do not elucidate is the interstitial space between activities that take place within the home and activities and conversations that occur in the public sphere. Unpacking the link between private and public practices is an overlooked and vital component of the study of sustainable consumption – and the focus of this chapter. Practices that connect private and public spheres may do so by articulating the importance of sustainable consumption and infusing related practices (for example, shorter showers, better light bulbs) with a sense of efficacy for cultivating socio-ecological change. The first aim of this chapter is to draw attention to that work, which we label 'environmental civic practices'. Our second objective is to consider whether shedding light on the nature of environmental civic practices can help researchers and practitioners understand contemporary resistance to civic and political engagement.

Although the notion of individualized behavior is aptly charged with being too simplistic, similarly the premise of relying on spending patterns to effect sustainable outcomes warrants skepticism. Looking past the debate about whether private acts of consumption are self-interested or not, several findings foreground our discussion of their importance for civic and political engagement. First, acts such as recycling and purchasing local food can mask untenable levels of resource consumption. Kennedy et al. (2015) found the highest levels of environmental impact exist among households also likely to adopt pro-environmental behaviors. Secondly, some scholars argue that pursuing social change through shopping decisions displaces collective political consciousness (Maniates 2001; Shah et al. 2012; Szasz 2007). Finally, regardless of whether sustainable consumption is positive or negative for projects of social change, the proliferation of such responses to collective action problems is indicative of daily contemporary life, and therefore a topic well suited to theories of social practice.

At the nexus of social practice theories and sustainable consumption, existing research has focused on energy, water, and food consumption. For instance, Spaargaren (2011) identifies six domains (or 'fields') relevant to sustainable consumption: food, leisure, dwelling, mobility, personal care, and hobbies. In contrast to the robustness of research into household practices, there is comparatively little environmentally-oriented social practice theoretical scholarship on civic and political engagement on environmental issues. This is a surprising oversight given that a rich theoretical and empirically informed body of research on social movements illuminates the importance of collective mobilization and resistance work for projects of social change (see Wright and Boudet 2012 for an overview). Given the myriad established barriers to living sustainably (from price premiums to cultural norms), civic and political engagement are central to framing the importance of sustainable consumption and drawing attention to the power relations, favored access, and privileged discourses that obfuscate efforts to live within our planetary means (Freudenberg 2005).

The study of environmental civic practices might be informed by overlapping with existing scholarship on organizations and social movements.[1] This work can provide a foundation for seeing ways to synthesize individual and collective approaches to sustainable consumption. For example, Dubuisson-Quellier's (2013) research highlights how a social movement organization can advance its agenda for collective social change by encouraging individuals to adopt pro-social and pro-environmental purchasing practices. Similarly, Middlemiss (2011a) demonstrates that individual involvement in environmental community organizations leads to greater uptake of environmental behaviors in the home. However, it cannot be convincingly argued that ethical consumption leads to political activity; Dubuisson-Quellier et al. (2011) show that creating spaces or opportunities for ethical consumption does not necessarily lead to political action or awareness. Instead, they contend that consumption opportunities are imbued with distinct meanings for people depending on whether they are concerned primarily with personal health, a connection to rural livelihoods, or to complex projects of consumer-citizenship.

This chapter focuses on the space between individual and collective actions related to sustainable consumption. We first describe the study context and data sources and then turn our lens on the transitional space between individual and collective actions using qualitative data collected from eat-local movements in three Canadian cities. We conclude the chapter with insights into the potential for future research and a summary of the knowledge gained through this particular study.

THEORIZING COLLECTIVE ACTION: SOCIAL PRACTICE THEORIES AND BEYOND

Examining individual and household environmental behaviors from the perspective of social practice theories draws attention to the contextual parameters of social life, including everything from cultural norms (Giddens 1984; 1987) to physical infrastructure (Spaargaren 2003). From a social practices standpoint, we can understand the range of social, cultural, political, and institutional orders that foster some behaviors and make others much more difficult to perform. Consider, for example, consumption of bottled water: Szasz (2007) observed that amid concerns that water quality was declining in the United States, the most pronounced change in social practice was seen in personal water consumption. Thus a collective identity emerged among consumers that, in turn, fostered individualized approaches to environmental protection (bottled water). This rise in personal bottled water consumption has been reliant on collectively acquired knowledge of contaminants in tap water, cultural norms asserting that it is each person's responsibility to protect herself against external risks (Beck 1992; Taylor 2004), and widespread accessibility of plastic water bottles (in terms of price, know-how, and retail availability). In this way, our shared collective contexts encourage individualized responses. Szasz argues that one of the obvious limitations of this approach to risk management is that many contaminants cannot be kept at bay through individual consumption choice and rather require state regulation – consider for example air pollution or radiation.

Scholarship on social practice theories has yielded other important advances to the study of human–environment interactions. For instance, Shove (2003) used historical analysis to show that water consumption remains (often unsustainably) high due to social norms for cleanliness and housing infrastructure like indoor plumbing and high-flow showers, while Spaargaren (2003) developed a case study of utility providers in the Netherlands to demonstrate the importance of supportive policy and technical systems in the uptake of renewable energy. A review of the literature on social practice theories applied to sustainable consumption shows a great deal of work on the structuration of household-level actions such as bathing and driving (see for instance Shove 2003; Warde 2005). Even studies that document the transition from individual- to community-level practices tend to focus on the impact of the community level on the individual level (for example, Middlemiss 2011a; Shove and Pantzar 2005) rather than on those practices that might foster civic and political engagement. In contrast to rich work on the structuration of household consumption (for example, Doyle 2014; Sahakian and Wilhite 2014), comparatively little research has applied social practice theories to environmentally significant political mobilization.

At the nexus of sustainable consumption and social practice theories, few efforts have been devoted to understanding the interstitial space between individual and collective approaches to sustainability. Of the few examples, Middlemiss' (2010; 2011a; 2011b) work is of relevance, as it explores the impact that membership in a community of interest has on individuals' sustainable household practices. This example illustrates the power of shared norms but is relatively silent on what some authors suggest is a more transformative role for collectivities: 'the building of power through collective action' (Bunyan 2012, p. 129). This is a topic central to the study of social movements but largely unconnected to environmental social practice theories. Nonetheless, Middlemiss' research indicates that there exists fertile terrain between private practices and civic and political engagement by cultivating shared norms.

To inform a more thorough understanding of the link between private and public spheres, we briefly discuss the types of studies that are of relevance. The first example focuses on the role of social movements. From a social movements perspective, much work exists on ethical consumption that highlights the role of communities and organizations. For example, Weber et al. (2008) demonstrate how individual preferences for grass-fed meat and dairy products proliferate through the activities of social movement organizations. These organizations challenge mainstream cultural meanings, forge connections between producers and consumers, and support identity-building work that allows consumers and producers to shift toward grass-fed products. Other examples can be found in the area of food studies, where scholars have engaged similar questions at the periphery of social practice theories and sustainable consumption. Goodman et al. (2012, p. 4) argue that activists working in alternative food networks 'are mapping different ways forward by creating new economic and cultural spaces for the trading, production, and consumption of food [with] . . . ethical "qualifications" [that] distinguish them from [conventional] products'. Again, this work points to the active construction of opportunities for individualized expressions of citizenship. Finally, research in environmental justice has demonstrated that action on environmental threats is often a response to two feelings: first, that no one else will step forth to address the issue and, secondly, that the issue cannot be tackled alone (Cable and Shriver 1995). This third example moves toward better understanding the nature of those practices that synthesize private and public spheres.

Social practice theories within the topic of sustainable consumption have focused almost exclusively on household-level actions. Even the rare analyses of civic and political practices are studied with an eye to estimating individuals' ability to reduce their own impact, rather than their ability to collectively overcome the myriad barriers to sustainable practices across multiple domains (Spaargaren 2011). For instance, Shove and Pantzar's (2005) work shows how communities of interest (for instance in Nordic walking) can increase how commonly a behavior is practiced by individuals in a particular area. Middlemiss (2011b) offers a similar finding: that people who are members of environmental communities of interest (such as a church group trying to encourage sustainable lifestyles) can change their household consumption habits. Without discounting the significance of this scholarship, the current chapter aims to open up new theoretical territory for the study of sustainable consumption. We use a social practices perspective to explore the discourse and actions that link civic and political sustainability acts to shifts in household consumption and to assess why individual actions dominate the contemporary environmental imagination.

ENVIRONMENTAL CIVIC PRACTICES

Civic practices are a key sensitizing concept for understanding the space between individual and collective actions. Drawing from her ethnographic study of voluntary associations in the United States, Eliasoph (1996; 1998) describes civic practices as integrating discourse and action in the pursuit of creating spaces and opportunities for collective identities. Civic practices foster cultural norms that encourage active citizenship; they generate precedent for getting involved in public life. To offer an example: in a context where civic practices are supportive of active citizenship, concern with contaminants in drinking water might foster public discussion about the need for regulatory reform, pricing of environmental externalities, and transparency to reveal the most egregious polluters rather than induce people to consume bottled water. Eliasoph (1996) observed that in the absence of supportive civic practices, political consciousness evaporates, as there is no cultural infrastructure to foster debate and discussion on the common good. Environmental civic practices, which we will discuss in the next section, can populate the space between individual and collective action by opening up opportunities to awaken latent political consciousness and generate options and pathways to civic action.

We introduce the term 'environmental civic practices' to refer to actions that use formal and informal conversations, and visible practice of alternative low-consumption practices, to cultivate an environmental imagination. Environmental civic practices synthesize the transitional space between private (for example, household) and public (for example, media, town meetings) spheres. In some contexts, environmental civic practices might simply be introducing a sustainable consumption practice to a new setting, thereby instilling a sense that seemingly private practices have a public orientation. For instance, starting a community garden can develop a discursive and physical space to invite formerly private practices into a semi-public space (McClintock 2014). Environmental civic practices may be commonplace, but without a lens to identify such practices and evaluate their impact, the potential that they hold to confront socio-ecological problems could escape scholarly and practical attention.

STUDY SETTING AND METHODS

In Canada, where the qualitative data for this chapter were collected, evidence suggests that group-centered political engagement is not an integral part of daily life for most people. While an increasing proportion of Canadians have volunteered over the past decade, rising from 32–34 percent in 1998–2003 to 42 percent in 2008 (Statistics Canada 1998; 2000; 2003; 2008), this increase is taking place alongside a rise in individualized responses to socio-ecological issues (for example, boycotting, searching for information on an issue). Accompanying this prominence of

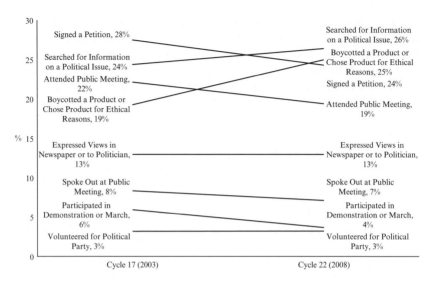

Source: Statistics Canada (2003; 2008).

Figure 3.1 Percentage of respondents engaged in eight political activities

individual-focused action has been a decline in and lack of group-oriented political activities such as attending a public meeting or participating in a political demonstration (Figure 3.1). These macro-level trends are suggestive of a context (likely not limited to Canada) that fosters and maintains a choice-based attitude to political engagement. That is, even political action is becoming more individualized.

To understand the space between individual and collective efforts to foster more sustainable consumption practices, we examined environmental civic practices in data collected between May 2013 and May 2014. With the help of two research assistants, we collected interview and participant observation data from three Canadian cities: Edmonton, Toronto, and Victoria. Our focus was on how people involved in reaching beyond private ethical consumption and production choices became engaged in trying to reduce the environmental and social costs of the food system. In each city, our sampling frame included farmers; municipal, provincial, and federal employees; entrepreneurs; community members; and employees of non-profit organizations. We recruited participants through the use of knowledgeable insiders: residents of the city who were part of established networks of individuals seeking to transform the food system to be more locally resilient. We supplemented this approach with participants recruited through a more formal process. Using popular food-related email listservs in each city, we posted a recruitment flyer explaining our aim to hear from people working to promote sustainable food systems in their work or volunteer time.

The interviews ranged in length from 45 minutes to three hours. Most meetings were held at cafés or restaurants, though some were conducted at farms, community gardens, and offices. The interviews were professionally transcribed and entered into qualitative data organization software (NVivo 10). We conducted 22 interviews in Edmonton, 19 in Toronto, and 16 in Victoria, resulting in 57 interviews in total. In each study site, we attended food-related events as participant observers. We visited farmers' markets, community gardens, food banks, permaculture gardens, and municipal food-strategy meetings. In all, we recorded over 30 hours of interactions at public events. Observers wrote up field notes to document and summarize these proceedings and the field notes were also entered into NVivo 10. We coded the data using the constant comparison method: once themes were established, we created codes that represented their breadth and the relationships among them. We continued to conduct interviews until theoretical saturation was reached, as indicated by repetition of themes rather than the development of new themes.

Bearing in mind the retreat of traditional political participation and the rise of individual approaches to civic and political engagement in Canada, we look now to the environmental civic practices that synthesize individual and collective responses to socio-ecological issues. Using the qualitative data we collected from key leaders in local food movements, we introduce here examples of these civic practices to develop a greater understanding of the conditions under which environmental civic practices arise, as well as their potential limitations.

WHAT ARE ENVIRONMENTAL CIVIC PRACTICES? HOW ARE THEY STRUCTURED?

As modes of engagement that foster an environmental imagination, environmental civic practices generate responses to problematic human–environment interactions. In this way, environmental civic practices are different from individual and collective actions – they synthesize the individual and the collective. Each of the participants whom we observed and with whom we spoke provided us with examples of environmental civic practices. These practices differed in some senses – such as whether the practice was based in discourse or action, or whether it engaged like-minded individuals or sought to expand support by engaging new audiences. Regardless, environmental civic practices share an emphasis on creating contexts for citizen engagement.

Environmental civic practices involve a complex constellation of thoughts, speech acts, and activities. Dana, who volunteers her time to work with a community-organizing group in Edmonton, is constantly fostering and maintaining strategic relationships. She will take people out for coffee and listen to their concerns and their interests, and connect individuals with shared interests to one another in her pursuit of stronger civic collective action. Dana says that she sees her most significant role as a facilitator, connecting people who want to create a more sustainable food system and convincing others not yet committed. This is an environmental civic practice, in that Dana is trying to create spaces for citizens' concerns to take a less ethereal form and foster or add to public debate. As a practice, her approach comprises different activities. Here is Dana's description of her actions:

> First of all I just try to be curious and listen, and I'm always on a talent search. I'm looking for the people who seem to have a following. Not necessarily the movers and shakers – what I'm looking for is those leaders who have a following who are building things with others, not a one-man show. I can engage people by email and phone perhaps, but I also make direct phone calls. I've got a very long list of contacts. So that's the model, I'm always trying to build that team and looking for the organizers and those who are open to listening.

Dana's civic practices entail bodily activities (going to meetings, making telephone calls), mental activities (keeping track of who's who, assessing their leadership abilities), things (a well-used notebook with endless contacts and details, an agenda to coordinate her volunteer and work schedules), know-how (cultural knowledge of how to approach people, how to listen), and knowledge about states of emotion and motivational knowledge. Taken together, her work is particularly important for developing community organizing by connecting disparate individuals working at similar goals.

Environmental civic practices can also foster institutional reform. In the next example Blair, who works for a non-profit organization in Toronto but was previously employed by government, explains his sense that the policy impact of local food work is limited by activists' approaches to reaching the ears of policy makers. Like Dana, many of the activities that comprise Blair's environmental civic practices are based on communication and networking. Being part of a civil society organization *and* understanding the logic of the state allows him to play the role of translator. By explaining the passion of food-movement activists in a way that civil servants can understand, he is creating a context for change-oriented conversations related to human–environment interactions:

> I have a skillset that this movement lacks. By hopping outside government and civil society, I'm dragging both sides together. I had a senior government bureaucrat say to me, 'You know, I'm not set up to deal with the [food] movement. I get what you're saying and I get all of this energy on the food movement, but we're institutionally not set up to deal with it.'
>
> By me having a lot of knowledge of the processes and people, and being able to frame issues in a way that government understands, I'm continuing on the work that I did [in the government] but I'm able to mentor people . . . I'm like a plumber and if you don't know how to do plumbing, it's just a mystery. You look at this collection of pipes and you go, I don't understand what to do here. I'm trying to give them the tools.

Blair's explanation brings to the fore many concepts central to theories of social practice. He is articulating his *sens practique*, or sense of the game (Bourdieu 1977) and making clear that knowing the rules of the game in various institutional contexts can provide an avenue for individuals' socio-ecological concerns to influence institutional reform. By creating a space for conversations that hitherto were stuck in institutional silos, Blair's environmental civic practice is bridging individual and collective subjectivities. His specific skills include knowing how to adopt language that conveys the needs of the local food movement in a way that seems important and relevant to policy for government bureaucrats, and his aptitude as a mentor teaching other activists how to communicate their message.

Another example of environmental civic practices based in language is from Brian, a government employee in Edmonton. He explains that in his workplace, local food production and consumption are viewed as marginal activities. Brian feels its location at the periphery of policy constitutes a barrier to expanding the prevalence of local food and he uses linguistic environmental civic practices to overcome the barrier. His practice includes identifying those in positions of authority and reminding them about local food in non-threatening ways:

> I'm constantly popping my head in to remind [those in charge] about new developments in local food or possibly synergistic projects. I have to go about promoting local food through collaboration, creating an 'us versus them' situation won't help. It's not easy to bring the issues up with people who may see local food in a certain light so I use language that integrates different values, like I say 'stakeholder' rather than 'industry' and 'producer' instead of 'farmer'. That sort of lets them see that local food fits with their worldview too.

These rhetorical practices create new opportunities to cultivate greater production and consumption of local food and draw in potential allies.

Brian's discursive civic practices are creating contexts for collective mobilization and building an incremental approach to institutional reform, by establishing the groundwork for policies that support local food. Linguistic environmental civic practices like Brian's were common among local food advocates who were surrounded by individuals whose schema of food consumption excluded locally produced food on economic, cultural, or political grounds. Thus we heard about similar practices from a former city councilor in Victoria trying to encourage the development of community gardens on municipal lands and a farmer in Edmonton who was among the first in the area to take up organic agriculture. In each of these cases, the speaker recounted toeing the line between pushing for change and drawing attention to similarities between their environmental practice and the mainstream practice.

An additional example of environmental civic practices is teaching – most frequently used to promote individual actions. Reckwitz (2002) explains that lack of knowledge and know-how is a significant barrier to changing practices. Our respondents intuited these obstacles and found ways to create public and semi-public contexts to transfer their knowledge about local food production, preservation, and consumption to others (a large number of participants (43/57) integrated knowledge-based environmental civic practices into their daily lives). Examples of these civic practices included an aquaponics expert who staged demonstrations at malls in Edmonton to reach beyond the usual scope of local food proponents, and community gardeners in all cities who hosted workshops on canning, visited local schools to teach children about growing food, and dropped by local senior centers to cook shared meals from communal gardens. Nikki, a community gardener in Victoria, explains how she used formal and informal teaching in her daily life as a tool to expand the practice of local food:

> I try to go to places where not everyone is a gardener. When you talk to them not only about how to grow but also how to eat, usually people try. I think that's why I'm involved in those organizations and I'm always talking about food. For ten years I've talked about food. I started by organizing dinners with sustainable farmers once a month and some of the people I met back then are now teaching other people to start growing food.

As with Brian's linguistic civic practice, Nikki's teaching practices seek to reach beyond the audiences already in support of local food. Her approach is to position growing food as a practice that can enhance the health of individuals, communities, and the soil rather than rely strictly on personal benefits because she says improvements in individual health are rarely immediately apparent and people may lose interest in the practice.

Most of our respondents recognized that eating local food is not the 'default option' but a more complicated consumption choice often demanding more time, more money, and more know-how, particularly for those growing their own food. In reaction, participants use environmental civic practices to overcome barriers to the practice of eating local food (such as fighting for affordable land for farmers, starting community gardens, teaching others to grow food). However, we were surprised that we rarely heard participants use environmental civic practices to encourage resistance efforts or challenge cultural meanings that stand in the way of more widespread urban agriculture. A significant ideological barrier might include acquiescence to municipal governments' perceived need for economic growth (Logan and Molotch 1987). Other significant practical barriers to the expansion of urban agriculture may be the combination of skills needed to grow food and the money required to purchase local produce. To use the language of Dowie's (1996) environmental imagination, we see environmental civic practices regularly encouraging 1) collective adoption of individual actions, 2) community organizing to support local food production and consumption, and 3) some evidence of reform to policy barriers. We saw little evidence of efforts to encourage more substantive institutional reform such as challenging cultural barriers, political and economic interests, or the mainstream practices of conventional agriculture.

HOW DO ENVIRONMENTAL CIVIC PRACTICES SHAPE COLLECTIVE ACTION?

In addressing this question, we first comment on how practitioners are recruited to environmental civic practices, and then discuss how these practices can lead to collective action. In our interviews and observations, we identified two conditions that encourage practitioners to pursue environmental civic practices. The first condition is when an activity that has been deemed to be valuable by a cohort of people (for example, growing food in community gardens) is threatened by the state, the market, or civil society. The second is when individual actions are perceived as ineffective to overcome the challenge in question. We will illustrate these conditions with an example.

In this illustration, the valued activity is local, organic food production. Consumers can generally support this activity by buying organic food at farmers' markets, through community-supported agriculture, and from direct sales. In many ways, infrastructural barriers to local food are being challenged, and almost always through collective action: new farmers' markets open each year, community gardens now have waiting lists, and grocery stores have adopted local and organic food labels. Despite the successes related to creating local food infrastructure, confrontation with economic institutions (in this case, the residential and commercial development industry) limits the potential growth of local food production and consumption practices. For example, in one of our study sites, the city council announced plans to rezone a large expanse of high-quality agricultural land for residential development. Using the physical and virtual spaces created through the environmental civic practices described in the previous section, a wave of community mobilization staked a strong position against the rezoning through newspaper, television, and blog posts, as well as protests at multiple council meetings (for more details, see Beckie et al. 2013). A valued activity (local food production) was threatened by residential and commercial development and a broad swath of citizens engaged in an ongoing series of public debates and protests.

Damon, an entrepreneur and community organizer, describes a similar experience in Toronto. In this particular case, the food-related practice is community gardening, which was proliferating and strongly supported by local residents. In this example, an unsanctioned community garden was threatened when the parks division of the municipal government decided to remove the garden. Despite the fact that there are very few food-related protests in Toronto, the potential of closure galvanized community-gardening proponents, even leading to another protest:

> There was a protest last year, when the Parks Department took out this community garden that people planted at Queens Park. This garden had been put there without sanction but it was very public and supported. Other groups partnered with the people who wanted to keep their garden. A good amount of people from different backgrounds came out and this led to another community protest that was very interesting. There was another community garden that was having problems starting up in a mixed-income neighborhood that had food-access problems. After the Queens Park group held their protest, a big group of people went to City Hall. I was walking up to it and was like, 'Oh crap, there are all these neighbors who are against the garden', but then when I got there, everybody had signs reading, 'We support community gardens for all.' They all got together and it was really nice to see. It's interesting, because a lot of the food policy work is usually more behind the scenes.

In this excerpt, Damon's description draws attention to public support, an outside threat, and a collective sense that a united voice constituted a more effective challenge than individual actions. To reiterate, environmental civic practices recruited greater numbers of people under two conditions: first, when an activity that a cohort of people felt should play a role in their lifestyles was challenged by infrastructural constraints, policies, or a perceived lack of social awareness; and, secondly, under a strong sense that individual efforts were insufficient to tackle the barrier. Under these conditions, people took steps beyond their individual actions to make it easier for others to adopt particular food-related practices. Whether this response would have been as forthcoming and effective without environmental civic practices, like those Dana implemented to create the groundwork for community action, is not certain. However, relational work – rarely captured in surveys of pro-environmental behaviors or lists of ways to 'save the planet' – is an extremely important practice for synthesizing individual and collective actions (O'Shaughnessy and Kennedy 2010). With a critical mass of citizens finding a space to manifest their political consciousness into action, environmental civic practices provide a bridge between individual and collective identities.

SYNTHESIZING INDIVIDUAL AND COLLECTIVE ACTION

For environmental social scientists and other researchers interested in human–environment interactions, it is important to understand how a society reacts to a threat to its socio-ecological sustainability. The popularity of individualized actions vis-à-vis community organizing and institutional reform is reflected in social practices. At the outset of this chapter, we stated our aim to identify and describe environmental civic practices, as we believe these forms of engagement can synthesize individual and collective actions by creating opportunities for engaged citizenship. Our qualitative inquiry focused on identifying environmental civic practices and the conditions under which they can arise.

Environmental civic practices do indeed create space for people to talk about and/or take action on their concerns for the socio-ecological impacts of mainstream daily practices. These practices are not synonymous with community organizing or institutional reform; rather, they help to create the groundwork for such collective responses. In Eliasoph's (1998) terms, they establish an 'etiquette' that allows individuals to discuss concerns in public settings. On a positive note, the environmental civic practices we observed create opportunities for collective political activity, such as fundraising for new campaigns, building networks of support to call upon for civic protest, and offering a place for citizens to air their concerns and find common cause.

Our second objective was to evaluate the potential for these civic practices to unsettle the structures that individualize environmental responsibility, and here our findings are somewhat less optimistic. Rather than cultivate an environmental imagination that challenges socially mainstream approaches to food consumption, environmental civic practices among local food advocates are more typically employed to work *with* powerful elites to convince them that local food is a non-threatening practice that could complement the industrial food system. Though such allegiances ensure more widespread consumption and production of local food, forging alliances with individual and institutional interests committed to maintaining the status quo ultimately props up unjust and unsustainable modes of eating. Environmental civic practices that are used to open up new opportunities to vote with one's dollar reinforce the common wisdom that individual action is the most effective way to support change and that dismantling problematic institutions is the job of conscientious consumers. Critics of individualized strategies for change argue that the state is better positioned to defend the public good (Fraser 1992; Perrin 2006). For while our participants are indeed creating opportunities for individuals to ground their political consciousness in discourse and action, the most common practices create opportunities primarily for political consumerism rather than a broad array of engagement tactics such as community organizing, political campaigning, or public protest.

There are many structures in everyday life that preclude greater community organizing and institutional reform, from the demands of the labor market to how cities, towns, neighborhoods, and homes are designed. Yet perhaps most prominently a robust environmental imagination is hampered by an economic system predicated on constant growth. The environmental civic practices we identified do not overtly challenge these barriers, but seek to circumvent many of them through the creation of social networks and a defense and reinforcement of sustainable household practices. Thus we see the need to distinguish between community organizing intended to bring a collective dimension to individual consumption practices and community organizing aimed at cultivating strategies to resist powerful interests and political and economic inequality. In our sample, we witnessed a dominance of the former type and little direct engagement with issues of power and inequality in both conventional and local agriculture. The reticence to discuss injustice is concerning for advocates of sustainability given evidence that efforts to protect the environment in the absence of justice are not tenable (Alkon and Agyeman 2011). Putting aside the question of whether or not the environmental practices we observed are effective, our data show that when an activity (such as community gardening or organic farming) is associated with positive emotions and associations *and is* constrained by systems of provision and social norms, barriers to the practice can recruit participants into a space created through environmental civic practices. Collective responses are more likely to result when people sense that individual action is insufficient to address the barriers in question (in our case, barriers to local food consumption and production).

When applied to the topic of sustainable consumption, social practice theories have thus far drawn attention to daily practices with direct consequences for material consumption. Meanwhile, environmental sociologists and others have illustrated the limits of consumption and other individual actions in the home as a social movement strategy (Dubuisson-Quellier 2013; Johnston 2008). Thus, while scholars of sustainable consumption have developed social practice accounts of bathing, cooking, home heating, and transportation, this chapter has identified a need to understand the everyday practices that can provide a place for political consciousness to challenge the cultural, political, and economic barriers that prevent sustainable practices from becoming a default option.

Given the efficacy of targeted and sustained civic engagement for tackling barriers to socially and environmentally beneficial practices, it is fitting for social practice theorists to interrogate environmental civic practices. In conclusion, we call for new scholarship at the juncture of social practice theories and sustainable consumption that uses the flexibility of an agency/ structure dualism to understand the rise of individualized actions and to account for emergent collective responses to environmental issues. Future studies of environmental civic practices would do well to develop greater understanding of how these transitional practices can cultivate spaces to engage in environmental politics beyond the marketplace. Environmental civic practices warrant the same scrutiny as showering or driving, for these are the actions that connect disparate pro-environmental individual actions with a collective orientation. Theories of social practice have the potential to explore the liminal space that synthesizes private and public spheres, and this space offers the potential to cultivate substantial pro-environmental change.

NOTE

1. These two areas of scholarship are relevant to the current area of study but beyond the scope of this chapter.

REFERENCES

Alkon, Alison H. and Julian Agyeman (eds) (2011), *Cultivating Food Justice: Race, Class, and Sustainability*, Cambridge, MA: MIT Press.

Beck, Ulrich (1992), *Risk Society: Towards a New Modernity*, Thousand Oaks, CA: Sage.

Beckie, Mary A., Lorelei L. Hanson, and Deborah Schrader (2013), 'Farms or freeways? Citizen engagement and municipal governance in Edmonton's food and agriculture strategy development', *Journal of Agriculture, Food Systems, and Community Development*, **4** (1), 15–31.

Bourdieu, Pierre (1977), *Outline of a Theory of Practice*, translated by Richard Nice, New York: Cambridge University Press.

Bunyan, Paul (2012), 'Partnership, the big society and community organizing: between romanticizing, problematizing and politicizing community', *Community Development Journal*, **48** (1), 119–133.

Cable, Sherry and Thomas Shriver (1995), 'Production and extrapolation of meaning in the environmental justice movement', *Sociological Spectrum*, **15** (4), 419–442.

Dowie, Mark (1996), *Losing Ground: American Environmentalism at the Close of the Twentieth Century*, Cambridge, MA: MIT Press.

Doyle, Ruth (2014), 'Washing', in A.R. Davies, F. Fahy and H. Rau (eds), *Challenging Consumption: Pathways to a More Sustainable Future*, New York: Routledge, pp. 135–157.

Dubuisson-Quellier, Sophie (2013), 'A market mediation strategy: how social movements seek to change firms' practices by promoting new principles of product valuation', *Organization Studies*, **34** (5–6), 683–703.

Dubuisson-Quellier, Sophie, Claire Lamine, and Ronan Le Velley (2011), 'Citizenship and consumption: mobilisation in alternative food systems in France', *Sociologia Ruralis*, **51** (3), 304–323.

Eliasoph, Nina (1996), 'Making a fragile public: a talk-centered study of citizenship and power', *Sociological Theory*, **14** (3), 262–289.

Eliasoph, Nina (1998), *Avoiding Politics: How Americans Produce Apathy in Everyday Life*, New York: Cambridge University Press.

Fraser, Nancy (1992), 'Rethinking the public sphere: a contribution to the critique of actually existing democracy', *Social Text*, **25/26**, 56–80.

Freudenberg, William R. (2005), 'Privileged access, privileged accounts: toward a socially structured theory of resources and discourses', *Social Forces*, **84** (1), 89–114.

Giddens, Anthony (1984), *The Constitution of Society*, Malden, MA: Polity Press.

Giddens, Anthony (1987), *Sociology: A Brief but Critical Introduction*, 2nd edn, Orlando: Harcourt Brace Javanovich.

Goodman, David, E. Melanie DuPuis, and Michael K. Goodman (2012), *Alternative Food Networks: Knowledge, Practice, and Politics*, New York: Routledge.

Kennedy, Emily H., Harvey Krahn, and Naomi T. Krogman (2015), 'Are we counting what counts? A closer look at environmental concern, pro-environmental behaviour, and carbon footprint', *Local Environment*, **20** (2), 220–236.

Johnston, Josée (2008), 'The citizen-consumer hybrid: ideological tensions and the case of the whole foods market', *Theory and Society*, **37** (3), 229–270.

Logan, John R. and Harvey L. Molotch (1987), *Urban Fortunes: The Political Economy of Place*, Berkeley: University of California Press.

Maniates, Michael F. (2001), 'Individualization: plant a tree, buy a bike, save the world?', *Global Environmental Politics*, **1** (3), 31–52.

McClintock, Nathan (2014), 'Radical, reformist, and garden-variety neoliberal:

coming to terms with urban agriculture's contradictions', *Local Environment*, **19** (2), 147–171.

Middlemiss, Lucie (2010), 'Reframing individual responsibility for sustainable consumption: lessons from environmental justice and ecological citizenship', *Environmental Values*, **19** (2), 147–167.

Middlemiss, Lucie (2011a), 'The effects of community-based action for sustainability on participants' lifestyles', *Local Environment*, **16** (3), 265–280.

Middlemiss, Lucie (2011b), 'The power of community: how community-based organizations stimulate sustainable lifestyles among participants', *Society & Natural Resources*, **24** (11), 1157–1173.

O'Shaughnessy, Sara and Emily Huddart Kennedy (2010), 'Relational activism: reimagining women's environmental work as cultural change', *Canadian Journal of Sociology*, **35** (4), 551–572.

Perrin, Andrew J. (2006), *Citizen Speak: The Democratic Imagination in American Life*, Chicago: University of Chicago Press.

Reckwitz, Andreas (2002), 'Toward a theory of social practices: a development in culturalist theorizing', *European Journal of Social Theory*, **5** (2), 243–263.

Sahakian, Marlyne and Harold Wilhite (2014), 'Making practice theory practicable: towards more sustainable forms of consumption', *Journal of Consumer Culture*, **14** (1), 25–44.

Shah, Dhavan V., Lewis Friedland, Chris Wells, Young Mie Kim, and Hernando Rojas (2012), 'Communication, consumers, and citizens: revisiting the politics of consumption', *The Annals of the American Academy of Political and Social Science*, **644** (1), 6–19.

Shah, Dhavan V., Douglas M. McLeod, Lewis Friedland, and Michelle R. Nelson (2007), 'The politics of consumption/the consumption of politics', *The Annals of the American Academy of Political and Social Science*, **611** (1), 6–15.

Shove, Elizabeth (2003), *Comfort, Cleanliness and Convenience: The Social Organization of Normality*, New York: Berg.

Shove, Elizabeth and Mika Pantzar (2005), 'Consumers, producers and practices: understanding the invention and reinvention of Nordic walking', *Journal of Consumer Culture*, **5** (1), 43–64.

Spaargaren, Gert (2003), 'Sustainable consumption: a theoretical and environmental policy perspective', *Society & Natural Resources*, **16** (8), 687–701.

Spaargaren, Gert (2011), 'Theories of practices: agency, technology, and culture', *Global Environmental Change*, **21** (3), 813–822.

Statistics Canada (1998), *Public Use Microdata File: General Social Survey – Time Use Survey (Cycle 12)*, Ottawa: Statistics Canada.

Statistics Canada (2000), *Public Use Microdata File: General Social Survey – Access to and Use of Information Communication Technology (Cycle 14)*, Ottawa: Statistics Canada.

Statistics Canada (2003), *Public Use Microdata File: General Social Survey – Social Engagement (Cycle 17)*, Ottawa: Statistics Canada.

Statistics Canada (2008), *Public Use Microdata File: General Social Survey – Social Networks (Cycle 22)*, Ottawa: Statistics Canada.

Stern, Paul C. (2000), 'Toward a coherent theory of environmentally significant behaviour', *Journal of Social Issues*, **56** (3), 407–424.

Szasz, Andrew (2007), *Shopping Our Way to Safety: How We Changed from Protecting the Environment to Protecting Ourselves*, Minneapolis: University of Minnesota Press.

Taylor, Charles (2004), *Modern Social Imaginaries*, Durham, NC: Duke University Press.

Warde, Alan (2005), 'Consumption and theories of practice', *Journal of Consumer Culture*, **5** (13–14), 131–153.

Weber, Klaus, Kathryn L. Heinze, and Michaela DeSoucey (2008), 'Forage for thought: mobilizing codes in the movement for grass-fed meat and dairy products', *Administrative Science Quarterly*, **53** (3), 529–567.

Willis, Margaret M. and Juliet B. Schor (2012), 'Does changing a light bulb lead to changing the world? Political action and the conscious consumer', *The Annals of the American Academy of Political and Social Science*, **611** (1), 160–190.

Wright, Rachel A. and Hilary Schaffer Boudet (2012), 'To act or not to act: context, capability, and community response to environmental risk', *American Journal of Sociology*, **118** (3), 728–777.

4. Italy's Solidarity Purchase Groups as 'citizenship labs'

Francesca Forno, Cristina Grasseni, and Silvana Signori

INTRODUCTION

Contemporary Western societies have been identified as particular variants of advanced capitalism due to the shift from the primacy of production to consumption, and the fact that the 'consumer' has become a central societal figure vis-à-vis the declining relevance of the 'citizen' (Clarke et al. 2007). This is a process that, as is often pointed out, has favored the individualization and fragmentation of contemporary society (Bauman 2007). In fact, while the notion of the 'citizen' may be strongly linked to the notion of the 'common good', the term 'consumer' evokes primarily personal and instrumental preferences that are typically associated with the 'private good'.

Given the centrality of consumption in late capitalist societies, it should come as no surprise that many contemporary social movements have started to appeal to individuals in their role as consumers and have identified 'political consumerism' as an important form of action through which to bring about social change. Examples include groups devoted to protecting the environment, to ameliorating poverty, to overcoming corporate power, to resisting war, and to challenging organized crime (Forno and Graziano 2014). Political consumerism refers to the purchasing of goods and services based not only on price and product quality, but also on the evaluation of producers' behavior and production methods with respect to environmental sustainability, labor justice, and human rights. This mode of citizen participation stresses the importance of individual responsibility for the common good through acknowledgment that the act of consumption is a fundamental part of the production process (Micheletti 2009).

Although not new, since the mid-1990s the political use of consumption has experienced significant growth, even in contexts where it has long been a niche phenomenon, such as in southern Europe (Ferrer-Fons 2006;

Koos 2012). Throughout the Western world, there has been considerable increase in market demand for food, manufactured goods, and services from companies that ensure codes of conduct respectful of workers' rights and the environment. This development indicates that political consumerism today enjoys favorable cultural, political, and economic opportunities.

Perhaps not surprisingly, the growth of political consumerism has generated a great deal of scholarly interest. Many studies on the topic, however, have analyzed this phenomenon mainly from the perspective of individual consumers (Forno and Ceccarini 2006; Micheletti 2003; Stolle et al. 2005), while less attention has been paid to social movement organizations that promote a political vision of consumption and try to mobilize consumers in favor of their cause (Alexander and Ussher 2012; Balsiger 2010; Grasseni 2013; Graziano and Forno 2012; Sassatelli 2006).

This chapter specifically reflects on the recent rise of political consumerism in Italy. Rather than investigate this activity from a microeconomic point of view, considering consumers as individual actors in a value-neutral market, we analyze the expansion of political consumerism by connecting it to new social movement organizations, and by identifying it as a specific form of collective action. In Italy, the *Gruppi di Acquisto Solidale* (GASs or Solidarity Purchase Groups) have grown significantly over the last decade (Carrera 2009; Grasseni 2013; Graziano and Forno 2012; Rebughini 2008). Due to their numbers, GAS members constitute a viable sample for investigating the decision-making processes and organizational practices through which provisioning is being critically reinvented.

Our analysis shows that in such experiences alternative provisioning moves beyond individualized political consumerism and brings diverse collectives together. These collectives develop strategies of economic intervention in the name of the common good and critiques of commonly held conceptions of 'growth' as synonymous with 'development'. Unlike traditional consumer organizations that seek to protect customers from corporate abuse (such as unsafe products, predatory lending, or false advertising), GAS groups create a space for civic learning, building social capital, and considering opportunities for political mobilization, often counteracting or aiming to substitute inefficient governance in the realms of environmental stewardship and labor protection.

The chapter is structured as follows. We next provide a general description of GAS groups in Italy before proceeding to describe our research framework and data-collection process. The fourth section discusses the most relevant findings, focusing particularly on the socio-economic characteristics of GAS participants and the motivation behind their involvement, the structure and organization of GAS groups, and the ability of the groups to function as new socio-pedagogic laboratories where attitudes are translated into concrete behavior.

WHAT IS A GAS?

Although the first GAS in Italy was established during the mid-1990s, this particular type of buyers' group became increasingly common during the following decade when it spread to all of the Italian regions. This system, though, maintains its highest concentrations in the northern and central regions of the country. According to data provided by the website of the national GAS network, the number of self-registered GASs has risen from 153 in 2004, to 394 in 2008, to 518 in 2009, and to 977 in 2014 (see Figure 4.1).[1] However, these figures, as argued below, are likely significant underestimates of the real number of existing groups.

The GASs are mutual systems of provisioning, usually set up by groups of people who cooperate to buy food and other commonly used goods directly from producers at prices that are equitable to both parties. The organizations may collectively buy bread, pasta, flour, milk, dairy products, oil, fish, meat, detergents, wine, preserves, juices and jams, fruit and vegetables, and other items of everyday use (such as basic toiletries). They also increasingly purchase textiles and 'alternative' services such

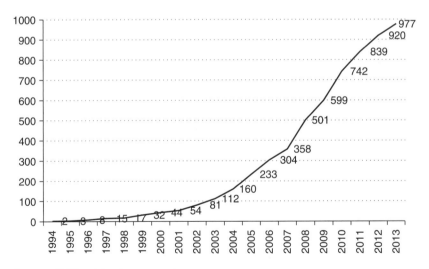

Source: GAS registered on www.retegas.org.

Figure 4.1   Growth trend of GAS in Italy, 1994–2013

as renewable energy and sustainable tourism. For GAS groups, the term 'solidarity' represents a sort of guiding principle in the choice of products and producers. This means that, unlike other collective purchasing groups, GASs do not simply strive to get the cheapest price, but instead choose their products and producers with the explicit goal of building a viable alternative to the 'consumer society', which they tend to regard as a societal model based on the exploitation of human and natural resources.

These criteria generally lead to a preference for local products as a way to minimize the environmental impact of transportation, but this approach also supports regional economies and increases the transparency of the food chain. Other criteria favor organic agriculture for environmental reasons, fair-trade goods out of an effort to assist disadvantaged producers by promoting their human rights, and reusable or eco-compatible goods to promote a sustainable lifestyle. Rather than as an end to itself, collective purchasing by GAS groups represents a way to foster awareness of environmental and social problems. Furthermore, this mode of provisioning constitutes a first step toward building a more just society. In this sense, GASs may be seen as a type of social movement as defined by della Porta and Diani (2006, p. 20) as 'distinct social processes, consisting of the mechanisms through which actors engage in collective action [through which they] are involved in conflictual relations with clearly identified opponents; [and through which they] are linked by dense informal networks; [and] share a distinct collective identity'.

As we shall see, compared with other 'alternative food networks' that have emerged in affluent countries over the last decade – such as the French AMAP (*Associations pour le Maintien d'une Agriculture Paysanne*) or the American CSA (Community-Supported Agriculture) – being part of a GAS requires a higher level of commitment and involvement. Members are in fact usually asked to participate actively in the organization of their group by taking part in the creation of norms, the management of financial and logistical activities, and the planning of convivial and informational activities. This is because GASs, unlike CSAs, are largely consumer- rather than producer-driven. Moreover, at the local level, once these groups achieve a critical mass, they sometimes assemble themselves into *Distretti di economia solidale* (Districts of Solidarity Economy) that are roughly similar to the Anglo-Saxon transition town movement and have explicit governance objectives (Grasseni 2013; Grasseni et al. 2015).

Our contention is that experiences in GASs move beyond political consumerism as a form of merely individual responsibility (Micheletti 2009) to develop collective, citizenship-driven alternative styles of provisioning. These groups facilitate both the circulation of resources (information, tasks, money, and goods) and common interpretations of everyday life, thus simultaneously providing a framework for collective action and enabling the actual deployment of alternative lifestyles. For example, each member of the group usually buys one item (e.g., pasta) in bulk on behalf of everyone else and then distributes it to other members of the GAS. This activity entails collecting orders from other group members, checking availability with the provider, traveling to pick up the order, paying in advance for everyone else, and arranging a time and place for other members to come by, pay up, and collect their share. However seemingly inefficient, this time-consuming method forces every member to be proactive, to participate in the group with equal responsibilities, and to engage in intensive processes of socialization (the making of telephone calls and sending of emails, the partaking in visits that inevitably lead to follow-up invitations to cultural and political events of common interest, the circulation of relevant readings and news on the group mailing list, and the opening up of space for discussion and exchange of mutual information on how to provision 'alternatively').

Within a GAS, political consumerism becomes much more than a way to compensate for the inability of institutions to pursue pro-environmental policies and human-rights protection through a so-called 'politics of the self' or 'life politics' (Giddens 1990). The GASs are collective experiences, designed to co-produce the common good by (re)building reciprocity and trust among diverse subjects operating in the same territory, directly intervening in local food provisioning chains, and reintroducing social and environmental sustainability issues in regional economies, sometimes with the explicit aim of participating in the governance of the territory.

RESEARCH DESIGN AND DATA COLLECTION

Between 2011 and 2013, the CORES Lab project *Inside Relational Capital* gathered detailed data about GAS groups in the northern Italian region of Lombardy through a two-tiered questionnaire, combined with qualitative insights from participant observation.[2] The aim of the research was to better understand the mechanisms and processes behind the diffusion of GAS groups in Italy, exploring individual decisions to join, as well as their internal organization and action strategies.

Lombardy, with approximately 10 million inhabitants, is the most densely populated Italian region and the part of the country estimated to have the highest concentration of GAS groups.[3] The informality that characterizes these groups, as well as their rapid spread since 2005, required us first to generate an accurate map of these organizations as a prerequisite to the implementation of our survey. A pilot project in and around the town of Bergamo mapped approximately twice the number of previously known GAS groups.[4]

The mapping of Lombardy-based GAS groups was enabled by close collaboration between the research team and individual GAS activists.[5] An internal 'facilitator' was identified for each of the 12 provinces of Lombardy (Bergamo, Brescia, Como, Cremona, Lecco, Lodi, Mantua, Milan, Monza, Pavia, Sondrio and Varese). Under the supervision of the research team, a member of the GAS movement compiled a list of groups in his/her own province on the basis of personal knowledge and access to peers. The local facilitators not only helped to build an accurate register of the active groups, but also made first contact with each GAS group in his/her province to explain the objectives of the research and to stimulate participation in the online survey.

Data collection took place via two online questionnaires. We designed an initial survey for completion by the representatives of each individual GAS that was aimed at gathering information about the operational characteristics of the group such as its internal organization, logistics, and means of communication. A supplementary questionnaire was intended for individual members of each group. The main objective of this part of the survey was to collect information about the features and motivations of the *gasistas*, such as their socio-economic profile, educational and professional background, reasons for joining, and perceived achievements.[6]

In both cases, we employed a closed-ended structure in the design of the questionnaires, with each consisting of 52 questions. The research team sent a letter to each facilitator asking him/her to disseminate the announcement of the survey to each GAS group in their respective geographic area. The surveys were administered online and completed directly by the GAS coordinators (one per group) and by *gasistas* (one per family in a group).

GAS activists are targeted for a large number of inquiries due to the attention that the organizations receive from political associations, media, and market-research companies. We thus arranged for prominent figures from the national GAS network (Tavolo RES) to endorse the research announcement so that the initiative would be perceived as a collaborative venture between GASs and university researchers, not as a top-down investigation into GAS activism. Internal access and support from the national network ensured a high degree of participation and valid results.

RESULTS

It is reasonable to presume that the profile of GAS members varies regionally due to historical, socio-economic, and political divisions in Italian society.[7] However, the high presence of GAS groups in Lombardy makes this area a particularly interesting case. The region has always been characterized by a broad range of active civic associations, a fact that has often been linked to the economic development of this region, which is the richest and most populous in Italy (Putnam 1993).

When we launched our research, some information about the internal organization of the GAS groups (as well as about the profile of their members) was already available. A handful of qualitative studies had already been published (Carrera 2009; Rebughini 2008) and all the CORES researchers had direct experience with alternative provisioning as members of different GAS groups. What was missing, however, was a quantitative study capable of producing a systematic empirical investigation of this social phenomenon. The survey gathered previously unavailable data to measure GAS characteristics, together with their presence and impact on local and regional economies.

The first significant finding of the research was that the number of GAS groups turned out to be much higher than the number of self-registered groups. Table 4.1 compares the number of formally registered groups with those detected through the CORES Lab project. We identified a total of 429 GAS groups in Lombardy through our outreach and mapping. Among these groups, 204 group coordinators and 1658 *gasistas* completed the online questionnaire.[8] Collaboration with local GAS leaders and the nationwide Tavolo RES ensured an exceptionally high turnout, reaching 48 percent among coordinators and 23 percent among individual *gasistas* throughout Lombardy.[9]

The survey provided an initial estimate of how much money families spend through a GAS. Total annual household expenditures are approximately €742 (US$941) per household. Considering that each group enrolls an average of 25 families of four people, each GAS would cater to the needs of around 100 consumers. Projecting these data onto the number of GAS groups in Lombardy (the 429 identified), the economic weight of these groups would account for about €8 million (US$10.2 million).

But what are the characteristics of the people who participate in these groups? What are the reasons for joining a GAS? How are these groups organized and how do they spread? Moreover, and perhaps most importantly, does participation in these groups really bring about changes in lifestyles and consumption patterns, or do GAS groups rather strictly aggregate individuals who already have certain values and habits?

Table 4.1 GAS surveyed in the provinces of Lombardy

Province	GAS self-registered	No. GAS detected through CORES Lab mapping	No. GAS completing the survey	% of coordinators completing the survey	No. of families in the mapped groups	No. of individual GAS members completing the survey	% of individual GAS members completing the survey
Milano	95	153	51	33.33	1851	368	19.88
Bergamo	24	62	44	70.97	1032	299	28.97
Brescia	23	50	22	44	704	198	28.13
Como	14	46	14	30.43	264	42	15.91
Varese	18	40	17	42.5	607	152	25.04
Monza e Brianza	23	33	23	69.7	763	224	29.36
Lecco	8	17	10	58.82	540	85	15.74
Pavia	7	11	9	81.82	392	70	17.86
Cremona	8	7	5	71.43	374	74	19.79
Mantova	4	4	3	75	115	39	33.91
Lodi	1	3	3	100	355	90	25.35
Sondrio	2	3	3	100	225	17	7.56
TOTAL	227	429	204	47.55	7122	1658	23.28

Source: CORES Lab project, 'Inside Relational Capital'.

Who Participates in GASs and Why?

The socio-economic profile of individuals who participate in GAS groups appears to be similar to those identified by other empirical research on political consumers (Forno and Ceccarini 2006; Micheletti 2003; Stolle et al. 2005). The GAS participants tend to be more often female (62 percent), confirming the tendency that women are more involved than men in political consumerism (either individual or organized) and neither very young nor very old.[10] Among those who responded to the question-naire, 49.6 percent were aged between 30 and 44 and 42.9 percent aged between 45 and 60. Our findings also revealed that GASs are made up mostly of families with children (71.8 percent), 25.6 percent of which have at least one child under five years old.

Among *gasistas*, the percentage of university graduates is also con-siderably higher than the national average (49.5 percent of those who completed the questionnaire had a university degree, compared with the national average of 13.5 percent recorded by the 2011 National Institute of Statistics census). *Gasistas* more frequently held white-collar jobs or were teachers (60.1 percent). By contrast, the percentage of blue-collar workers is limited (4.4 percent), as is the share of the unemployed (2.7 percent) and pensioners (4.1 percent). Although characterized by rather high 'cultural capital', families that participate in GAS groups (families made up of an average of four members) do not comprise particularly high income earners: 22.3 percent declared a net monthly income of less than €2000 (US$2537), 56 percent an income of between €2000 (US$2537) and €3500 (US$4440). Only 20 percent said they had an income of over €3500 (US$4440) (1.7 percent did not answer this question). This finding seems to suggest that, in contrast with individualized forms of political consumerism (cf. Forno and Ceccarini 2006), GAS groups may not attract members of the 'dominant class' or the bourgeoisie (Bourdieu 1984), but rather that fraction of the middle class that possesses high amounts of cultural capital but relatively little financial capital.

Gasistas are also usually engaged citizens and the majority of our respondents declared an interest in politics: 69.8 percent of them claimed to be very or fairly concerned about political issues. To keep up to date, *gasistas* use various channels of information such as the Internet (91.1 percent) or radio or television news (84.3 percent). They also often discuss political issues with friends and colleagues (79.1 percent). This finding is indicative of how social and political issues are part of the daily lives of these individuals.

The high interest in politics recorded among *gasistas* is however accompanied by relatively low confidence in certain institutions. Less than 25 percent trust political parties at all (only 8 percent of our sample replied that they trust political parties 'very much' or 'somewhat'), television (2.8 percent), the World Bank (3.4 percent), Parliament (7.7 percent), or industrial associations (23.4 percent). In the middle, with rates scoring between 25 and 75 percent, is trust in the Catholic Church (29.5 percent), trade unions (32.6 percent), the European Union (45.6 percent), municipal administrations (48.4 percent), and the police (64 percent). Definitely high (above 75 percent) is the trust that *gasistas* have in consumer groups (75.1 percent), the judicial system (77.2 percent), and social cooperatives (80.9 percent). All of these features indicate that people who participate in GASs may be classified as 'critical citizens' (Norris 1999); in other words, individuals characterized by a specific socio-economic profile, usually with a higher level of education and income and a particular demonstrated willingness to bear the costs (in terms of both time and money) of experimenting with innovative forms of action and participation in the promotion of the common good.

Our data also revealed that most of the *gasistas* have had prior associational experience. Only 7 percent of respondents indicated that they had never previously participated in any association. This finding is particularly important as it underlines that GASs often work as secondary networks, explaining, as we will discuss below, how these groups initially form. *Gasistas* tend to come from diverse civic and associational backgrounds, often having been members of a wide range of organizations, from environmental and pacifist groups to sports, cultural, and religious associations. Furthermore, among individuals participating in these entities, there is an equal distribution between people who claim to be religious and to attend church regularly and those who do not claim to follow any religion.

Not only do *gasistas* come from various associational backgrounds but their motivations for joining a GAS are also diverse. Some may look for a GAS group out of self-interest, for example to gain access to organic produce at an affordable price or to improve their own health or that of their family. Others want to contribute to social or collective causes – such as supporting small producers to oppose food standardization. As Figure 4.2 shows, the opportunity to consume healthier food and the willingness to support small local producers get very similar response rates (respectively 82 percent and 79.6 percent). Moreover, more than half of our respondents replied that the main motivation behind their decision to become a member of a local GAS was a desire to participate with a concrete action in common causes (63.5 percent), an opportunity to build new relationships (63.7 percent), or an increasing concern about environmental problems (56.2 percent). As the data point out, 'saving money' received less

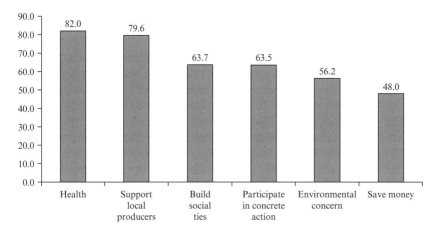

Source: CORES Lab project, 'Inside Relational Capital'.

Figure 4.2   Motivation for joining a GAS (% strongly agree/agree)

preference than other motivations (48 percent). However, this point was still mentioned by half of the respondents, confirming that while financial motivation is not the main factor behind the decision to join these groups neither is it totally irrelevant.

As will emerge more clearly over the following subsections, rather than just a way to save money, GAS groups represent innovative participatory spaces within which individuals experience new forms of action, imagining, and experimenting with practical alternatives to an economic system perceived as increasingly unjust and unsustainable. Overall, these networks offer common ground for various people to liaise through novel and collaborative projects, starting with the basic act of food provisioning.

Structure and Organization of GAS Groups

Setting up a GAS is not effortless, and managing its activities, as we will see, can be very time-consuming. Most of the GAS groups that we analyzed originated as spontaneous initiatives among groups of friends (39.4 percent), and in a further 21.2 percent of cases they stemmed from preexistent GAS groups. As will be argued in more detail below, members' interdependence constitutes a core relational resource which GAS groups continually attempt to encourage and reproduce through a series of strategies. These include initiatives to stimulate participation and to attract new

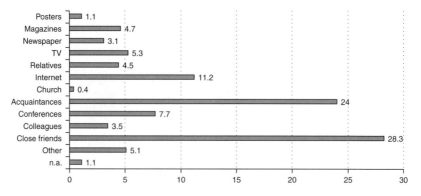

Source: CORES Lab project, 'Inside Relational Capital'.

Figure 4.3   Primary media through which participants discover GASs (%)

members, but also lengthy internal discussions to avoid the risks of 'professionalization' (Grasseni 2014).

As Figure 4.3 highlights, respondents heard about their GASs from close friends (28.3 percent) and acquaintances (24 percent). Also Internet news (11.2 percent) and conferences/meetings (7.7 percent) were mentioned by a significant number of *gasistas* as ways of getting to know about GASs. Of minor importance, by contrast, were television programs (5.3 percent), print magazines (4.7 percent), relatives (4.5 percent), colleagues (3.5 percent), newspaper articles (3.1 percent), posters (1.1 percent), and the Catholic Church (0.4 percent).

Groups may also be very diverse with regard to their size. Among the 204 GAS groups that participated in the survey, 34.4 percent consisted of fewer than 20 families, 44.8 percent of between 20 and 40 families, 10.4 percent of 40 to 60 families, and another 10.4 percent of more than 60 families. Despite this diversity, GASs appear to have quite similar internal organizations. In fact, unlike other initiatives aimed at promoting the commercialization and dissemination of eco-friendly or fair-trade products (such as farmers' markets and organic box schemes), all members of GAS groups are, as a rule of thumb, required to manage orders as explained above. Group members may propose a product or producer to the rest of the group, or 'inherit' contacts from previous members and groups, but in any case it is expected that they will contact the producers and deliver the produce to other members. Noncompliance with this requirement (whether formalized or not) may be sanctioned with expulsion from the GAS.

The majority of the GAS groups that we analyzed opt for an egalitarian division of labor. For instance, 72 percent of the 204 groups split

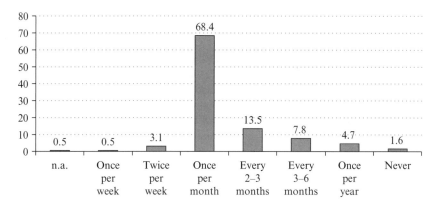

Source: CORES Lab project, 'Inside Relational Capital'.

Figure 4.4 Frequency of GAS plenary meetings (%)

up responsibilities for the collection and distribution of orders among members so that there was one contact person for each product. In only 19.7 percent of cases was there a distinct group of people within the GAS that organized purchases, and only in 4.7 percent of cases were the orders managed by an external cooperative.

Although not all GAS groups have formal rules (only a minority are registered associations), choices regarding purchases, producers, and, more generally, the mission of each group is discussed collegially during general assemblies. As may be seen from Figure 4.4, in most of the groups (68.4 percent) this meeting is held on a monthly basis; in other cases every 2–3 months (13.7 percent), and in others every 3–6 months (7.8 percent). Only in a few cases are assemblies held on an annual basis, and only a very small number of groups (1.6 percent) do not organize general membership meetings at all. In general, then, *gasistas* discuss and scrutinize products and production methods collegially. Producers are often invited to participate and present not only their merchandise but also their vision with respect to the social responsibility of the company, including its environmental stewardship and solidarity with workers. Thus critical consumption is exercised collectively and face to face, which has the effect of (re)socializing citizens into many aspects of logistics, distribution, and production. *Gasistas* call this work of rethinking logistics, 'co-production'.

Gasistas are directly involved in rethinking logistics. Families in particular usually provide space for receiving and distributing goods themselves. Once there is agreement on the producers from which to source, orders of each product (greens, fruit, pasta, jam, olive oil, but also such products as

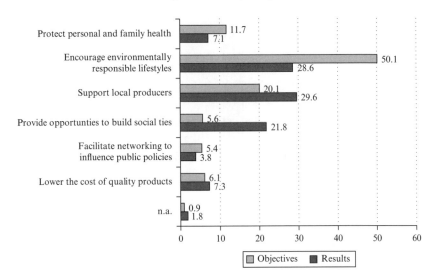

Source: CORES Lab project, 'Inside Relational Capital'.

Figure 4.5   Main objectives and results of GAS groups (%)

meat, fish, flour, snacks, cheese, yoghurt, and eggs) are usually posted to a website or mailing list by one of the members, who then collects orders at announced deadlines. The GASs often produce specific company documentation so all the members (old and new) have a full overview of the reasons that led the group to select a particular supplier.

Choosing products and manufacturers occupies most of the time in GAS discussions. However, if shopping remains, on the one hand, the central activity of GASs, on the other hand, the main perceived result of participating in these groups is to move beyond collective buying per se. Interesting in this regard is Figure 4.5, which shows the differences that *gasistas* themselves identified regarding the main objectives and results achieved by GAS groups. For half of our respondents, the main objective of the groups was to encourage more environmentally responsible lifestyles (50.1 percent). Among the major achievements of the groups, however, has been the concrete support that *gasistas* give to local producers (29.6 percent) as well as the opportunities that members have to build new social ties (21.8 percent). The GAS practices facilitated meeting new people as the groups offer a common ground to discuss topics of mutual interest.

In other words, GAS activities help to build or extend networks, across which knowledge travels. This knowledge-building process engenders trust among GAS groups, thus facilitating, for instance, feedback about producers. Such cooperation, however, often extends to new activities beyond shopping: barter fairs, reading groups, cooking workshops, cultural events such as book presentations and seminars, and responsible-consumption fairs (not only of food but also of textiles) are all examples of initiatives organized by networks of GAS groups. Thus the roles of consumers and citizens cross-fertilize, and collaboration between consumers and producers finds new spaces, for example in setting up farmers' markets and 'citizenship markets' (Forno 2013; Grasseni 2013). The GAS activists maintain that they not only exercise ethical or critical consumption as individuals or groups, but that they 'co-produce' a common wealth. In short, political consumerism is not *the objective*, but rather *the result* of engaged practice.

GASs as Socio-pedagogic Laboratories

In addition to the markets and swapping clubs that GASs often organize, they also convene events of public instruction about the workings of global finance and supply chains and their alternatives, offer school classes, convene conferences, and host festivals. In this cultural mobilization of civil society, collaboration with other associations is often facilitated by GAS members who simultaneously belong to one or more citizens' organizations. By virtue of their double affiliation, they usually play a key role in bridging different networks and discourses, thus facilitating a shared language and contagious mobilization in the case of specific events. This was the case in Italy's referendum against the privatization of water supplies in June 2011.

As is apparent in Figure 4.6, initiatives organized by GAS groups cover a wide range of themes, including producers' presentations (57 percent), sustainable agriculture (49.7 percent), commons management (39.4 percent), local issues (38.9 percent), nutrition education (36.8 percent), and alternative energy (35.8 percent). Other matters were the upcoming referendum of 2011 (32.6 percent), fair trade (29.5 percent), homesteading (25.9 percent), ethical finance (25.4 percent) and, although to a lesser extent, the role of the Mafia in the economy (17.6 percent), degrowth (16.6 percent), types of quality certifications (13 percent), and car-pooling (3.1 percent).[11]

The referendum against the privatization of water supplies also marked a milestone in GAS political awareness. As our survey revealed, some 80 percent of *gasistas* declared they had participated in the mobilization preceding the referendum. Several referenda had failed in the past because the outcome did not reach the mandatory quorum of 50 percent plus one of those having the right to vote. The fact that about 55 percent of registered voters actually cast a vote – almost 26 million people – to express their

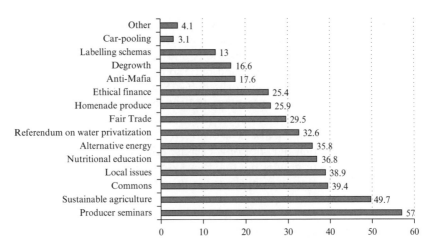

Source: CORES Lab project, 'Inside Relational Capital'.

Figure 4.6   Initiatives organized by GASs, by topic (%)

dissent for decentralizing and privatizing the water supply was interpreted then as a result of the grassroots campaign brought forward by civic action groups, including GASs.

GASs are, therefore, simultaneously involved in two diverse, but inter-related, practices. On the one hand, these organizations try to reduce the information deficit among citizens about the environmental and social issues of global supply chains, by way of seminars and other public events. On the other hand, through collective purchases, they experiment with new solutions, intervening directly in local food-provisioning chains, identifying critical issues pertaining to delegation, representation, participation, and labor division. They, in effect, function as socio-pedagogic laboratories, facilitating learning processes and the sharing of knowledge, that in turn play an important role in translating attitudes into behavior (see Chapter 8 in this volume).

As Tables 4.2, 4.3 and 4.4 show, the *gasistas'* shopping baskets, their consumption styles, and even styles of civic participation changed, sometimes dramatically, after joining a GAS.

Consumption of local (80.6 percent), organic (79.4 percent), and seasonal (68.1 percent) food increased, while the consumption of meat decreased (42.5 percent). Membership in a GAS also increased participation in recycling (32.5 percent) and reduced the consumption of electricity (29.3 percent) and water (28.6 percent). In sum, GAS practice facilitated the adoption of more sustainable lifestyles in the private sphere. Looking to the public sphere, membership also fostered the diffusion of more

Table 4.2   Changes in consumption habits of GAS members (%)

	Increased	Decreased	Introduced	No change	n.a.	Total
Vegetable	50.4	0.4	0.7	47.4	1.2	100
Organic	79.4	0.2	7.7	11.6	1.1	100
Wholemeal	52.9	0.6	10	35.2	1.4	100
Legumes	38.5	0.5	3.7	56.3	1.1	100
Local	80.6	0.2	5.4	12.6	1.1	100
Seasonal	68.1	0.1	2.8	27.8	1.2	100
Cereals	45.1	0.3	12.8	40.5	1.3	100
Meat	3.1	42.5	0.2	52	2.2	100
Fair trade	39.6	1.4	5.6	51.8	1.5	100
Mafia-free	44.6	0.6	14.7	38.5	1.5	100
Ecological	41.4	0.6	25	31.9	1.1	100

Source: CORES Lab project, 'Inside Relational Capital'.

Table 4.3   Changes in lifestyles of GAS members (%)

	Yes	No	Already did	n.a.	Total
Decreased purchasing pre-cooked food	24.8	5.1	69.4	0.7	100
Decreased shopping in supermarkets	41.4	47.9	9.7	0.9	100
Increased purchases in local shops	27.5	33	37.9	1.6	100
Started producing food at home	38.3	31.9	29	0.9	100
Started growing vegetables	16.2	54.8	27.6	1.4	100
Started to use the car less	17.6	46.9	34.5	1	100
Increased recycling	32.5	6.7	60	0.9	100
More attention to energy consumption	29.3	22.9	46.3	1.4	100
More attention to water consumption	28.6	6.1	64.3	1	100

Source: CORES Lab project 'Inside Relational Capital'.

collaborative attitudes (39.7 percent), cultivated interest in politics among participants (in particular local politics, 26 percent), and enhanced their sense of social efficacy (23.9 percent).

CONCLUSION

Although limited to a minority of people in Italy, there is no doubt that GAS practice is helping collectives develop strategies for economic and

Putting sustainability into practice

*Table 4.4   Changes in civic and political participation of
             GAS members (%)*

	Yes	No	Already was	n.a.	Total
More interested in problems concerning my town of residence	26	30.3	42.5	1.2	100
More interested in politics in general	7.9	35.8	55	1.3	100
More able to cooperate with people in general	39.7	16.1	42.9	1.4	100
Feeling more able to influence public policy	23.9	60.8	13.8	1.6	100

Source: CORES Lab project 'Inside Relational Capital'.

political intervention which often fill the gap left by inefficient governance in the fields of environmental management or labor protection. In this regard, our research shows that these groups represent important examples of grassroots innovation. However constrained in scope, they demonstrate the will to develop local and regional solutions to sustainability problems (Brunori et al. 2011; Migliore et al. 2014). Our claim is that, despite their limited capacity to change global food systems directly, GAS groups work as 'citizenship labs', namely as spaces of aggregation and workshops for collective practice on the part of consumers. On the GAS shop floor, so to speak, people practice hands-on what it means to develop a direct relationship with producers, some proximate and others more distant (*gasistas* in Lombardy order their oranges from Sicily, 1000 kilometers away). It is this practice of collective self-provisioning that develops awareness about the complexity and flaws of the global food system. A fair amount of effort is needed to find local producers that meet the solidarity criteria and/or to collect orders and redistribute produce. On the basis of this novel recognition, more responsible lifestyles ensue, and a sense of collective direction about resilience, sufficiency, and sustainability is developed as a group.

Thus, in many respects, GAS groups represent new spaces for people who not only view the consumer society as unjust but also want to search for practical alternatives. Although GAS members may hold different political and religious convictions, they come to these groups with various motivations and are impelled by a desire to share a critical approach to the global economic model and consumerist lifestyles. Within their GAS groups, members find more than information and reciprocal support. The ongoing networking among *gasistas* facilitates social learning, building social capital and multiplying the potential of individuals to act. This is evident from the way in which many groups feel the need to evolve, expand,

and set up more complex initiatives than collective purchasing among a small group of friends.

The emerging picture thus seems to highlight that GASs are not simply a new type of consumer organization, but rather an innovative form of political participation in an overall context of high levels of distrust in traditional channels of participation (e.g., political parties). Although their overall economic impact seems to be limited, we focus on their societal, relational, and political roles as spaces of apprenticeship for a new type of consumer citizenship. Through these groups, people do more than satisfy 'liberal guilt' by shopping ethically; they join together to try to make a difference to environmental and social justice issues. In our individualized and fragmented societies, these groups thus represent an important way for people to bond together. As seen, starting from the basic act of food provisioning, GASs help citizens to start asking questions not only about quality, sustainability, and the costs of goods *as consumers*, but also about municipal services, schools and education, pollution, and so forth *as citizens* whose economic needs must be met with a view to sustainability and solidarity. After all, the call for a sustainable eco-economy requires not only a radically different system of production and distribution, but also different collective styles of consumption, which need to be based on new civic values as well as novel forms of participation.

NOTES

1. These numbers refer to the GAS groups that have decided to self-register voluntarily. See http://www.retegas.org (accessed 15 December 2014).
2. The data presented here are part of a wider research project entitled *Dentro il capitale delle relazioni* (Inside Relational Capital), carried out by the CORES Lab under the scientific direction of the authors. The CORES Lab is an interdisciplinary research group, officially established in 2012 at the University of Bergamo, with the aim of investigating the mechanisms and processes underpinning the contemporary rise and growth of grassroots economic practices. See http://www.unibg.it/cores for further details (accessed 15 December 2014). The study discussed here was endorsed by the Italian Solidarity Economy Network and carried out in collaboration with Davide Biolghini and Giuseppe Vergani of the Tavolo group within *Rete Italiana di Economia Solidale* (Italian Solidarity Economy Network).
3. See http://www.retegas.org (accessed 20 March 2014).
4. A parallel initiative in Rome found proportionally similar results (Fonte et al. 2011).
5. A pilot study carried out in Bergamo established a protocol that was extended to the rest of Lombardy, and is currently being applied to other Italian regions – notably Sicily and Friuli Venezia Giulia – in collaboration with facilitators *in situ* that have in-depth knowledge of the local contexts.
6. Members of GAS groups call themselves *gasista* and we use here the term *gasistas*, the gender-neutral plural form of the word which is in fact a neologism in Italian.
7. Citizens' organizations and civic associations in Italy have historically developed in close proximity with one or another political party. This 'collateral' relationship

between political parties and civil society organizations has resulted in distinctive 'territorial political subcultures' (Communist subcultures in the central Italian regions and Catholic/Christian-Democratic ones in the northeast of the country; see Messina 2012). These relationships still play a critical role in forging and disseminating novel, but distinctive, forms of civic involvement, such as political consumerism (Forno and Ceccarini 2006).

8. Data are as of March 2013.
9. Web-based surveys usually have a much lower response rate than other survey modes (Manfreda et al. 2008).
10. In the request to participate in the survey, only the person who did most of the GAS-related work in each family was asked to fill out the questionnaire. It is, though, important to view these data with some caution. Even though we sought to ensure that the most active member of the household completed the questionnaire, this figure could also be due to the fact that women are more prone than men to take the time to respond to such inquiries. Our ethnographic observation, however, confirms this finding (Grasseni 2013).
11. *Gasistas'* motivations are thus in line both with those who believe that more sober lifestyles can benefit the planet, but also that rethinking consumption is in their immediate and long-term self-interest.

REFERENCES

Alexander, Samuel and Simon Ussher (2012), 'The Voluntary Simplicity Movement: a multi-national survey analysis in theoretical context', *Journal of Consumer Culture*, **12** (1), 66–86.

Balsiger, Philip (2010), 'Making political consumers: the tactical action repertoire of a campaign for clean clothes', *Social Movement Studies*, **9** (3), 311–329.

Bauman, Zygmunt (2007), *Consuming Life*, Malden, MA: Polity Press.

Bourdieu, Pierre (1984), *Distinction: A Social Critique of the Judgment of Taste*, Cambridge, MA: Harvard University Press.

Brunori, Gianluca, Adanella Rossi, and Vanessa Malandrin (2011), 'Co-producing transition: innovation processes in farms adhering to solidarity-based purchase groups (GAS) in Tuscany, Italy', *International Journal of Sociology of Agriculture and Food*, **18** (1), 28–53.

Carrera, Letizia (2009), 'I gruppi di acquisto solidale: una proposta solida nella società liquida' ('Solidarity purchase groups: a solid proposal in a liquid society'), *Partecipazione e Conflitto*, **3** (28), 95–122 (in Italian).

Clarke, John, Janet Newman, Nick Smith, Elizabeth Vilder, and Louise Westmarlan (2007), *Creating Citizen-Consumers: Changing Publics and Changing Public Services*, Thousand Oaks, CA: Sage.

della Porta, Donatella and Mario Diani (2006), *Social Movement: An Introduction*, 2nd edn, Malden, MA: Blackwell.

Ferrer-Fons, Mariona (2006), 'Il consumerismo politico in Europa: le differenze nazionali tra dimensione politica e livello micro' ('Political consumerism in Europe: the differences between national political dimension and micro level'), in Simone Tosi (ed.), *Consumi e Partecipazione Politica: Tra Azione Individuale e Mobilitazione Collettiva* (*Consumption and Political Participation: Between Individual Action and Collective Mobilization*), Milan: Franco Angeli, pp. 109–131 (in Italian).

Fonte, Maria, Mariella Eboli, Ornella Maietta, Brunella Pinto, and Cristina

Salvioni (2011), 'Il consumo sostenibile nella visione dei Gruppi di Acquisto Solidale di Roma' ('Sustainable consumption in the vision of fair trade groups in Rome'), *Agriregionieuropa*, **7** (27), http://www.agriregionieuropa.univpm.it (in Italian) (accessed 8 October 2014).

Forno, Francesca (2013), 'Cooperative movement', in D. Snow, D. della Porta, B. Klandermans, and D. McAdam (eds), *Blackwell Encyclopedia of Social and Political Movements*, Malden, MA: Blackwell, pp. 278–280.

Forno, Francesca and Luigi Ceccarini (2006), 'From the street to the shops: the rise of new forms of political actions in Italy', *South European Society and Politics*, **11** (2), 197–222.

Forno, Francesca and Paolo R. Graziano (2014), 'Sustainable community movement organisations', *Journal of Consumer Culture*, **14** (2), 139–157.

Giddens, Anthony (1990), *The Consequences of Modernity*, Palo Alto, CA: Stanford University Press.

Grasseni, Cristina (2013), *Beyond Alternative Food Networks: Italy's Solidarity Purchase Groups*, London: Bloomsbury.

Grasseni, Cristina (2014), 'Seeds of trust: alternative food networks in Italy', *Journal of Political Ecology*, **21** (1), 178–192.

Grasseni, Cristina, Francesca Forno, and Silvana Signori (2015), 'Beyond Alternative Food Networks: Insights from Italy's Solidarity Purchase Groups and US Community Economies', in P. Utting (ed.), *Social and Solidarity Economy: Beyond the Fringe?*, London: Zed Books, pp. 185–201.

Graziano, Paolo R. and Francesca Forno (2012), 'Political consumerism and new forms of political participation: the *Gruppi di Acquisto Solidale* in Italy', *Annals of the American Academy of Political and Social Science*, **644**, 121–133.

Koos, Sebastian (2012), 'What drives political consumption in Europe? A multi-level analysis on individual characteristics, opportunity structures and globalization', *Acta Sociologica*, **55** (1), 37–57.

Manfreda, Katja Lozar, Michael Bosnjak, Jernej Berzelak, Iris Haas, and Vasja Vehovar (2008), 'Web surveys versus other survey modes: a meta-analysis comparing response rates', *International Journal of Market Research*, **50** (1), 79–104.

Messina, Patrizia (2012), *Modi di Regolazione della Sviluppo Locale: Una Comparazione per Contesti di Veneto ed Emilia Romagna* (*Modes of Regulation of Local Development: A Comparison of Contexts of Veneto and Emilia Romagna*), Padua: Padua University Press (in Italian).

Micheletti, Michele (2003), 'Why more women? Issues of gender and political consumerism', in M. Micheletti, A. Follesdal, and D. Stolle (eds), *Politics, Products, and Markets: Exploring Political Consumerism Past and Present*, New Brunswick, NJ: Transaction Press.

Micheletti, Michele (2009), 'La svolta dei consumatori nella responsabilità politica e nella cittadinanza' ('The consumer turn in political responsibility and citizenship'), *Partecipazione e Conflitto*, **3** (25), 17–41 (in Italian).

Migliore, Giuseppina, Giorgio Schifani, Giovanni Dara Guccione, and Luigi Cembalo (2014), 'Food community networks as leverage for social embeddedness', *Journal of Agricultural and Environmental Ethics*, **27** (4), 549–567.

Norris, Pippa (ed.) (1999), *Critical Citizens*, New York: Oxford University Press.

Putnam, Robert (1993), *Making Democracy Work: Civic Traditions in Modern Italy*, Princeton, NJ: Princeton University Press.

Rebughini, Paola (2008), 'Costruire nuovi spazi di consumo: i gruppi di acquisto e il sogno della trasparenza' ('Building new spaces of consumption: purchasing groups and the dream of transparency'), in L. Luisa and R. Sassatelli (eds), *Il consumo critico* (*Critical Consumption*), Rome-Bari: Laterza, pp. 34–61 (in Italian).

Sassatelli, Roberta (2006), 'Virtue, responsibility and consumer choice: framing critical consumerism', in J. Brewer and F. Trentmann (eds), *Consuming Cultures, Global Perspectives: Historical Trajectories, Transnational Exchanges*, New York: Berg, pp. 219–250.

Stolle, Dietlind, Marc Hooghe, and Michele Micheletti (2005), 'Politics in the super-market: political consumerism as a form of political participation', *International Political Science Review*, **26** (3), 245–269.

PART III

Collective dimensions of household practices

5. Beyond behavior change: social practice theory and the search for sustainable mobility

Stewart Barr

INTRODUCTION: SMARTER CHOICES?

We have all seen the signs, pinned up as they are on lamp posts and competing for space among the plethora of other icons that adorn our highways: 'Try car sharing' or 'Be smart and use the bus'. These appeals to our supposedly better nature are ones that have become as much a part of everyday life to drivers as signs showing the speed limit or the distance to the next filling station. And therein lies a problem: appeals to change our behaviors have largely become ones that are dismissed and lost among the overwhelming infrastructure that supports the very actions they are trying to move us away from: the normality, care-free, and supposed freedom afforded by the motorcar.

James Howard Kunstler's (1994; 1998) commentary on the development of an automobile culture in North America highlights the embeddedness of driving as a practice that is a necessity for living a normal life in the twenty-first century. This has not emerged because we have become addicted to the motorcar *per se*, but rather because we have designed a living arrangement (beginning in the 1920s) that necessitates driving to fulfill economic, social, and cultural goals. As Kunstler (1994) highlights, such goals are deeply rooted in a generations-old suspicion of the city as an urban living arrangement, one that has its roots partly in the poverty, disease, and slumdom of the industrial cities of the nineteenth century. Kunstler conjectures that people at this time desperately wanted to attain some of the freshness and freedom of the countryside, with all the civilized affordances of the city. And thus was born the idea of the suburb: a living arrangement that appeared to offer the space for expansionist movement, while doing so in such a way that provided access to the necessities of urban life.

Initially conceived of as 'streetcar suburbs' or 'Metroland', the invention of the motorcar rapidly enabled land speculators and developers to begin the process of building the vast suburban sprawls that we are so familiar with today in North America and, to a lesser degree, the United Kingdom (UK). In line with such developments, the suburbs became a rapidly desirable place to live as spaces that embodied the freedom of a liberal and individualized society, with access to all services provided by private motor transport. By contrast, such developments have progressively witnessed the decline of urban centers and the flight of retail and entertainments outlets to vast shopping malls and strip malls, adorned with the icons of our postmodern economic model, all of which encourage us to consume . . . and to be happy about it.

What this brief (and necessarily generalized) description highlights is the intricate but often overlooked relationship between so-called individual travel behaviors (often regarded as travel mode choices) and the broader social contexts of mobility and society's relationship with place. As such, the question of why we travel in the way that we do is a fundamentally geographical one, concerned with our relationship to place and the ways in which such relationships have shifted over time.

Yet this recognition is not one that currently holds much sway within communities of practice that have sought to reduce our reliance on the motorcar. Driven by efforts to reduce global carbon emissions to tackle anthropogenic climate change, reducing reliance on the motorcar has been regarded as a key priority. However, the approach to achieving this objective has largely centered on developing communications-based messages and behavioral change strategies that focus either on the climate change 'problem' or the alternative 'choices' available to car drivers. Such an approach is one that mirrors several other behavioral change strategies, and in this chapter I will unpack some of the assumptions underlying what has become a pervasive and permeating discourse within national and local government. In so doing, I will argue that behavioral change approaches have become stuck in an instrumentalist, individualized, and unambitious consensus that largely ignores the possibilities for envisioning mobility in different ways. To do this, a clearer understanding of how mobility has developed over time and how it is related to social, economic, and physical infrastructures is required. In this way, I will explore how social practice theories can facilitate an alternative approach to studying and changing mobility practices – one based on understanding the relationships among place, mobility, and the individual.

In the next section, I examine the apparent consensus within communities of practice that has adopted behavior change as the main strategy for reducing reliance on the private motorcar. In so doing, I explore the underpinning theories that have driven this agenda, focusing on the social psychology of travel behavior and emergent ideas of 'nudge' (Thaler and Sunstein 2008) and social marketing. I then examine the ways in which scholars have begun to unpack the assumptions underlying such approaches by exploring the political basis for behavioral change strategies, focusing in particular on the ways in which states have adopted particular forms of soft paternalism to achieve policy goals. I then use empirical research on transport and mobility to explore the alternative possibilities for shifting mobility practices, highlighting three key areas for attention: physical choice architectures, socio-economic choice architectures, and the politics and planning of the urban landscape. Through these lenses I conclude that social practice theories can assist in understanding mobility through their focus on both historical antecedents and wider infrastructures that mold practices.

BEHAVIOR CHANGE: 'NUDGING' INDIVIDUALS

Individuals in contemporary industrialized societies tend to accept almost without question that to achieve certain policy goals – be they reducing car use or promoting healthy eating – the focus of attention should be the individual. Yet it was not always so. Within the environmental realm, the notion that individual citizens are responsible for ecological damage is a relatively new phenomenon of the 1990s, with nation states and commercial organizations being regarded as those that should regulate and manage such issues (McCormick 1989). The shift towards individual responsibility has therefore been relatively recent and can be related to the broader changes in the political economy of nation states. Giddens (1991) highlights the ways in which the shift toward a neo-liberal economic and political model, particularly in North America and the United Kingdom, has fundamentally changed the relationship between the state and citizens. Rose and Miller (1992) characterize this transformation in their argument that as the nation state has been rolled back, the prominence and role of individuals has increased, through both the provision of greater economic choices afforded by deregulation and reliance by the state on individuals to deliver certain policy goals through these choices.

These shifts have supported the development of what Clarke et al. (2007) have termed the 'consumer-citizen' construct; an individual who simultaneously exercises the choices and freedoms bestowed by a neo-liberal economic model, but does so in a way that is socially, economically, and environmentally responsible. The notion of the citizen-consumer is one that has received considerable academic attention in the past ten years (e.g., Johnston 2008; Scammell 2000; Slocum 2004) and has manifested into a particular form of policy making known as 'behavior change'. In this model, the philosophy and techniques of the market are used to create opportunities for shifting behaviors regarded as problematic to ones that meet prescribed policy goals. A useful example of this is the UK Department of the Environment, Food and Rural Affairs' (DEFRA's) 2008 *Framework for Environmental Behaviours*, in which 12 behavioral goals are set for individuals on the basis of existing climate change targets. Examples include reducing the use of private motor transport for short journeys, reducing reliance on short haul flights, and increasing walking and cycling (Darnton and Sharp 2006).

In attempting to use behavior change to meet these specific goals, a particular interpretation of existing approaches has been adopted by scholars and practitioners. Within the UK, this has been dominated by perspectives from behavioral economics and social psychology (Whitehead et al. 2011) and has attempted to move beyond many of the pitfalls that have befallen previous attempts to encourage behavioral change through the simple provision of information (McKenzie-Mohr 2000). The particular focus on the individual and the notion that it is behavior that constitutes 'the problem' has therefore afforded researchers from academic disciplines like economics and psychology the ability to gain purchase within the policy community, offering as they do some of the certainties and quantifiable evidence for understanding and potentially changing behavior.

Within travel behavior research, studies of psychological determinants of individual decision making have tended to follow the trajectory of scholars examining other pro-environmental behaviors (such as recycling, energy conservation, and water saving), by focusing on particular theoretical models of behavior, doing so via large quantitative survey instruments and by paying most attention to the environmental 'determinants' of behavior through examining attitudes and values. Accordingly, authors such as Anable (2005), Bamberg et al. (2003), Dallen (2007), Götz et al. (2003), and Heath and Gifford (2002) have utilized Ajzen's (1991) theory of planned behavior as the basis for delineating between key constructs including attitudes, social norms, perceived behavioral control, behavioral intention, and behavior through the use of questionnaire surveys of publics. As Whitehead et al. (2011) highlight, such research aligns well with the implicit values held by policy makers, who have come to value research that utilizes large samples, measures constructs quantitatively and with reference to theory, and, in a quantifiable sense, research that can be replicated reliably.

The popularity afforded by the apparent certainties and robust evidence basis of social-psychologically informed research has been carefully adopted and deployed by policy makers seeking to understand travel behaviors and reduce private car use, alongside other pro-environmental behaviors. First, within the UK, the Behavioural Insights Team of the Cabinet Office has been instrumental in the assimilation of nudge theory into UK behavior change policy making. Based on Thaler and Sunstein's renowned book (2008, p. 8), nudge theory is defined as:

> [A]ny aspect of the choice architecture that alters people's behaviour in a predictable way without forbidding any options or significantly changing their economic incentives. To count as a mere nudge, the intervention must be easy and cheap to avoid. Nudges are not mandates. Putting the fruit at eye level counts as a nudge. Banning junk food does not.

Within this definition are the two key constructs of the citizen-consumer: the maintenance of free choice within a particular context, but the definitive prescription of the 'right' choice as a good citizen, concerned for one's own and society's welfare. Nudge theory has gained so much purchase in part because it has utilized many of the theoretical understandings of individual behavioral decisions that social psychology has highlighted as significant for shifting behaviors, based on the notion of the individual as the primary unit of decision making.

This use of the free market to prescribe and promote particular choices has been developed through the adoption of a second approach known as social marketing. Once again, this has been enthusiastically adopted as a pragmatic tool by both national and local governments in countries like the UK and focuses on three key components that likewise draw on understandings of individual behavioral decisions (French et al. 2009; McKenzie-Mohr 2000). First, specific behavioral goals are required to establish the basis for a social marketing campaign, often described by the use of targets. Secondly, consumer segmentation is critical for examining the different motivations and barriers for participation in the desired behavior. For example, for a behavior like car driving, there will be multiple segments that are defined by demographic, economic, social, and cultural attributes, alongside social-psychological constructs, such as attitudes and norms. Finally, to make an effective campaign, social marketers rely on an effective marketing mix that is attuned to particular population segments and their characteristics.

As an approach, social marketing draws heavily on conventional marketing perspectives to create a relationship between individual consumers and the behaviors being promoted. As such, it is heavily dependent on market intelligence about particular consumer groups. Accordingly, a range of national and local government departments have invested considerable time and money in developing understandings of key pro-environmental behaviors, and these are illustrated in segmentation models developed by

DEFRA (2008) and the Department for Transport (2004; 2011a; 2011b) in the UK. For example, DEFRA's (2008) segmentation model defines seven key groups within the UK population, from 'Positive Greens', who exhibit both a willingness and ability to perform a range of environmental behaviors, to the 'Honestly Disengaged', who are those least convinced about the merits of acting in an environmentally friendly manner.

Accordingly, as the House of Lords Science and Technology Committee (2011) has argued, behavior change has become the approach of choice for practitioners wishing to achieve a range of outcomes, from reducing carbon emissions to the promotion of healthy eating. Yet behavior change is bound up with a set of assumptions and epistemological traditions that require some explicit unpacking, particularly when it comes to the promotion of more sustainable mobilities. It is to this critique that I now turn.

BEYOND BEHAVIOR CHANGE: UNPACKING THE 'BLACK BOX'

Although it is readily acknowledged that behavior change has its roots within the neo-liberal scripting of a rolled back nation state eager to afford individuals the right to choose (Clarke et al. 2007), the impact of such a philosophy on the outcomes that behavior change seeks to generate has only received attention in recent years. Here there are two major strands of critique, which have focused on the political construction of behavior change as a project and the epistemological assumptions that surround the understanding and application of behavioral change.

To begin with the epistemological basis of such research, which has foregrounded much of the political adoption of behavioral change as a strategy, there have been persistent and vociferous critiques of the social-psychological assumptions underlying the notion of behavior change and individual decision making. Both Owens (2000) and Shove (2010) identify some of the most basic questions surrounding the assumptions of such research, including the underlying logic that suggests behaviors are rational choices, exercised through the combination of measurable and verifiable constructs in linear models that can ultimately use statistical procedures to predict behavior. Moreover, within the travel behavior literature, De Groot and Steg (2007), Verplanken and Aarts (1999), Verplanken et al. (1997) and Møller (2002) have highlighted the role of habit formation as a key driver of travel practices, one that is not determined by individual and everyday choices, but rather developed through learned behaviors over time and related to specific situations. In this way, sociologists of mobility have strongly argued for a focus on the social as a key construct of intellectual focus. Thus Cresswell (2011), Freudendal-Pedersen (2009), and Urry (2007) argue for a research agenda that recognizes the relationship between movement and broader social and economic structures – a phenomenon that is intricately related with the living of everyday life, rather than the overtly conscious decision making of individuals about specific pro-environmental travel behaviors.

Alongside these epistemological and methodological arguments, recent commentaries have asserted that behavior change also represents a fundamentally unambitious approach to pursuing and providing a vision for different, more optimistic sustainable futures (Dobson 2010; Seyfang 2005). In her well-known critique of what she terms the 'ABC' of behavior change (Attitude–Behavior–Choice), Shove (2010) contends that such approaches are based on narrowly defined instrumentalist policy goals that crowd out opportunities for debate and deliberation over the changes that would be required to create the basis for major shifts in behavior. This is because, she argues, the focus on individual behaviors takes no account of the wider trajectory of social practices that shape what we regard as manifested individual choices. As social practice theorists argue (Shove et al. 2012), there is a need to explore the wider trajectories of historically rooted practices and their relationship with physical and economic architectures that shape practices. In this way, the so-called choice architectures of mobility are defined and narrowed by a particular focus on very specific ways of determining what constitutes sustainable travel and whose role it is to deliver on such a political goal.

The political critique of behavior change has therefore gained currency in recent years, with Jones et al. (2011a; 2011b) arguing that the individualization of pro-environmental policy agendas represents a form of soft paternalism in countries like the UK, in which non-regulatory policies are enacted to direct citizen behaviors toward particular and prescribed 'right' choices. Alternatively termed libertarian paternalism, behavior change reflects the need of nation states to enable citizens to exercise free choice over their consumption habits, while carefully guiding them as to what appropriate choices should be for the 'good' citizen.

The political critique of such paternalist approaches is matched by a pragmatic questioning of the role and effectiveness of incrementalist strategies to promote shifts in practices that will have a fundamental environmental impact. Crompton and Thøgersen (2009) argue that to meet the aspirational climate change targets set by the UK and other governments, behavioral change as it is currently framed will only have a marginal impact, in large part because current behavior change policies are focused on small changes to lifestyle practices at the individual level and do not tackle the shifts necessary to challenge habitualized (over)consumption.

Indeed, Peattie and Peattie's (2009) critique of social marketing approaches highlights the limitations of adopting a fundamentally consumption-based approach to the promotion of *reduced* consumption without the broader context required to shift practices.

What these critiques highlight is the heavily contested nature of research and practice that surrounds the promotion of sustainable practices and the ways in which policy makers have adopted one particular interpretation of social science research, one that largely ignores both wider sociological understandings of mobility and, more specifically, one that regards travel behavior as an individualistic set of decisions based on psychological attributes. By contrast, there is mounting evidence that suggests a practice-orientated approach to travel and mobility can offer an alternative and more rewarding perspective from which to view how we understand and potentially promote sustainable mobility, one that draws on the relationship among the individual, mobility as a social practice, and the structure of the places around us in which we live.

MOBILITY AS SOCIAL PRACTICE

The research on which this chapter is based was undertaken through a series of projects from 2005 until 2012, which aimed to examine the ways in which publics engaged in sustainable mobility practices and how such practices mapped onto existing understandings of travel behavior and public responses to exhortations to reduce car and air transport use to reduce carbon emissions. Within the UK, the publication of DEFRA's (2008) *Framework for Pro-environmental Behaviours* crystalized existing attempts to encourage a range of behaviors, one component of which was sustainable travel behavior, in the form of reducing car use by encouraging more walking, cycling, and public transport use, alongside less reliance on short-haul flights for business and leisure travel. Based on a social marketing approach and utilizing a segmentation model, the framework drew heavily on research intelligence from behavioral economics and psychology, and it is these assumptions that the empirical research in this chapter will unpack.

The research reported in this chapter utilized both quantitative and qualitative methods to examine both the veracity of existing approaches to understanding mobility practices through testing the assumptions of segmentation models based on social marketing approaches (Barr et al. 2010; 2011a) and the potential for using a practices approach for understanding the shifts necessary to promote sustainable mobility (Barr et al. 2011b). This chapter will focus on this second theme and does so by highlighting three key attributes of mobility practices that present opportunities for further research into the ways in which practice theory can contribute to understandings of sustainable mobility. The quotations used are all taken from focus groups and in-depth interviews that took place in and around the city of Exeter, in which a range of transport and mobility issues were explored with participants drawn from members of the public. Exeter is a provincial Cathedral city in the county of Devon in the South West of the UK, with a population of around 120,000 inhabitants surrounded by a mainly rural hinterland. The focus groups and in-depth interviews were designed to examine the broad context of personal mobility and to explore the ways in which participants discussed the potential for behavioral change. The study areas for the research were selected to represent different residential environments (Polsloe: high density inner city; Pennsylvania: low density inner city; St. Loyes: low density city fringe; Cullompton: small town suburban commuter settlement; Crediton: small market town). These study areas enabled the research team to examine the ways in which different types of planned landscape related to mobility practices and perceptions of future mobilities.

In adopting a practices approach, the research followed a tradition within environmental sociology that has highlighted several key components of Reckwitz's (2002) conceptualization, in which body, mind, things, knowledge, discourse, structure/process, and the agent are components in understanding practices. Pragmatically, the research of Shove and Warde (2002), Shove (2003), and Shove et al. (2012) has tended to focus on practices that are sets of shared behaviors or routines that develop through time and space and which are intricately related to particular consumption contexts. Within the travel and mobilities realm, the following definition was adopted for the research reported in this chapter:

> Social practices are conceived as being routine-driven, everyday activities situated in time and space and shared by groups of people as part of their everyday life . . . Social practices form the historically shaped, concrete interaction points between, on the one hand actors, with their lifestyles and routines, and on the other hand, modes of provision with their infrastructures of rules and resources, including norms and values. (Verbeek and Mommaas 2008, p. 634)

Accordingly, the practices approach in this research focused on the interaction points between actors and the wider architectures of choice that act as modes of provision. Critically, these are shaped by historical context, in which mobility practices emerge through time. In adopting this method, I want to emphasize the ways in which practices become learned and reinforced and the tensions that emerge in both time and space when dominant practices are challenged by exhortations to change modes of mobility.

Moreover, I want to illustrate how we might utilize the findings from this research to explore how a practices approach can contribute to an alternative framing of sustainable mobility that exploits the relationships between the individual, mobility practices, and new forms of living arrangement. In so doing, I am not able to provide a very positive view of the future unless some of the very basic but essential assumptions about how we consider our relationship to place are examined and re-visited. In the following three sections, I draw from empirical data to illustrate my argument, focusing on three key elements concerning the interaction of practices with physical choice architectures, socio-economic choice architectures, and the politics and planning of the urban.

Physical Choice Architectures

One of the key components of behavioral economics and the politics of nudge is the emphasis placed on the role of choice architectures. It is argued that the goals of behavioral change can be achieved in part if the surroundings in which people operate are conducive to the behavior being promoted. So, within a mobilities context, the provision of bicycle racks, secure cycle storage, and showers might all be components of a choice architecture that promotes greater levels of bicycling to the workplace (Department for Transport 2011b). Set within the behavioral goal of encouraging more bicycling, these changes to the physical landscape seem eminently sensible and, for the most part, few would quarrel with such positive change. Yet the research undertaken in and around the city of Exeter indicates that mobility practices are far more embedded and related to wider physical choice architectures than the provisioning of specific technologies for achieving behavioral goals:

> Our towns . . . we are still planning and building our town of Exeter around the car, we haven't stopped that. You know *Toys R Us* [toy superstore] has just opened in Sowton, which is clearly built for the car isn't it; you know you can't walk there or cycle there as a family. It's built a big car park: you are going to drive there [and] park up. (Matt, Polsloe)

In this way, the very structure of the built environment sends signals about the ways in which mobility ought to be performed and the expectations that are placed on individuals about such performances. As a result of decades of planning focused around the car, mobility practices have developed within these physical choice architectures that necessitate long commutes, weekly shops by car, driving to schools to drop off children, and generally planning life around the affordances of the car:

> I think society has got so dependent on the convenience and everything else that even if things were improved and other forms of transport were improved I think there still would be a lot of people . . . who would cling to that car because it means so much to them now. (Tim, Cullompton)

A sense that the car affords convenience illustrates the complex interaction of mobility with contemporary living arrangements, because in large part it is the planning of physical infrastructure around the car that has made it the most convenient mode of transport. Indeed, such physical choice architectures play a critical role in reinforcing practices and suppressing other visions of what different mobilities and different places might look like:

> But to achieve [sustainable mobility] in the existing city I mean is, is so expensive, so radical, that I mean somewhere like Exeter you could only do it, like I say, by pulling down houses, well almost rebuilding the city. (Thomas, St. Loyes)

There was a clear sense from the research that, as Tim from Cullompton argued, '[T]he predominance of the car in life for all of us and everything, shopping, whatever it is, is kind of designed in as time goes on, around the use of the car'. Accordingly, the challenge for promoting sustainable mobility practices starts with the physical landscape, with an acknowledgement that trying to persuade populations to reduce car use within infrastructures that are designed around car use is highly problematic. While a major challenge, the possibilities for shifting social practices by redesigning places without the car as a central feature is eminently possible, as both European and New Urbanist North American examples highlight (Glaeser 2011). Yet there are challenges in translating both the culturally embedded notion of the café society and pedestrian cultures of continental Europe and the still largely token examples of New Urbanist forms into what we might call the mainstream (Glaeser 2011; Glaeser and Shapiro 2001). Indeed, as Lund (2003) has pointed out, where such changes do occur, they tend to be led and often colonized by homogenous groups of middle-class incomers, with the vast majority left in the suburban sprawl. Accordingly, as one of the research participants highlighted, the task of wholesale urban change for sustainable mobility is enormous and one that is about shifting the values associated with planning places to live and work to those that encourage dwelling rather than movement. What a practices perspective reveals is that the basis and historical roots of the current values underlying planning are fundamentally orientated toward promoting movement, and movement that gives priority to the individual and the private – in short, the single-occupancy automobile.

Socio-economic Choice Architectures

If the physical choice architectures of planning have conspired to create landscapes that promote private motor transport, then the socio-economic underpinnings of mobility practices are ones that relate closely to how our towns and cities look and feel. Within the research, participants charted the shifts in society that have occurred, which encourage the individual use of cars. Notably, one participant highlighted the historical shift from consolidated workplaces, often providing mass transit for workers, and the emergence of smaller businesses, often located in out-of-town business parks:

> When we were not such an insulated society, for example, people who worked at Dagenham, Fords of Dagenham or somewhere like that, they ran car clubs, because they all worked at the same place and they all started at the same time, or whatever shift there was, the cars were then loaded with guys 'it's your turn to drive' that doesn't work. More people today live alone. Now young people your age who have their own house are not part of anything like that, they have their own transport, they do everything on the Internet. So there's no society as it was like that. No nuclear family, . . . or large[r] family, people don't work like that anymore. That's the big change. (Thomas, Cullompton)

Accordingly, contemporary mobility practices can be understood as representative of shifting relationships between the state, economy, society, and individuals (Clarke et al. 2007; Giddens 1991; Rose and Miller 1992). One consequence of these dynamic relationships is that fulfilling social expectations places great strain on personal and working lives, with the need to be mobile, and to be individually mobile, attaining greater significance:

> [W]ell I feel guilty about the pollution of the car but I just have to [use the car] . . . with the nature of my work, because I am self-employed I can work anything between 80 and 60 hours a week and very flexible hours. So you know I might need to pop into [town for] two hours, I might need to come back later, I might need to have a passenger, I might need to go on to hospital. It's just absolutely impossible to do by bus. (Cheryl, Crediton)

A practices approach to studying mobility can therefore highlight the reflective nature of mobility practices of dominant socio-economic conditions. Within a country like the UK, economic growth is regarded as an objective that can be attained by greater mobility, in a 24-hour, on-demand and highly individualized context. Mobility practices reflect this shift to a speeded-up society (Urry 2007), one where the competitive nature of economic activity necessitates greater and greater willingness to travel and to do so at speed. Accordingly, a second contribution of practice theory to understanding sustainable mobility is to highlight the contradictory nature of behavioral change programs that seek to shift behaviors toward modes of travel that run counter to the economic model being operated. A useful example of this phenomenon is the debate currently ongoing in the UK concerning the construction of a second high speed rail line, between London and Birmingham. Opponents argue that the greater mobility afforded by the new line will encourage more travel between cities and a continued trend for London to become the place 'to do business', further marginalizing regional centers that are in need of regeneration and development. Yet the proponents argue that greater economic activity and national growth can be promoted through enabling people to travel further and faster. This second viewpoint runs contrary to the notion of the sustainable mobility paradigm advocated by Banister (2008), in which the goal is to slow travel down, encourage the notion of 'reasonable travel times', and see mobility as valued rather than wasted time. In Banister's (2008) framework, sustainable mobility involves reducing the need to travel by making the places where people live economically viable and vibrant. In this way, mobility practices are shaped by the expectations and political framings of travel that shape our economic discourse.

The Politics and Planning of the Urban

A final contribution of practice theory to the understanding of mobility is the focus that needs to be placed on the possibilities for change. As noted earlier in this chapter, behavioral change is a fundamentally unambitious project because it bounds the possibilities of change to a small set of incremental changes in people's lives, without considering the underlying physical or socio-economic architectures that frame practices. Accordingly, there is a political dimension to the promotion of sustainable mobility that a practices approach can reveal, by highlighting the ways in which the possibilities of urban renewal and democratic reform are constrained by contemporary policy making and planning. This partly emerges through the ways in which we understand how publics perceive the planning system as it stands:

> I think it's totally confused actually. I mean I don't think the Government has a consistent policy, particularly going through the economic situation we are, where on one hand the Government wants more and more cars to be sold, and on the other hand they are saying they want people to use public transport, not cars. (Thomas, St. Loyes)

What the quotation above highlights is the expectation that politicians ought to provide a greater scope for promoting change through consistent policy making. Indeed, participants recognized that practices were often rooted deep in the political economy of energy supplies that have afforded much of the economic growth and development in recent years. As one respondent noted, 'If you just look at the way it's going, we are governed by basically fossil fuels and if we could find another source of energy it would make things easier' (Thomas, Cullompton).

It therefore seems that practices are also framed by what we might call a politics of fatalism, a sense that we are locked into the ways we behave and that these are both sanctioned and restricted by the forms of politics in which we can engage, a politics of high-energy-dependent consumption, of individualism, and of the status quo. This has important implications for the ways in which we all see the opportunities for change in the future. There are two points to note here. First, the rise of the language of choice architectures has unfortunately restricted much of the discussion on change to the incrementalism of behavioral change. In other words, 'choice' has been constructed in a narrow and unambitious way, crowding out opportunities to reflect on what underlying choice architectures exist. Yet it is clear that practices do form within social, historical, and political contexts that comprise loose architectures that shape such practices. A new politics of mobility and the urban therefore needs to have a much broader political agenda that is radical and open-ended (Dobson 2010). Secondly, the process of exploring social change needs to draw upon the critiques of authors like Owens (2000) who have argued against expert-led approaches to decision making that operate within particular epistemic frameworks and promote hegemonic ways of thinking about the world that suppress innovation. As Johnston (2008) has noted, the current political framing of the consumer-citizen is one that promotes passive individuals, operating within a limited framework of highly individualized action.

CONCLUSION: CHALLENGING BEHAVIORAL CHANGE THROUGH SOCIAL PRACTICE THEORY

When I was invited to write this chapter, one of the comments I received from the editors was, quite understandably, that I should try to emphasize the pragmatic ways in which practice theory can contribute to an understanding of sustainable mobility. Part of the problem with practice theory is that it tends to reveal more about the challenges of a given set of practices than afford opportunities for short-term change or resolution. Indeed, it is the vast attention that has been paid to behavioral change that may have artificially raised expectations about the potential for short-term 'solutions' to the challenges of sustainable mobility in an age dominated by the private motorcar. Accordingly, what I offer by way of conclusions are not policy recommendations or articulations of easy steps for shifting behaviors, but rather three pathways for the use of practice theory to dislodge the dominance of short-term, incrementalist, and individualistic thinking on sustainable mobility.

First, in considering how we might want to promote sustainable mobility, we need to consider what makes people need or want to move in the first place. Here we need to look at both the socio-economic and physical choice architectures that I discussed earlier in the chapter. Mobility has emerged as a key practice in our advanced societies only relatively recently because economic growth has become reliant on the rapid movement of things and people and because we have exploited the affordances of cheap oil to the extreme, by developing transport networks and living arrangements that rely on this versatile but ultimately finite resource (Dennis and Urry 2009; Kunstler 1994). Accordingly, any major shifts in mobility practices will need to be foregrounded by changes in the underlying influences on mobility.

Secondly, a practices approach affords a very real and pragmatic way of shifting away from the research praxis of behavior change. Here there are questions of how the environmental social sciences deal with the challenges presented by global environmental change. It is certainly the case that many researchers have followed the trajectory of social-psychological approaches that have tended to focus on the incremental changes that policy makers have advocated at an individual scale. Yet, as Jones et al. (2011a; 2011b) and Whitehead et al. (2011) have argued, this agenda follows a particular interpretation of behavior and how we might envision social change. A practices approach looks at this from a different perspective, highlighting the role of learned practices through time and the complex outworking of behaviors as interactions between actors and structures. In this way, studying social practices inhabits a place where social science can be utilized to uncover the broader underpinnings of unsustainable practices.

Finally, to effect social change means developing a form of politics that enables discussion of practices rather than behaviors. This means debate about how our cities and towns are planned, about the role and function of the motorcar, about the role of pedestrian space, and about the hypermobility that our current economic system relies upon (Banister 2008). These are currently issues that are politically contentious at a national level, yet they are vital to address if we are to adopt meaningful social practices for promoting sustainable mobility. Such practices are vital to develop and adopt because in a future marked by climate change and higher fuel prices, incremental behavior change is unlikely to be sufficient to withstand the radical shifts in lifestyles that living in a resource-scarce and climate-changed world will depend on.

ACKNOWLEDGEMENTS

The author would like to thank the Economic and Social Research Council for financial support to undertake the research reported in this chapter (Grant No. RES-061-25-0158) and for the comments of three anonymous referees in helping to make revisions to the chapter.

REFERENCES

Ajzen, Icek (1991), 'The theory of planned behavior', *Organizational Behavior and Human Decision Processes*, **50** (2), 179–211.

Anable, Jillian (2005), '"Complacent car addicts" or "aspiring environmentalists"? Identifying travel behaviour segments using attitude theory', *Transport Policy*, **12** (1), 65–78.

Bamberg, Sebastian, Daniel Rölle, and Christoph Weber (2003), 'Does habitual car use not lead to more resistance to change of travel mode?', *Transportation*, **30** (1), 97–108.

Banister, David (2008), 'The sustainable mobility paradigm', *Transport Policy*, **15** (2), 73–80.

Barr, Stewart, Gareth Shaw, and Tim Coles (2011a), 'Times for (un)sustainability? Challenges and opportunities for developing behaviour change policy', *Global Environmental Change*, **21** (4), 1234–1244.

Barr, Stewart, Andrew Gilg, and Gareth Shaw (2011b), 'Citizens, consumers and sustainability: (re)framing environmental practice in an age of climate change', *Global Environmental Change*, **21** (4), 1224–1233.

Barr, Stewart, Gareth Shaw, Tim Coles, and Jan Prillwitz (2010), 'A holiday is a holiday: practicing sustainability, home and away', *Journal of Transport Geography*, **18** (3), 474–481.

Clarke, John, Janet Newman, Nick Smith, Elizabeth Vidler, and Louise Westmarland (2007), *Creating Citizen-Consumers: Changing Publics and Changing Public Services*, London: Sage.

Cresswell, Tim (ed.) (2011), *Geographies of Mobilities: Practices, Spaces, Subjects*, Aldershot: Ashgate.

Crompton, Tom and John Thøgersen (2009), *Simple and Painless? The Limitations of Spillover in Environmental Campaigning*, London: WWF-UK.

Dallen, Jamie (2007), 'Sustainable transport, market segmentation and tourism: the Looe Valley branch line railway, Cornwall, UK', *Journal of Sustainable Tourism*, **15** (2), 180–199.

Darnton, Andrew and V. Sharp (2006), *Segmenting for Sustainability, Reports 1 and 2*, Didcot: Social Marketing Practice.

De Groot, Judith and Linda Steg (2007), 'General beliefs and the Theory of Planned Behavior: the role of environmental concerns in the TPB', *Journal of Applied Social Psychology*, **37** (8), 1817–1836.

Dennis, Kingsley and John Urry (2009), *After the Car*, Cambridge: Polity Press.

Department of the Environment, Food and Rural Affairs (DEFRA) (2008), *Framework for Pro-environmental Behaviours*, London: DEFRA.

Department for Transport (2004), *Smarter Choices: Changing the Way We Travel.*

Final Report of the Research Project: The Influence of 'Soft' Factor Interventions on Travel Demand, London: DfT.

Department for Transport (2011a), *Climate Change and Transport Choices. Segmentation Model: A Framework for Reducing CO$_2$ Emissions from Personal Travel*, London: DfT.

Department for Transport (2011b), *Creating Growth, Cutting Carbon: Making Sustainable Local Transport Happen*, Command Paper 7996, London: The Stationery Office.

Dobson, Andrew (2010), *Environmental Citizenship and Pro-environmental Behaviour: Rapid Research and Evidence Review*, London: Sustainable Development Research Network.

French, Jeff, Clive Blair-Stevens, Dominic McVey, and Rowena Merritt (2009), *Social Marketing and Public Health: Theory and Practice*, Oxford: Oxford University Press.

Freudendal-Pedersen, Malene (2009), *Mobility in Daily Life*, Aldershot: Ashgate.

Giddens, Anthony (1991), *Modernity and Self-Identity: Self and Society in the Late Modern Age*, Cambridge: Polity Press.

Glaeser, Edward L. (2011), *The Triumph of the City: How Our Greatest Invention Makes Us Richer, Smarter, Greener, Healthier, and Happier*, London: Pan Macmillan.

Glaeser, Edward L. and Jesse Shapiro (2001), 'Is there a new urbanism? The growth of U.S. cities in the 1990's', Cambridge, MA, National Bureau of Economic Research Working Paper No. 8357.

Götz, Konrad, Willi Loose, Martin Schmied, and Stephanie Schubert (2003), 'Mobility styles in leisure time', paper presented at the 10th International Conference on Travel Behaviour Research, Lucerne, 10–15 August.

Heath, Yuko and Robert Gifford (2002), 'Extending the theory of planned behavior: predicting the use of public transportation', *Journal of Applied Social Psychology*, **32** (10), 2154–2189.

House of Lords Science and Technology Committee (2011), *Behaviour Change, Second Report of Session 2010–12*, HL Paper 179, London: The Stationery Office.

Johnston, Josée (2008), 'The citizen-consumer hybrid: ideological tensions and the case of Whole Foods Market', *Theory and Society*, **37** (3), 229–270.

Jones, Rhys, Jessica Pykett, and Mark Whitehead (2011a), 'The geographies of soft paternalism in the UK: the rise of the avuncular state and changing behaviour after neoliberalism', *Geography Compass*, **5** (1), 50–62.

Jones, Rhys, Jessica Pykett, and Mark Whitehead (2011b), 'Governing temptation: changing behaviour in an age of libertarian paternalism', *Progress in Human Geography*, **35** (4), 483–501.

Kunstler, James Howard (1994), *The Geography of Nowhere: The Rise and Decline of America's Man-Made Landscape*, New York: Simon and Schuster.

Kunstler, James Howard (1998), *Home from Nowhere: Remaking our Everyday World for the 21st Century*, London: Simon and Schuster.

Lund, Hollie (2003), 'Testing the claims of new urbanism: local access, pedestrian travel, and neighboring behaviors', *Journal of the American Planning Association*, **69** (4), 414–429.

McCormick, John (1989), *Reclaiming Paradise: The Global Environmental Movement*, London: Belhaven.

McKenzie-Mohr, Doug (2000), 'New ways to promote proenvironmental behaviour:

promoting sustainable behaviour: an introduction to community-based social marketing', *Journal of Social Issues*, **56** (3), 543–554.

Møller, Berit (2002), 'Travel mode choice as habitual behaviour: a review of the literature', Working Paper 02-1, Aarhus: Aarhus School of Business.

Owens, Susan (2000), 'Engaging the public: information and deliberation in environmental policy', *Environment and Planning A*, **32** (7), 1141–1148.

Peattie, Ken and Sue Peattie (2009), 'Social marketing: a pathway to consumption reduction?', *Journal of Business Research*, **62** (2), 260–268.

Reckwitz, Andreas (2002), 'Toward a theory of social practices: a development in culturalist theorizing', *European Journal of Social Theory*, **5** (2), 243–263.

Rose, Nikolas and Peter Miller (1992), 'Political power beyond the State: problematics of government', *The British Journal of Sociology*, **43** (2), 173–205.

Scammell, Margaret (2000), 'The internet and civic engagement: the age of the citizen-consumer', *Political Communication*, **17** (4), 351–355.

Seyfang, Gill (2005), 'Shopping for sustainability: can sustainable consumption promote ecological citizenship?', *Environmental Politics*, **14** (2), 290–306.

Shove, Elizabeth (2003), *Comfort, Cleanliness and Convenience: The Social Organization of Normality*, Oxford: Berg.

Shove, Elizabeth (2010), 'Beyond the ABC: climate change policy and theories of social change', *Environment and Planning A*, **42** (6), 1273–1285.

Shove, Elizabeth and Alan Warde (2002), 'Inconspicuous consumption: the sociology of consumption, lifestyles, and the environment', in R.E. Dunlap, F.H. Buttel, P. Dickens, and A. Gijswijt (eds), *Sociological Theory and the Environment: Classical Foundations, Contemporary Insights*, Lanham, MD: Rowman and Littlefield, pp. 230–251.

Shove, Elizabeth, Mika Pantzar, and Matt Watson (2012), *The Dynamics of Social Practice: Everyday Life and How It Changes*, London: Sage.

Slocum, Rachel (2004), 'Consumer citizens and the cities for climate protection campaign', *Environment and Planning A*, **36** (5), 763–782.

Thaler, Richard H. and Cass R. Sunstein (2008), *Nudge: Improving Decisions about Health, Wealth, and Happiness*, New Haven, CT: Yale University Press.

Urry, John (2007), *Mobilities*, Cambridge: Polity Press.

Verbeek, Desirée and Hans Mommaas (2008), 'Transitions to sustainable tourism mobility: the Social Practices Approach', *Journal of Sustainable Tourism*, **16** (6), 629–644.

Verplanken, Bas and Henk Aarts (1999), 'Habit, attitude, and planned behaviour: is habit an empty construct or an interesting case of goal-directed automaticity?', *European Review of Social Psychology*, **10** (1), 101–134.

Verplanken, Bas, Henk Aarts, and Ad Van Knippenberg (1997), 'Habit, information acquisition, and the process of making travel mode choices', *European Journal of Social Psychology*, **27** (5), 539–560.

Whitehead, Mark, Rhys Jones, and Jessica Pykett (2011), 'Governing irrationality, or a more than rational government? Reflections on the rescientisation of decision making in British public policy', *Environment and Planning A*, **43** (12), 2819–2837.

6. Disentangling practices, carriers, and production–consumption systems: a mixed-method study of (sustainable) food consumption

Julia Backhaus, Harald Wieser, and René Kemp

INTRODUCTION

More than three decades ago, cultural anthropologist Mary Douglas coined the expression 'food is not feed' (1982, p. 124). Douglas analyzed links among food, public policy, and social change and studied food as a system of communication and as an art form, asserting that food 'always has a social dimension of the utmost importance' (p. 82). She hoped to establish recognition of 'how food enters the moral and social intentions of individuals' and how it is used to 'create and maintain . . . social relations' (Douglas 1984, p. 10). Undoubtedly, food and practices related to its provision, obtainment, preparation, and consumption carry many dimensions, including economic, political, social, and cultural significance. At the same time, food is tied to family traditions and individual taste, nutritional needs, and preferences.

We focus in this chapter on food consumption and scrutinize how far practice-based approaches aid in developing a better understanding of human behavior, both conceptually and analytically. Reminiscent of Reckwitz's (2002) frequently cited definition of a practice as 'a routinised type of behaviour which consists of several elements, interconnected to one other' (p. 249), we attempt to unpack these elements, yet refrain from focusing solely on the constituents of practices. We contemplate whether additional elements that are conceptually better assigned to practice-carriers or to the production–consumption systems in which practices are embedded can help to explain practice variations that otherwise remain insufficiently understood. The elements of practices, understood to be materials, meanings, and competences (Shove et al. 2012), might engulf individual values or exclude systemic factors that give rise to particular divergences in practice performances. Therefore, we examine, on the one

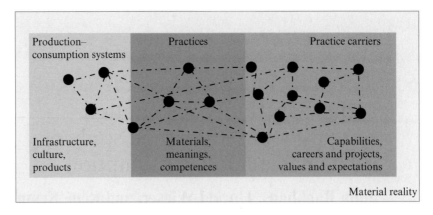

*Figure 6.1   A web of entangled elements across practices, their carriers,
and production–consumption systems*

hand, the role of diversified production–consumption systems that accommodate or even facilitate a wide array of possible practice performances and, on the other hand, elements on the part of individual carriers that interactively give rise to a very diverse, yet patterned, range of observable practices in everyday life. We thus propose a conceptual framework that can cope with practice variations. To this end, we develop the notion of 'webs of entangled elements' across production–consumption systems, practices, and their carriers (Figure 6.1).

Using detailed empirical data derived from several in-depth interviews and a survey of over 1200 respondents (as carriers of practices) in three European countries (Austria, Hungary and the Netherlands as examples of differing production–consumption systems), we trace the role of a number of elements in bringing about variation or supporting stability in practice performances. Though the list of the elements we examine is not exhaustive, it is comprehensive and inspired by prior research (Gram-Hanssen 2011; Reckwitz 2002; Schatzki 1996; Shove et al. 2012; Warde 2005).

We first elaborate our conceptual approach and framework and then describe our methods. These specifications are followed by description of the data and presentation and analysis of our results. We conclude with some reflections on our findings.

CONCEPTUAL APPROACH AND FRAMEWORK

While practice-based approaches for understanding people's everyday behaviors have a long history (Nicolini 2013), they have experienced an interesting and academically demanding revival in recent years, especially with respect to theory development and application (see Chapter 1 of this volume). Faced with the challenges of our times, such as climate change, resource scarcity, and social inequality, practice researchers in the consumption domain (cf. Shove 2010; Warde 2005) promise more appropriate theorizing that seeks to overcome overly individualistic or structural approaches and to develop a better understanding of how to more sustainably organize everyday life. In line with these intentions, this chapter explores the instrumental and operational use of practice theories in studying and conceptualizing diversity of and change in food-consumption practices.

Interesting work has been carried out to date on the emergence of new practices (Shove and Pantzar 2005), the persistence and stability of practices over space and time (Bourdieu 1990), the operationalization of continuity and change in the performance of practices (Gram-Hanssen 2011; Warde 2005), and the nature of individuality (Schatzki 1996). Nevertheless, practice-inspired empirical work faces difficulty capturing the diversity of and change in practices while studying particular (forms of) practices and (configurations of) their constituent elements. In more recent empirical work, Halkier and Jensen (2011) describe instabilities in consumption processes, yet admit that their typology of practices fails to capture these characteristics. They propose to empirically study practice variability through practice performances and performativity. We follow a similar route but focus our efforts on developing a conceptual framework that captures reasons for change and stability in practices.

In this chapter we investigate how entangled and mutually constitutive elements across production–consumption systems, practices, and their carriers give rise to diversified patterns of practices (and hence consumption). The focus is on the integrative practice (Schatzki 1996) of food purchasing, which not only involves a number of dispersed practices such as planning, questioning, examining, and imagining, but is also intricately linked with several other integrative practices including working, moving or traveling, cooking, and eating. To establish our argument we narrow our gaze to a number of specific aspects of the practice of food purchasing, namely the purchasing of processed food, (organic) meat, and (regional, seasonal, and organic) produce. In addition to theoretical or conceptual reasons for choosing this focus, we also strive to contribute to sustainability research on reductions in the consumption of meat and processed food, as well as the use of organic meat and regional, seasonal, and organic fruit and vegetables.

Our conceptual approach draws on the work of Anthony Giddens (1979; 1984) and his notion of the duality of structure. In addition, and in common with other practice theorists, we assert that practices can be understood as nexuses of doings and sayings (Schatzki 1996). Reckwitz (2002) enumerates the following interconnected elements as constituting a practice: 'forms of bodily activities, forms of mental activities, things and their use, a background knowledge in the form of understanding, know-how, states of emotion and motivational knowledge' (p. 250). Consistent with this list of factors, we agree that routinized and conventionalized ways of understanding 'are necessary elements and qualities of a practice in which the single individual participates, not qualities of the individual' (Reckwitz 2002, p. 250). Further, we follow others who emphasize the role of 'the physical', be it in the form of bodies and the tacit knowledge they encapsulate (Polanyi [1958] 1998) or in the form of material objects that are part and parcel of (ensembles of) practices (Shove et al. 2012). The objects, materials, and infrastructures that are necessary for the performance of practices, and thereby also shape practices-as-entities, have been usefully conceptualized as forming part of production–consumption systems.

We would, however, like to refrain from a conceptual understanding of the production–consumption system as an external backdrop against which practices are staged (Spaargaren 2003) or as forming a dynamic setting malleable to and somehow part of practices (Shove et al. 2012). Rather we view production–consumption systems as being constituted by practices, yet considered from the perspective of a single practice or a single carrier as relatively static. Further, despite the appearance of stasis, production–consumption systems are diversified, enabling and constraining a range of performances. Practice-carriers navigate these possibilities at their discretion, yet they are bound by experiences, expectations, and expenditures, among other things. This conceptual approach allows us to test the extent to which the empirically observable patterned variation of practices can be explained by systemic or individual factors without falling into the abyss of determinism. Additionally, the framework helps us understand why certain practice performances are more popular than others.

With these conceptual starting points established, we can advance the following framework, which consists of webs of entangled elements that form part of a practice, its carriers, and production–consumption systems. All elements are embedded in physical reality encompassing resources, objects, infrastructures, and bodies.

As others have demonstrated (Geertz [1973] 2003; Royal Commission on Environmental Pollution 2006), the concept of a web is useful in signifying interrelations and the mutual constitutiveness of its components. Although there is room for flexibility, creativity, and improvisation – or agency – in the performance of every practice, practices come with a set of material objects, necessary knowledge, know-how, competences, understandings, and meanings (Shove et al. 2012). These constituents present themselves to (potential) practice-carriers as elements that need to be mastered to perform a practice (Gherardi and Nicolini 2002). For our research on sustainable food consumption, we conceptualize practices as constituted of and entangled with elements that support, or even facilitate, some variation while simultaneously forming a net or web providing rules, offering guidance, and restricting certain actions or possibilities. We thus closely follow Giddens' (1979; 1984) theory of structuration and understand the mutually dependent and entangled elements as 'webs of drivers and constraints' for a diverse, yet patterned range of practices. Attributing some elements to the central practice considered, other elements to individual carriers, and yet still others to production–consumption systems allows us to profit from the strengths of practice-based approaches. At the same time it enables us to apply these strengths to a detailed analysis of various factors at play that are not necessarily part of the practice considered but are nonetheless influential to its performance.

Empirical work is needed to determine these influential factors. Since the primary purposes of this exploratory study are the development and testing of our conceptual framework, we pre-identified a number of key factors that give rise to patterns of food-purchasing practices (see Table 6.1). With respect to practices, we follow Shove et al. (2012) in considering materials, meanings, and competences. Other elements included are inspired by consumption research or emergent from our data. Concerning the production–consumption system, three elements are notable: infrastructure, culture, and products and services. These constituents encompass the physical environment relevant for the practice of interest (e.g., supermarket, parking space), the products and services available in this environment, and the dominant customs and traditions in society.

Consistent with Reckwitz (2002), we view carriers as 'the unique crossing points of practices' (p. 256). The success of a practice to 'recruit' (Shove and Pantzar 2005) a carrier depends on the individuals' capabilities, career, ongoing projects, and the values and expectations of how a practice is to be performed. An individual's capabilities can be broadly understood as the capacity to adopt a practice and are strongly linked to acquired social, cultural, and economic capital (Bourdieu 1986), as well as to physical and mental abilities. The concept of the career refers to past practices an individual has carried out and the notion of dominant projects denotes the various practices in which an individual is engaged at a specific point in time (Shove et al. 2012). Values and expectations do not delimit the general possibilities of individuals, but in accordance with Schatzki (1996) they 'are threatening transgressors with sanctions' (p. 162) and thereby render particular practice performances more likely than others. Our framework

Table 6.1   Elements of production–consumption systems, practices, and carriers

Production–consumption Systems	Practices	Carriers
Infrastructure	Materials	Capabilities
Culture	Meanings	Career (past practices) and dominant projects (current practices)
Products and services	Competences	Values and expectations

thus invites the empirical investigation of nine (groups of) elements or factors that relate to the (sustainable food-purchasing) practices under scrutiny, their carriers or the production-consumption system they are embedded in (see Table 6.1).

METHODS AND DATA

To explore relevant elements of practices, their carriers, and production–consumption systems that shape sustainable food-purchasing practices, we collected qualitative and quantitative data through semi-structured interviews and a questionnaire survey. Although social practices are our primary unit of analysis we also include features of practice-carriers and production–consumption systems as secondary units of analysis that shape everyday practices.

Some students of practices who doubt people's ability to reflect meaningfully about practices view both methods of data collection we used critically. This concern is based on the quality of practices as involving tacit knowledge, which eludes consciousness and leads to a tendency for individuals to rationalize their behaviors when asked to reflect on them (Mirosa et al. 2011). Hence, practice theorists often prefer ethnographic methods to 'less direct' forms of data collection. However, participant-observation data also do not simply present the observed but comprise the observers' interpretations and representations (Atkinson and Coffey 2003). Like Halkier and Jensen (2011), we contend that qualitative data can capture social performances or enactments, allowing for the study of 'doings' and 'sayings' and therefore offering insight into the 'organizing elements' of practices (p. 111).

Similar to Hitchings (2012) we found that respondents do not report naively but that they critically reflect on utterances, often without having (yet) been asked to do so. Based on these experiences, we assert that interviews can be used to tap into discourses about sustainable food-purchasing practices. Conversations and stories are key components of the dissemination and entrenchment of practices (Hitchings 2012; Nicolini 2013; Schatzki 1996).

If interviews are viewed as a 'less direct' method of data collection than participant observation, a quantitative survey can provide an additional mediating instrument. In our view gathering data on the reported behaviors of respondents and their socio-demographic backgrounds, values, and interests offers at least three advantages: 1) a broad-scoped and varied picture of practices and their carriers can be obtained; 2) cross-national and cross-socioeconomic group comparisons are possible; and 3) the popularity and coverage of certain practices, also in relation to one another, can be determined. As Kennedy et al. (2013) have convincingly argued in their study of transportation practices, regression analyses help to show how circumstantial factors have a bearing on consumption practices.

Following the above considerations and our own experiences, we deem both methods – qualitative interviewing and quantitative data collection – capable of uncovering insights about practices if they are applied in a reflective way and if they are triangulated and analyzed with caution. On one hand, the survey data enable us to learn about 'typical performers' as well as the spread of particular food-purchasing practices among certain social groups. Qualitative in-depth interviews, on the other hand, offer information on respondents' reflections on their life circumstances and other relevant elements shaping the food-purchasing practices that we consider here, such as meanings, competences, information, and infrastructure. For instance, due to the predictive power of age in our quantitative model we took care to interview representatives from all age groups in each country. In Hungary, where the survey sample was skewed toward the younger age groups, we took care to recruit two interviewees above the age of 60. Although the number of interviews (n = 15) is dwarfed by the number of survey respondents (n = 1217), each dataset offers valuable insights to this explorative study.

Our large-scale, web-based questionnaire survey forms the quantitative basis of this chapter and was completed by Austrian, Hungarian, and Dutch citizens (n = 1217) with a minimum age of 18 between December 2013 and January 2014.[1] In addition to a wide range of questions about people's behavior in the food, mobility, and housing domains the survey contained a section on respondents' socio-demographic backgrounds as well as a number of statements probing their attitudes and values.[2] The survey section on food consumption asked respondents to report their dietary habits, the percentage of all food purchases that comprise regional, seasonal, and processed food, and how much organic meat and fish they consume.

The Dutch and Austrian samples are representative in terms of age and education and the Austrian sample is also representative with respect to gender. Notable recruitment difficulties arose in Hungary, where Internet use is most prominent among younger generations and people with higher levels of education. These circumstances resulted in overrepresentation of respondents who hold a university degree or higher. The Hungarian sample is representative only in terms of gender.[3]

To better understand the connections between agency, practices, and structures, we conducted ordinal and multinomial logistic regressions. The regression analyses were performed in SPSS version 21. Regressions were used to determine which factors exert a statistically significant influence on the share of food that is seasonal, regional, processed, or organic and the frequency of meat or fish consumption. Logistic regression analysis is an appropriate method when the dependent variable has an ordinal scale because it assumes a specific link function between the dependent and independent variables. All regressions were tested for their model fit, outliers, multicollinearity, dispersion, and the parallelity of lines or proportional odds, respectively. In the case of meat or fish consumption the parallelity of lines was rejected wherefore a multinomial logistic regression is used. Socio-demographic variables, the planning of meals ahead, and a measure for environmental concerns were included in all regressions. Responses to the following questions and statements were taken to define the measure for environmental concerns: 'I feel a (spiritual) connection with nature', 'I like spending time in nature', 'Mankind is over-exploiting natural resources', 'Natural resources need to be preserved for mankind's future generations', 'Natural resources need to be preserved because they are irreplaceable', 'Do you think that future generations will be economically less well-off than present generations as a result of resource depletion?', and 'Do you think that future generations will experience a reduction in general well-being due to resource depletion?' A categorical principal component analysis suggests that environmental concerns are reliably measured (Cronbach's alpha = 0.75).

In addition to the survey, we conducted 15 semi-structured interviews in April and May 2014, with five respondents from each of the three countries, either via telephone or face to face, and lasting on average for 47 minutes. For the analysis, all interviews were transcribed and coded. During the interviews, we invited respondents to describe their food-purchasing practices and subsequently probed into issues that were of specific interest to us, such as the regionality and seasonality of purchased produce. Further, we asked questions about people's emotions, associations, and competences with respect to their food-purchasing practices and the meanings that they attach to particular food characteristics, including organic, regional, or seasonal. Finally, we asked respondents for reflections on how their practices shifted over time and which people, experiences, or systemic aspects played a role in these changes. This technique helped us to avoid the problem of overly purpose-driven explanations typical of social psychological research. Interviewees were selected to capture diversity in terms of gender, age, education, living situation, and lifestyle. Particular attention was also paid to their level of environmental awareness or concern.

RESULTS AND ANALYSIS

To operationalize our focus on sustainable food-purchasing practices, we consider here exclusively the purchasing of regional and seasonal produce and (organic) meat or fish. Results of our statistical analyses, presented in Tables 6.2 and 6.3, depict the output of four ordinal and logistic regressions, where the share of regional food, seasonal food, processed food, and organic meat or fish are regressed on a number of socio-demographic variables as well as a measure of respondents' environmental values and concerns. Additionally, we include in the analysis a measure of the extent to which meals are planned ahead.

Our conceptual framework encourages us to structure the presentation and analysis of the research results around the three realms of (sustainable) food-purchasing practices, their carriers, and food production–consumption systems. As we will see, relevant elements interrelate across these analytically distinguished spheres and it is precisely these dynamics that we are seeking to disentangle. Table 6.4 provides a snapshot of the frequency of various practice performances, the details of which are examined in the ensuing parts of this chapter.

Sustainable Food-purchasing Practices: Materials, Meanings, and Competences

The first elements we disentangle relate to how people use competence to make sense of, give meaning to, and navigate material reality. First, infrastructure exists that facilitates delivery of products and services. These are the same for everyone at a given time and in a particular place and can be viewed as systemic elements. At the same time, these material elements tie practices together and have been considered part of practices (Shove et al. 2012).[4] In other words, particular practice performances are tied to certain places. For instance, regional and organic food is preferably bought at local markets that, in turn, are associated with better and healthier products.

Table 6.2 Buying regional, seasonal, processed food and organic meat or fish

	Regional food			Seasonal food			Processed food			Organic meat/fish		
	1= <10% 2= 10–30% 3= 30–50% 4= 50–80% 5= >80%			1= <10% 2= 10–30% 3= 30–50% 4= 50–80% 5= >80%			1= <10% 2= 10–30% 3= 30–50% 4= >50%			1= >75% 2= 50–75% 3= 25–50% 4= 10–25% 5= <10%		
Link function	logit			logit			logit			logit		
	B		OR	B		OR	B		OR	B		OR
	(SE)			(SE)			(SE)			(SE)		
Threshold												
1	**−1.969****		**0.14**	**−3.795****		**0.02**	0.335		1.40	−1.320		0.27
	(0.488)			**(0.625)**			(0.428)			(0.909)		
2	−0.713		0.49	**−1.897****		**0.15**	**1.856****		**6.40**	−0.225		0.80
	(0.480)			**(0.609)**			**(0.433)**			(0.908)		
3	0.203		1.23	−0.381		0.68	**3.326****		**27.83**	1.213		3.36
	(0.478)			(0.606)			**(0.456)**			(0.911)		
4	**1.067***		**2.91**	—		—	—		—	**2.566****		**13.02**
	(0.479)									**(0.912)**		
Country												
Austria	**0.352****		**1.42**	0.029		1.03	0.279		1.32	**1.848***		**6.35**
	(0.130)			(0.172)			(0.244)			**(0.804)**		
Hungary	**0.446****		**1.56**	−0.236		0.79	**0.361***		**1.43**	**3.826****		**45.90**
	(0.148)			(0.197)			**(0.159)**			**(0.824)**		
Netherlands	—		—	—		—	—		—	—		—

	Coef.	OR	Coef.	OR	Coef.	OR	Coef.	OR
Gender								
Men	**-0.225***	**0.80**	**-0.489***	**0.61**	0.150	1.16	-0.105	0.90
	(0.090)	—	**(0.126)**	—	(0.100)	—	(0.137)	—
Women	—	—	—	0.69	—	—	—	—
Age								
18–25	**-0.866***	**0.42**	—	—	**0.885***	**2.42**	-0.112	0.89
	(0.269)				**(0.304)**		(0.407)	
26–35	**-0.691***	**0.50**	—	—	**0.773***	**2.17**	0.247	1.28
	(0.216)				**(0.255)**		(0.318)	
36–45	-0.263	0.77	—	—	**0.557***	**1.75**	0.106	1.11
	(0.212)				**(0.254)**		(0.312)	
46–55	-0.132	0.88	—	—	**0.500***	**1.65**	0.467	1.60
	(0.208)				**(0.253)**		(0.311)	
56–65	0.009	1.01	—	—	-0.011	0.99	0.203	1.22
	(0.156)				(0.198)		(0.234)	
> 65	—	—	—	—	—	—	—	—
Age²	—	—	**0.058***	**1.06**	—	—	—	—
			(0.026)					
Education								
Secondary school	0.037	1.04	-0.386	0.68	**-0.415***	**0.66**	0.251	1.29
	(0.149)		(0.207)		**(0.168)**		(0.223)	
A levels/Abitur/baccalaureate	0.302	1.35	-0.235	0.79	**-0.391***	**0.68**	0.300	1.35
	(0.123)		(0.178)		**(0.139)**		(0.196)	
Vocational training	0.223	1.25	-0.209	0.81	**-0.347***	**0.71**	0.339	1.40
	(0.125)		(0.180)		**(0.140)**		(0.192)	
University degree or higher	—	—	—	—	—	—	—	—

Table 6.2 (continued)

	Regional food		Seasonal food		Processed food		Organic meat/fish	
	1= <10%		1= <10%		1= <10%		1= >75%	
	2= 10–30%		2= 10–30%		2= 10–30%		2= 50–75%	
	3= 30–50%		3= 30–50%		3= 30–50%		3= 25–50%	
	4= 50–80%		4= 50–80%		4= >50%		4= 10–25%	
	5= >80%		5= >80%				5= <10%	
Link function	logit		logit		logit		logit	
	B	OR	B	OR	B	OR	B	OR
	(SE)		(SE)		(SE)		(SE)	
Income								
<10,000€/year	−0.106	0.90	**−0.772****	**0.46**	0.135	1.14	0.490	1.63
	(0.162)		**(0.227)**		(0.185)		(0.257)	
10–20,000€/year	0.139	1.15	−0.265	0.77	0.228	1.26	**0.553****	**1.74**
	(0.131)		(0.179)		(0.147)		**(0.195)**	
20–30,000€/year	0.116	1.12	0.140	0.87	0.052	1.05	0.307	1.36
	(0.122)		(0.167)		(0.138)		(0.178)	
>30,000€/year	–		–		–		–	
Environmental score	0.010	1.01	**−0.180****	**0.84**	**0.114***	**1.12**	**0.375****	**1.46**
	(0.043)		**(0.060)**		**(0.047)**		**(0.176)**	
−2 log likelihood								
Intercept only	2166.264		2735.066		2027.529		2493.087	
Final	2086.431		2652.653		1903.371		2315.452	
R² Cox and Snell	0.107		0.085		0.126		0.182	

Note: The reference category is 'one day per week or less'; B = coefficients, SE = standard errors, OR = odds ratio; significant coefficients/odds ratios are shown in bold; a * (**) indicates that the coefficient is different from zero at a 5% (1%) level of significance.

Table 6.3 *Eating meat or fish: multinomial regression*

	Every day		4–5 days per week		2–3 days per week	
	B(SE)	OR	B(SE)	OR	B(SE)	OR
Constant	**3.007** (0.752)**	**20.23**	**2.712** (0.725)**	**15.06**	**1.578* (0.747)**	**4.84**
Country						
Austria	**−2.404** (0.480)**	**0.09**	**−0.914* (0.459)**	**0.40**	−0.031 (0.474)	0.97
Hungary	**−1.026** (0.499)**	**0.36**	−0.336 (0.485)	0.71	0.018 (0.506)	1.02
Netherlands	–	–	–	–	–	–
Gender						
Men	**1.453** (0.331)**	4.28	**1.166** (0.319)**	3.21	**0.930** (0.325)**	**2.53**
Women	–	–	–	–	–	–
Age						
18–25	0.368 (0.599)	1.44	0.368 (0.562)	1.45	0.039 (0.588)	1.04
26–35	0.388 (0.505)	1.47	−0.129 (0.485)	0.88	0.108 (0.496)	1.11
36–45	**1.221* (0.617)**	**3.39**	1.006 (0.597)	2.73	**1.239* (0.605)**	**3.45**
46–55	0.104 (0.538)	1.11	−0.206 (0.518)	0.81	0.555 (0.520)	1.74
56–65	−0.666 (0.475)	0.51	−0.758 (0.452)	0.47	−0.495 (0.467)	0.61
> 65	–	–	–	–	–	–
Education						
Secondary school	0.653 (0.599)	1.92	0.439 (0.585)	1.55	0.422 (0.592)	1.52
A levels or similar	**−1.034** (0.431)**	**0.36**	**−0.882* (0.410)**	**0.41**	**−0.846* (0.417)**	**0.43**
Vocational training	−0.243 (0.477)	0.78	−0.191 (0.459)	0.83	−0.234 (0.466)	0.79
University degree(s)	–	–	–	–	–	–
Income						
<10,000€/year	**−1.121* (0.539)**	**0.33**	**−1.187* (0.513)**	**0.31**	−0.534 (0.518)	0.59
10–20,000€/year	−0.723 (0.451)	0.49	−0.662 (0.430)	0.52	−0.447 (0.439)	0.64
20–30,000€/year	0.500 (0.517)	1.65	0.256 (0.506)	1.29	0.789 (0.511)	2.20
>30,000€/year	–	–	–	–	–	–
Environmental score	0.247 (0.148)	1.28	0.196 (0.141)	1.22	−0.009 (0.143)	0.99

Note: The reference category is 'one day per week or less'; B = coefficients, SE = standard errors, OR = odds ratio; significant coefficients/odds ratios are shown in bold; a * (**) indicates that the coefficient is different from zero at a 5% (1%) level of significance. Model fit: −2 log likelihood intercept only: 2472.902, final: 2219.039; R² (Cox and Snell) = 0.229.

Table 6.4   Overview of food-purchasing practice performances

Survey findings
• People report buying seasonal food more often than regional food
• Almost 45 percent of respondents report that more than 50 percent of produce they buy is seasonal
• More than a quarter of respondents indicate that at least 50 percent of produce bought is regional
• More than half indicate that at least 10 percent of produce they buy is processed
• Less than a third of respondents report eating meat every day
• More than 35 percent state they eat meat 4–5 times per week

For some respondents regional and organic food from supermarkets lacks authenticity. This is an example of how the meanings of food, a specific supply system, and a particular place are intertwined.

Our interviews also demonstrated how widely used terms such as 'regional', 'organic', and 'seasonal' food are variously interpreted. For instance, the respondents defined seasonal food in two related, but nevertheless strikingly different, ways. According to the first definition, seasonal food was intuitively thought to comprise those 'products which currently grow in the garden' (Claudia, 39, Austrian). The second definition is similar in so far as it focuses on the time period when a certain product is available. However, what is implicitly referred to is not the time period when a fruit or vegetable grows, but when it is actually made available in the supermarket. This latter interpretation of seasonal food may be indicative of the increasing distance between consumers and producers and the resulting loss of knowledge about the production process that occurs under these circumstances. Further, interpreting all fruits and vegetables that are available in the supermarket during a certain time period to be in-season dismisses the link between seasonality and regionality that several interviewees emphasized. Claudia, a person who greatly values locally produced food, elaborated that seasonal products from elsewhere are not actually seasonal. The crucial criterion for her is 'regionally seasonal' with the local region stretching across a few hundred kilometers in Austria and Germany. Despite this strong linkage between regionality and seasonality, the practices of purchasing regional or seasonal produce involve different 'sayings' and 'meanings'. While seasonality was frequently associated with freshness and fluctuating availability and prices, regionality was more often related to support for local farmers and the local economy, health (pesticides are more commonly used in Spain), or environmental issues

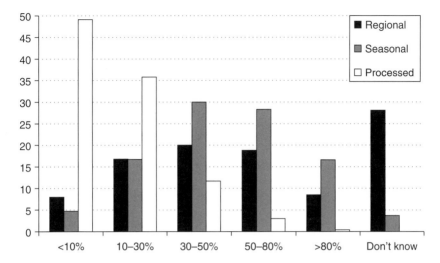

Figure 6.2   Reported frequency of the amount of regional, seasonal, and processed food bought across Austria, Hungary, and the Netherlands (in percentages; n = 1217)

(related to transportation distance). Further, our interviewees' definitions of 'regional' varied greatly from just a few kilometers away to the whole of Europe.

Based on our survey results, the quantitative pattern of food-purchasing practices displays a high consumption of regional, and even greater purchases of seasonal, produce (see Figure 6.2). While regionality was strictly defined in the survey, seasonality remained unexplained. Divergent understandings of seasonal products have certainly confounded the responses in untraceable ways. In contrast to the survey findings, our interviewees recognized little seasonal variation in their diets and explained that, since we live in times of abundance, seasonality is of little concern.

Being a competent carrier of a practice requires practical and general understanding. This can turn out to be problematic in the case of sustainable food purchasing. In general, people use a limited number of information sources to evaluate products. When pressed to explain how they knew whether food is regional or seasonal, for instance, respondents mentioned sign-posting, labeling, or market aisles designating regionality or the appearance of seasonal products for cheaper prices at a certain time of the year. The survey revealed high uncertainty around regional food, with nearly 30 percent of respondents stating they do not know how much of their food is regionally produced, while less than 5 and 0 percent claim the same for seasonal and processed food, respectively.

The most important finding is that while those interviewees who do not select food on the basis of strict criteria could not name a single difficulty with food purchasing, the more selective respondents shared several experiences when they felt they lack competence. People who prefer sustainable food alternatives report problems when either a lack or surfeit of eco-labels is provided. As an additional difficulty, not every sustainable food product is available in all supermarkets so people need to acquire detailed knowledge about where to find specific products. If they regard being informed about regionality, seasonality, or other food characteristics as important, our respondents indicated that they work to close knowledge gaps. This is exemplified by Annik and Jan (54 and 60, Dutch) who learned a lot about food in the aftermath of illness to navigate the complex terrain of product ingredients. Over time, this newly acquired knowledge became second nature to them and integral to their practices. According to prominent practice theorists, learning is as much a cognitive and bodily process (Polanyi [1958] 1998) as a social one involving belonging, engaging, and developing identities (Lave and Wenger 1991). The next subsection discusses personal factors in more detail.

Practice-carriers: Capabilities, Careers, and Projects, Values and Expectations

Elements that relate to practice-carriers and that shape and are shaped by practices include capabilities, careers and projects, and values and expectations. The analysis of socio-demographic factors (see Tables 6.2 and 6.3) is used to construct profiles of common or archetypical carriers of (sustainable) food-purchasing practices and reflects their capabilities. Most socio-demographic factors can be interpreted as proxies for the practices an individual has carried in the past and the ways someone is expected to behave. Educational background, for instance, roughly reflects the years a person spent at school and how much cultural capital was accumulated through this practice. This, in turn, may decrease or increase the capabilities of a person to carry a practice. Age, gender, and income level can be interpreted in a similar way. Age and gender also provide some insight into physical abilities.

Overall, the regression output reveals only a few significant factors for each sustainable food-purchasing practice, though some are very strong predictors. Age differences are particularly striking: older respondents are more likely to buy a greater number of regional and seasonal items but less processed food. Similarly, respondents with a high educational background (university degree or higher) are more prone to buy processed food, but consume less meat or fish than their counterparts who only completed secondary school. These findings are consistent with results reported in other studies (Diamantopoulos et al. 2003; Zepeda and Li 2006).

Further, interviewees explained how life circumstances like their family situation and time pressure play a role in the consumption of processed food. Different practices, such as the consumption of fresh vs. processed products, compete for performance. Candel (2001), Ragaert et al. (2004), and Jabs and Devine (2006) suggest that convenience is an important driver for consuming processed food. Accordingly, perceived time pressure, often caused by long working hours, makes people buy processed food and ready-made meals instead of spending the time to prepare a meal from fresh ingredients. One respondent Peter (41, Austrian) elaborated how his dietary habits tend to fluctuate. After periods of eating a lot of junk food and skipping breakfast there are times in which he is reportedly more reflective and switches to a 'holistic' diet. He attributes these changes to his self-employed working circumstances and ever-fluctuating working hours. Thus additional leisure time may, for some people, provide opportunity for critical reflection on and changes in their dietary habits. However, our regression results show that differences in the total number of hours people work per week cannot explain variations in the purchase of regionally seasonal or processed food.[5] Our respondents also suggested that time constraints are relevant for the purchase of regional produce and meat, though for different reasons. One interviewee considered meat as a rather simple and timesaving option or, in other words, a convenience good.

How might we explain these contradictory findings? Warde et al. (1998) reasoned that it is not working time that leads to increased consumption of processed food. In fact, working hours per person have remained constant or even declined in most European countries in recent decades. Yet, according to the authors, working hours are becoming increasingly scattered, which makes it difficult to synchronize time–space paths in everyday life. Convenience goods, including ready-made meals, help people to free up time for social activities. This may explain the insignificance of working time in the regression, while at the same time acknowledging the importance of time that we could trace in the interviews.[6]

The above compellingly shows that practice-carriers need to acquire competences to become carriers but practices also need to adapt to the life situation of their carriers. Changes in life circumstances thus provide fertile ground for practices to recruit new carriers and for new practices to emerge (Schäfer et al. 2012; Shove et al. 2012). If people face altered conditions, they are often forced to abandon certain habits and re-organize their life. Situations that typically lead (at least periodically) to persistent life-style changes, including with respect to food-consumption practices, are moving out of one's parental home (András, 30, Hungarian) or enrolling children in school (Annik, 53, Dutch).

However, whether changing conditions actually lead to the adoption of new food-buying practices also depends on values and expectations. Maria (74, Austrian), for example, almost exclusively buys seasonal and organic food from the region and has not changed her diet over the years, despite financially difficult periods. Her strong commitment to environmental conservation made her stick to her sustainable diet. Survey results also suggest that sustainable food-purchasing practices are more common among people who agree with statements such as 'I like spending time in nature' and 'I feel a (spiritual) connection with nature.'

In addition to values, the expectations of how a practice is to be performed also form an essential element in our proposed framework. Expectations depend as much on individual needs as on perception of how a practice is 'normally' performed. Further, products do shape the owner's expectations and may render the user incompetent if she is unable to live up to them (Shove et al. 2007). For example, shared expectations of food purchasing may explain the observed differences across age groups. Our older respondents often described food purchasing as a social activity and sought the contact with farmers while our younger interviewees highlighted the possibility to discover new products when shopping for food and the satisfaction of finding items that they like. Clearly, performances of the same practice vary congruently with elements related to individual carriers but are similar for cohorts comparable in terms of socio-demographics, values, or projects (life circumstances).

Production–Consumption Systems: Infrastructure, Culture, Products

Some of the factors that influence food-purchasing practices are located outside the sphere of individual consumers and we can consider them to be elements of the production–consumption system. As outlined above, these factors are not external to practices, but may be more appropriately conceptualized as forming part of other practices, such as policy making. For individual carriers and the practices in which they engage, these factors appear highly persistent and immutable.

Nearly all of our respondents questioned the reliability of information disclosed on product packaging about country or region of origin, production method, or ingredients contained. This uncertainty can contribute to a certain sense of powerlessness:

> When I buy some cold cuts or ham, for instance, it is very difficult at Billa [Austrian retail chain] to find out where the products are really coming from. In Austria, it is enough that the packaging is done in Austria to label it with an 'A'. Sometimes, a feeling of powerlessness comes up in such situations because one is actually unable to see the origin of the ham I buy. (Claudia, 39, Austrian)

Some respondents suspect capitalist motives to be the key factor determining the strategies of producers and retailers. The purchase of regional, seasonal, and organic products and the boycott of processed food are sometimes framed as a criticism of the prevailing food-provisioning system. At the same time, the purchase of such products may be interpreted as a reaction on the part of consumers to rebuild trust with producers (Sassatelli and Scott 2001).

The production–consumption systems differ, in the first place, with respect to infrastructures and availability of products. Austrian and Dutch consumers experienced the proliferation of modern supermarkets much earlier than their Hungarian counterparts. In 1993, the Hungarian food-distribution system was estimated to be 25 years behind the West (Mueller et al. 1993). Even though Hungarian food-provisioning processes have experienced rapid convergence toward western European standards, domestic demand for organic food remains negligible (see Table 6.3) and domestically produced organic produce is largely grown for export (Kjærnes and Torjusen 2012).

The strong cross-national variations evident in our survey, for example the substantially lower likelihood of Dutch respondents to buy regional food, may be due to the fact that this practice faces an unfavorable environment in the Netherlands. While only 47 percent of the population considers the geographical origin of food to be important – the lowest share among the EU-27 countries, the provenance of food is important to 78 percent of Austrians and 81 percent of Hungarians (Eurobarometer 2012).

Cross-national differences prevail in all of the aspects related to sustainable consumption addressed in our survey with the exception of the purchasing of seasonal food. These differences relate to cultural diversity as well as to varying provisioning systems which are, of course, intricately intertwined. Our survey indicates how individual practices vary but that observable patterns prevail. For example, Dutch food culture is usually associated with a practical attitude to food, where it is mainly valued for its functions like nutrition and health, rather than the pleasure of eating (de Borja et al. 2010). Further, consumption of simple snacks throughout the day and a cooked meal for dinner is typical in the Netherlands. In Austria and Hungary, lunch plays a more prominent role in everyday life. Such dominant food patterns are deeply rooted in society, passed on from one generation of carriers to the next, and typically remain relatively stable over time.

CONCLUSION

This chapter is part of an emerging literature on social practices which attends to entangled elements. Our research stands out by investigating the carriers of practices and the multitude of shaping factors in considerable detail with the help of in-depth interviews and the use of survey analysis. Our motivation to conduct a multi-method analysis of food-purchasing practices has been twofold. On the one hand, our study is driven by questions concerning which factors influence (more sustainable) practice performances and, on the other hand, by a desire to capture the diversity in these practice performances, both conceptually and analytically. The conceptual framework of a web of entangled elements that we developed for this purpose stretched beyond elements that form part of a single practice and included others related to practice-carriers and production–consumption systems.

It became apparent how some elements of food purchasing intersect with other practices and most notably with participation in the labor force. Further, we showed that broadening the analysis of relevant elements related to practice-carriers, as well as to systemic factors, highlights and systematizes the various reasons for practice variability. The main sources for innovation in practices are thus the confrontation of practices with new or changed carriers and production–consumption systems. Consequently, studying change or innovation requires the investigation of the factors we attribute to the production–consumption system (culture, products, infrastructure) and an understanding how practices are interrelated, including the past and present practices of individuals. By drawing attention to the influential factors that are usefully conceptualised outside of the focal practice(s) under scrutiny, our framework makes many sources for change visible that are not discussed in the literature on social practices (see Gram-Hanssen 2011).

Our discussion shows how looking at different elements from a practice, an individual or a systemic perspective offers new insights into how elements tie bundles of practices together. Material elements, for example, can be understood as a static backdrop (from a practice perspective), as a range of possibilities (from a carrier's perspective), or as a historically and culturally varying setting for activities (from a production–consumption system perspective). These findings open up practice research to more quantitative approaches for the analysis of how practices are interrelated, across space, time and individuals. The chapter also builds a bridge between practice and transition research by giving attention to 'landscape' factors (values, beliefs, and socio-demography) and regimes of practices (Hargreaves et al. 2013; McMeekin and Southerton 2012). We therefore experienced our focus on a set of (related) practices as empirically interesting and conceptually innovative (see also Bellotti and Mora 2014; Pullinger et al. 2013; Wieser et al. 2014).

Our survey findings offer insights into how various factors related to country-specific differences in production–consumption systems influence food-purchasing practices. As mentioned at the outset, we acknowledge that production–consumption systems can be conceptualized as a set of practices corroborated in customs and traditions, shared norms and values, legislation, or infrastructures. Our analysis of a particular set of practices related to food consumption has, however, proven to be more revealing by considering production–consumption systems as the rather static, yet diverse, settings with which practitioners engage in everyday life. Based on our interviews, this conceptualization allowed us to trace the material aspects to which people pay particular attention and the meanings they attach to places, products or practices that they consider to be important in navigating material and cultural systems.

In addition to delivering interesting insights into the geographical scope of particular practice performances, our survey also proved to be an appropriate method of choice for elaborating their socio-demographic scope. Supplemented by our interview findings, it became apparent how practice performances shift with changing life circumstances and time constraints, after a significant experience or simply due to information gleaned through the media. These shifts in performances, which otherwise are rather stable for longer periods of time, can be viewed as punctuated equilibria, with one and the same person being able to perform several equilibria, depending on which set of materials, meanings, and competences she is drawing. In addition, some aspects of practice performances, for example the personal commitment and dedication to eat regional food as much as possible, can remain stable over an entire lifetime despite changing circumstances.

With respect to shedding light on the practice of sustainable food purchasing itself, our survey and interview findings help to demonstrate how the materials, meanings, and competences tied to particular forms of this practice – buying regional, seasonal, or organic produce, or purchasing meat – interrelate. Further entanglements were found with other practices such as working or cooking. The practice we studied proved to be remarkably diverse, yet patterned similarities emerged.

Overall, our framework is conducive to identifying elements that can be attributed conceptually to production–consumption systems (infrastructure, culture, products, and services), to the individual practice-carrier (capabilities, career and projects, values and expectations) or to the particular practice under study (materials, meanings, competences). Not least due to their entanglement, the analytical attribution of certain elements to the practice under study, its carriers, or the production–consumption system is not always straightforward. Overall, our findings reinforce the value of a social practice perspective: socio-cultural and material contexts are deeply embedded in carriers of practice and recursively reproduced through the actions of everyday life. We found patterns of practices to be relatively stable at different levels of aggregation, across socioeconomic groups, and in various material settings. Shifts toward sustainable practices require engaging the web of entangled elements across (competing) practices, their carriers, and production–consumption systems.

NOTES

1. The survey was conducted in the context of the POLFREE project, funded as part of the European Union's Seventh Framework Programme (FP7/2007–2013) under grant agreement No. 308371. For a complete list of all questions and a report on all consumption domains addressed (food, housing, and mobility) refer to the POLFREE Report 1.6 available at http://www.polfree.eu/publications/publications-2014/individual-behavioural-barriers-to-resource-efficiency. The survey response rates for each country were: Austria 21.6 percent, Hungary 25.0 percent, and the Netherlands 61.0 percent. We devote attention to three countries because the associated project that gave rise to this work required a focus on several European countries. Selection of these three nations enabled the research team to economize on translation costs and facilitated cooperation with the project partners. In our view, the comparison of any three countries can be expected to bear interesting insights.
2. In our research, attitudes and values relate to cultural contexts and dominant socio-cultural meanings.
3. Detailed information on the sample can be found in Wieser (2014).
4. Furthermore, different people experience material elements differently and this invites an analysis of how the same product or place is variously viewed. For example, while some respondents consider food purchasing a necessary duty and avoid it as much as possible (András, 30, Hungarian), others feel a sense of achievement when making 'good choices' (Jan, 60, Dutch), and, yet again, others thoroughly enjoy it when visiting a farmers' market (Zsófia, 65, Hungarian).
5. Working hours per week was initially included in the regression analyses but found to be insignificant. Since the question on working hours only applied to employed people, the variable was dropped to better account for the differences among other occupational groups.
6. Another possible explanation is that food-related chores are shared among our respondents' household members in such a way that the effect of work time on food consumption is dampened.

REFERENCES

Atkinson, Paul and Amanda Coffey (2003), 'Revisiting the relationship between participant observation and interviewing', in J.F. Gubrium and J.A. Holstein (eds), *Postmodern Interviewing*, Thousand Oaks, CA: Sage, pp. 109–122.

Bellotti, Elisa and Emanuela Mora (2014), 'Networks of practices in critical consumption', *Journal of Consumer Culture*, published online before print, 26 May 2014. doi: 10.1177/1469540514536191.

Bourdieu, Pierre (1986), 'The forms of capital', in J. Richardson (ed.), *Handbook of Theory and Research for the Sociology of Education*, New York: Greenwood, pp. 241–258.

Bourdieu, Pierre (1990), *The Logic of Practice*, Malden, MA: Polity Press.

Candel, Math (2001), 'Consumers' convenience orientation towards meal preparation: conceptualization and measurement', *Appetite*, **36** (1), 15–28.

Diamantopoulos, Adamantios, Bodo Schlegelmilch, Rudolf Sinkovics, and Greg Bohlen (2003), 'Can socio-demographics still play a role in profiling green consumers? A review of the evidence and an empirical investigation', *Journal of Business Research*, **56** (6), 465–480.

de Borja, Juan, Lenneke Kuijer, and Walter A. Aprile (2010), 'Designing for sustainable food practices in the home,' paper presented at the ERSCP–EMSU Conference, Delft, The Netherlands, 25–29 October 2010.

Douglas, Mary (1982), *In the Active Voice*, New York: Routledge and Kegan Paul.

Douglas, Mary (1984), 'Standard social uses of food: introduction', in Mary Douglas (ed.), *Food in the Social Order: Studies of Food and Festivities in Three American Communities*, New York: Russell Sage Foundation, pp. 1–39.

Eurobarometer (2012), *Europeans' Attitudes Towards Food Security, Food Quality and the Countryside: Report*, Special Eurobarometer 389, Brussels: European Commission.

Geertz, Clifford ([1973] 2003), 'Thick description: toward an interpretive theory of culture', in Y. Lincoln and N. Denzin (eds), *Turning Points in Qualitative Research: Tying Knots in a Handkerchief*, Walnut Creek, CA: AltaMira Press, pp. 236–247.

Gherardi, Silvia and Davide Nicolini (2002), 'Learning the trade: a culture of safety in practice', *Organization*, **9** (2), 191–223.

Giddens, Anthony (1979), *Central Problems in Social Theory: Action, Structure and Contradiction in Social Analysis*, Berkeley, CA: University of California Press.

Giddens, Anthony (1984), *The Constitution of Society: Outline of the Theory of Structuration*, Berkeley, CA: University of California Press.

Gram-Hanssen, Kirsten (2011), 'Understanding change and continuity in residential energy consumption', *Journal of Consumer Culture*, **11** (1), 61–78.

Halkier, Bente and Iben Jensen (2011), 'Methodological challenges in using practice theory in consumption research. Examples from a study on handling nutritional contestations of food consumption', *Journal of Consumer Culture*, **11** (1), 101–123.

Hargreaves, Tom, Noel Longhurst, and Gill Seyfang (2013), 'Up, down, round and round: connecting regimes and practices in innovation for sustainability', *Environment and Planning A*, **45** (2), 402–420.

Hitchings, Russell (2012), 'People can talk about their practices', *Area*, **44** (1), 61–67.

Jabs, Jennifer and Carole Devine (2006), 'Time scarcity and food choices: an overview', *Appetite*, **47** (2), 196–204.

Kennedy, Emily, Harvey Krahn, and Naomi T. Krogman (2013), 'Taking social practice theories on the road: a mixed-methods case study of sustainable transportation', in M.J. Cohen, H.S. Brown, and P.J. Vergragt (eds), *Innovations in Sustainable Consumption: New Economics, Socio-technical Transitions and Social Practices*, Cheltenham and Northampton, MA: Edward Elgar Publishing, pp. 252–276.

Kjærnes, Unni and Hanne Torjusen (2012), 'Beyond the industrial paradigm? Consumers and trust in food', in G. Spaargaren, P. Oosterveer and A. Loeber (eds), *Food Practices in Transition: Changing Food Consumption, Retail and Production in the Age of Reflexive Modernity*, New York: Routledge, pp. 86–106.

Lave, Jean and Etienne Wenger (1991), *Situated Learning: Legitimate Peripheral Participation*, New York: Cambridge University Press.

McMeekin, Andrew and Dale Southerton (2012), 'Sustainability transitions and final consumption: practices and sociotechnical systems', *Technology Analysis and Strategic Management*, **24** (4), 345–361.

Mirosa, Miranda, Daniel Gnoth, Rob Lawson and Janet Stephenson (2011), 'Rationalising energy-related behaviour in the home: insights from a value-laddering approach', *European Council for an Energy Efficient Economy Summer Study Proceedings*, pp. 2109–2119, available at: http://proceedings.eceee.org/vis-abstrakt.php?event=1&doc=8-561-11 (accessed 11 February 2014).

Mueller, Rene Dentiste, James Wenthe, and Peter Baron (1993), 'Case note: the evolution of distribution systems: a framework for analysing market changes in Eastern Europe: the case of Hungary', *International Marketing Review*, **10** (4), 36–52.

Nicolini, Davide (2013), *Practice Theory, Work, and Organization: An Introduction*, New York: Oxford University Press.

Polanyi, Michael ([1958] 1998), *Personal Knowledge: Towards a Post-Critical Philosophy*, New York: Routledge.

Pullinger, Martin, Alison Browne, Ben Anderson, and Will Medd (2013), *Patterns of Water: The Water Related Practices of Households in Southern England, and Their Influence on Water Consumption and Demand Management*, Lancaster, UK: Lancaster University.

Ragaert, Peter, Wim Verbeke, Frank Devlieghere, and Johan Debevere (2004), 'Consumer perception and choice of minimally processed vegetables and packaged fruits', *Food Quality and Preference*, **15** (3), 259–270.

Reckwitz, Andreas (2002), 'Toward a theory of social practices: a development in culturalist theorizing', *European Journal of Social Theory*, **5** (2), 243–263.

Royal Commission on Environmental Pollution (2006), *26th Report: The Urban Environment*, available at: http://webarchive.nationalarchives.gov.uk/20060716005107/http://www.rcep.org.uk/urbanenvironment.htm (accessed 11 February 2014).

Sassatelli, Roberta and Alan Scott (2001), 'Novel food, new markets and trust regimes: responses to the erosion of consumers' confidence in Austria, Italy and the UK', *European Societies*, **3** (2), 213–244.

Schäfer, Martina, Melanie Jaeger-Erben, and Sebastian Bamberg (2012), 'Life events as windows of opportunity for changing towards sustainable consumption patterns? Results from an intervention study', *Journal of Consumer Policy*, **35** (1), 65–84.

Schatzki, Theodore (1996), *Social Practices: A Wittgensteinian Approach to Human Activity and the Social*, New York: Cambridge University Press.

Shove, Elizabeth (2010), 'Beyond the ABC: climate change policy and theories of social change', *Environment and Planning A*, **42** (6), 1273–1285.

Shove, Elizabeth and Mika Pantzar (2005), 'Consumers, producers and practices: understanding the invention and reinvention of Nordic walking', *Journal of Consumer Culture*, **5** (1), 43–64.

Shove, Elizabeth, Mika Pantzar, and Matt Watson (2012), *The Dynamics of Social Practice: Everyday Life and How it Changes*, Thousand Oaks, CA: Sage.

Shove, Elizabeth, Matt Watson, Martin Hand, and Jack Ingram (2007), *The Design of Everyday Life*, New York: Berg.

Spaargaren, Gert (2003), 'Sustainable consumption: a theoretical and environmental policy perspective', *Society and Natural Resources*, **16** (8), 687–701.

Warde, Alan (2005), 'Consumption and theories of practice', *Journal of Consumer Culture*, **5** (2), 131–153.

Warde, Alan, Elizabeth Shove, and Dale Southerton (1998), 'Convenience, schedules and sustainability', paper presented at the European Science Foundation Workshop on Consumption, Everyday Life and Sustainability, Lancaster University, Lancaster, UK, 27–29 March.

Wieser, Harald (2014), *Zooming In and Zooming Out on the Practice of Sustainable Food Shopping: Evidence from Austria, Hungary and The Netherlands*, Master's thesis, Vienna University of Economics and Business.

Wieser, Harald, Julia Backhaus, and René Kemp (2014), 'Exploring (in)consistencies and spillovers across sustainable food shopping practices', paper presented at the 5th International Conference on Sustainability Transitions, 27–29 August, Utrecht University, Utrecht.

Zepeda, Lydia and Jinghan Li (2006), 'Who buys local food?', *Journal of Food Distribution Research*, **37** (3), 1–11.

7. Getting emotional: historic and current changes in food consumption practices viewed through the lens of cultural theories

Marlyne Sahakian

INTRODUCTION

Social practice theory has brought new perspectives to 'sustainable consumption' studies in terms of both conceptual developments and rich empirical research. One appealing and shared understanding is that practices change over time, suggesting that shifts away from current unsustainable practices toward more environmentally sound and socially just alternatives are possible. Much work has focused on how to recruit new practitioners to more 'sustainable' practices (Jack 2013; Plessz et al. 2014; Shove 2012). What has been called the 'practice turn' in consumption studies, however, also represents a turning away from cultural readings of consumption. Cultural studies have tended toward a structuralist approach, from which practice theory purposefully breaks. Rather than assume that a pre-existent 'culture' is made visible in social life, through symbols and rituals, practice theory suggests that everyday practices are the stuff of which social life is made of and the object of social analysis.

There was good reason to shift away from cultural approaches in relation to 'sustainability'. Consumer culture tended to focus on conspicuous consumption and status goods, failing to grapple with much of our everyday, mundane activities that are inconspicuous yet environmentally significant (Shove and Warde 1998).[1] Spaargaren (2013; 2014) suggests that attention could be placed back on a cultural reading of consumption, as complementary to social practice theory. Building on the work of Collins (2004), Spaargaren proposes that the role of emotional energy, created during situated practices within specific contexts, could influence how practitioners are recruited by new practices. He calls for further research on the symbolic meaning of objects, or understanding how meaning is created and how it circulates, within practices and over space and time.

The goal of this chapter is to determine whether a cultural reading of consumption, focused on symbolic meaning and associated emotional energy, can enhance social practice theory approaches toward understanding opportunities for more 'sustainable' consumption patterns. Food consumption is an interesting theme to consider in this respect, as the practice of preparing food in the home has changed considerably over the past century. Looking at how practices evolved in the past, and comparing them with current efforts to sway consumption practices toward more sustainable patterns, could tell us something about how more sustainable forms of consumption might be possible in the future. With this in mind, I discuss and contrast two shifts in household food consumption in the European context: the diffusion of household appliances in the past and current trends toward community-supported agriculture (CSA).

Household appliances such as washing machines and air-conditioning units have transitioned from being novelties to becoming normal items over several decades (Cooper 1998; Sahakian 2014; Shove 2003). As access to electricity increased and appliances became more readily available, chores – such as washing laundry – that had been done in factories during the period of industrialization, found their way back into more households in the early 20th century. This 'industrial revolution in the home' (Cowan 1976) did not happen overnight and varied greatly between urban and rural regions, by social classes, and by country (Parr 1997). Appliances, including refrigerators, microwaves, bread machines, and the like, continue to change the way food is stored and prepared in the home.

Related to the prevalence of household appliances has been the acceleration of international trade, the expansion of industrialized agriculture and processed foods, and the creation of new systems of distribution such as supermarket chains. Increasingly, consumers in industrial societies are calling for food produced closer to home and through more sustainable practices (Princen et al. 2002). Efforts to promote local and organic agriculture through CSA have grown in importance since the 1970s, and are part of a wider trend toward alternative agrofood networks (Goodman et al. 2012). A CSA offers unique modes of provision and access to fresh produce that is bought on a contractual basis, thereby reducing or eliminating mainstream retail provisioning and packaged/processed foods. What appears in a CSA vegetable basket depends on the farmer, the natural environment, and the season, not on consumer choice.

In the section that follows, I briefly outline my methodology and then introduce the conceptual framework, drawing out key research questions that will guide my analysis. In the next section, I present both case studies and highlight my main arguments for each of them. I then discuss both cases in relation to the conceptual framework and draw some conclusions related to social practice theories and the usefulness of cultural readings of consumption.

METHODOLOGY

This chapter presents two case studies from Europe related to changing household food consumption practices toward greater sustainability.[2] Case-study research can be a relevant method when asking questions about 'how' and 'why' certain changes have taken place, while making use of multiple sources of evidence to investigate such an empirical topic. When more than one case is presented, cross-case conclusions can be drawn (Yin 2009). For the first case, I draw on secondary sources, including academic publications, as well as advertisements and other marketing materials, to understand how the shift toward the acquisition of new appliances in the home played out over time. For the second case study, I use existing literature to introduce the trend toward CSAs around the world and then focus on a particular CSA service offered in Switzerland, a country that has been a forerunner in the CSA movement.

For the CSA case, I conducted in-depth semi-structured interviews with 21 members of a Swiss CSA in 2014 to understand how practices associated with this type of food-provisioning system are playing out today. All respondents were clients of the same CSA service, which at the time had 135 members. They were contacted via the CSA provider through a regular weekly email correspondence and I arranged interviews with those members who agreed to participate either in their workplace, home, or neighborhood. Weekly observations also took place over a three-month period at the location where the CSA service is being offered: a restaurant and shop in Geneva. My interviews focused on the participants' perceptions regarding the CSA service and how it relates to their daily practices. I did not ask questions pertaining to values or beliefs directly, but rather this information came out in my analysis of the exchanges and through my observations. The respondents varied greatly in terms of socio-economic factors and their motivation for participating, from a young woman on a meager student budget motivated by environmental concerns, to a concierge concerned about her health, to a single mother of four seeking an affordable way to provide nutritious food, to a single male business executive happy to support local producers. All of the interviews were recorded, transcribed, and coded; respondents remain anonymous.

CONCEPTUAL FRAMEWORK

Douglas and Isherwood's (1979) seminal work begins with a critique of how classical economists approach consumption studies. More than three decades later the idea of consumers as rational, independent actors, meetings needs and basing decisions on price and information is still appealing to researchers and policy makers. When related to research and practice toward greater sustainability, in both environmental and social terms, this limited vision of consumption is buoyed by the view that technological advances (existing or imagined) will resolve environmental issues, and that individual consumers need only embrace these solutions to resolve environmental problems.

As a countertrend, approaches informed by social practice theories have been gaining in popularity among a growing group of researchers focused on current unsustainable consumption patterns and practices. Earlier developments in practice theory by scholars such as Bourdieu (1979) and Giddens (1984) sought to grapple with the dichotomy between human subjectivity and social structure without entirely forgoing human agency. Since then, Schatzki (1996) and Reckwitz (2002) have furthered these discussions, the former through a Wittgensteinian approach and the latter building on Bourdieu, Giddens, Taylor, and later works by Foucault (see Chapter 1 for an overview of social practice theories of sustainable consumption).[3] Contemporary researchers have differing perspectives on what constitutes a practice, and how practices play out in social life and over time, in relation to different resources and artifacts. The overarching question addressed in this chapter is whether cultural interpretations of consumption should be brought back into the practice theory discussion, noting the merits and challenges involved in doing so.

The idea of bringing culture back into the study of consumption stems from an earlier article by Wilk (2002), which makes the case for considering different theoretical readings of consumption divided into three categories – social, cultural, and individual approaches. While each approach may be flawed or partial, he argues that they may still have something to offer toward addressing global environmental problems. In relation to cultural theories, Wilk looks specifically at the role of mass media – including advertising – in terms of how cultural themes and meanings are 'hijacked' to make particular goods and services desirable. Spaargaren (2013) contributed to further revive the agency–culture debate, drawing mostly on the work of Collins (2004). Spaargaren suggests that researchers might return to objects, not solely as service providers, but as carriers of cultural meaning. For Collins, the main objects of sociological analysis are rituals, in a 'demystified' reading that includes all social gatherings where repeated enactments of a type of relationship between people take place (Kemper 2011). It is during these interactions that meanings and values are produced, around symbols and objects, and in a dynamic interaction among people, space, and artifacts. During a ritual, a type of 'collective effervescence' can occur – a term Collins borrows from Emile Durkheim. From that moment onward, people carry with them 'emotional energy' derived from that situation, embedded in individuals and associated objects.

Spaargaren argues that such a cultural approach to sustainable consumption is both innovative and relevant as it 'shows how norms, morals and awareness result from situated interactions in which eco-friendly symbols, objects and morals are used by individuals to gain energy and to "produce" sustainability' (2013, p. 244). Spaargaren suggests that the collective interactions discussed by Collins are similar to social practices and that the added element of emotional energy is another prism through which we can understand how people are recruited into new practices. Studying energy in terms of services and related practices has been useful (Sahakian and Steinberger 2011; Wilhite et al. 1996; Wilhite and Lutzenhiser 1999), but what about the cultural meaning and emotions associated with certain energy-intensive objects? For example, air-conditioning units are currently a status symbol among the growing middle classes in Southeast Asia (Sahakian 2014). Why is this the case and how could, say, photovoltaic panels come to generate the same positive emotional energy?

The notion of objects having cultural meaning builds on theoretical developments during the 1970s. Baudrillard (1968) proposed understanding objects as having 'symbolic value' in the attribution of meaning to an object, which then has 'sign value' in its ability to communicate this meaning to others. Douglas and Isherwood's (1979) cultural reading positioned consumption as a form of symbolic behavior with goods coded for communication, beyond their practical uses or functional purposes. While Douglas and Isherwood also proposed rituals as moments that give meaning to goods, they considered consumption as a form of classification that reflects an organized system of social relations or social hierarchy. Goods become a way for people to make sense of their universe and are a visible part of a seemingly pre-existing culture. Collins (2004) breaks with this structuralist approach in his work and indicates a practice approach when he says: 'My analytical strategy . . . is to start with the dynamics of situations; from this we can derive almost everything that we want to know about individuals, as a moving precipitate across situations' (p. 4). Culture is not the source of practices; attention is placed on the actual mechanisms of how situations play out, in specific contexts.

During a ritual, positive emotions – such as feelings of 'confidence, elation, strength, enthusiasm, initiative in taking action' (Collins 2004, p. 49) – are what motivate us, what set us in motion in relation to that ritual and beyond that moment, through 'interaction ritual chains'. Emotional energy also charges the objects involved in a ritual. It is during these emotionally charged encounters that collective symbols are generated, which Collins describes as the 'lenses through which we see', and which become the norms and values experienced by individuals and the group, even if 'the pathway to those experiences is deeply social' (2004, p. 374). Spaargaren (2014) relates this to practice theory, positing that emotional energy may be a key factor in attracting new practitioners to a practice. Further, emotional energy may help us understand how different practices hang together. According to Collins, people are not novelty seekers so much as they are emotion seekers. Spaargaren therefore suggests that by considering the symbolic meaning of certain practices, tied up with people, objects, and specific contexts, we could then better understand the type of emotional energy that is experienced. He suggests that linking emotional energy to more 'sustainable' practices could be one way of recruiting more practitioners to a practice.

As recent work relating practice theory to resource consumption has demonstrated, not all of our everyday actions are embedded with meaning and may not qualify as rituals. Turning on a light switch, for example, is a habit that is part of a certain routine, and that moment in itself may not be defined as a ritual – even if more than one person is present and the act is often repeated. It is an action within a practice, but if we relate that action to broader practices, we might uncover emotional energy. In certain cultures, lighting is an important factor in giving off feelings of comfort and coziness (Wilhite et al. 1996). In other contexts, keeping the lights on at night may have to do with feelings of safety (Sahakian 2010). While both Collins and Spaargaren seem to suggest that positive emotional energy is more attractive when recruiting new practitioners, negative emotional energy – such as fear or shame – might be an equally compelling factor. Emotions are related to contextual or societal norms, which are reproduced in everyday life, also through emotional energy – which for Collins is maintained over space and time through interaction rituals. It follows that a subdued or complete lack of emotional energy might lead to the breakdown of a practice, or that a change in ritual might also lead to changes in emotional energy.

Spaargaren (2013) proposes a research agenda premised on the consideration of objects and their cultural meanings to understand what kind of practices are associated with such objects, and how these objects flow through various practices and social interactions. Based on the conceptual framework discussed above, my analysis of changing food consumption practices in the home is focused on understanding what types of emotional energy are associated with certain objects – appliances and CSA produce – and whether such emotions are maintained. I consider how such emotional energy is manifest and how this translates into cultural and symbolic meaning, and assess how meaning diffuses over space and time. I uncover what meanings are tacitly accepted but left unspoken, and what meanings are explicit, in that they are visibly (and verbally) evident.

CASE STUDIES

A Historical Perspective: Household Appliances in Europe

The United States played an important role in deploying appliances to European households in the post-World War II era, not least through Marshall Plan propaganda that positioned appliances 'as symbols of the benefits that working-class people could enjoy if they abandoned Communism and bought into consumer capitalism' (Clarke 2012, p. 841). The 'promise of Americanization', Furlough (1993) tells us, was about breaking down gender distinctions with 'new women' accessing labor-saving goods through messages of 'efficiency and effortlessness' and toward a 'brighter and more managed future' (pp. 492–493). To some, the United States was 'a paradise of plenty and the model to follow' (Pantzar 2003, p. 83) or an 'irresistible empire' (de Grazia 2005).[4] Although most people living in Europe could not afford these products directly after World War II, Pantzar (2003) explains that appliances were already familiar to people through media exposure since the 1920s, promoting images of the American ideal, electrified home. Pantzar found that media played a central role in inventing, shaping, and normalizing the need for household appliances in Finnish society. Accordingly, the Finnish advertising industry, dominated by ties to American agencies and communication models, focused not on promoting products but on promoting new needs.

During the interwar period in France, political and commercial discourse converged around the notion that technological advances would benefit national economic growth and prosperity. As part of a 'modernist' movement, manufacturers promoted consumerism along with the 'liberatory possibilities of a technologically transformed social and political order' (Frost 1993, p. 111). During this period, selling appliances to the mass market meant positioning them as essential, practical things, rather than luxuries – as part of a normal standard of living that should be available to all classes (Clarke 2012). As such, they were necessary tools, not frivolous toys (Pantzar 2003).

The person who was to help achieve this 'agenda for growth and consumption beyond the great class divide' was to be 'a new woman who was simultaneously a worker, a housekeeper, and a prolific parent' (Frost 1993, p. 111). As Furlough (1993) states, '[T]he identification of femininity with consumer culture was a powerful cultural and economic construct that helped override national differences and served as a transfer point for structures and meanings of American consumer culture' (p. 510). The consumption of household goods became intertwined with notions of citizenship: women's and consumer organizations created a 'specifically feminine variant of citizenship while promoting their own influence by claiming that consuming skills did not come naturally, but through education and training, which they could provide' (Pulju 2011, p. 12). Consumer organizations hosted meetings to showcase appliances with women sharing in this collective and ritualized moment, and creating and reinforcing the main messages that using such appliances was part of being a good citizen and a good parent. The emotional energy we might imagine at these meetings is that of pride and excitement, at being part of something new and progressive, where women were seen as playing a key role.

Bringing people together in social gatherings – or rituals – was a key marketing and sales strategy for new appliances, and these events took place on a wider scale. Notions of progress and ideas around a liberated housewife were communicated at numerous fairs that sprang up across Europe. Inspired by the more 'rational' homes of the United States, Louis Breton launched the first Parisian *Salon des Appareils Ménagers* (Household Appliance Fair) in 1923. Manufacturers were invited to present their appliances and facilitate an 'encounter between practical and elegant appliances and the mass consumers' (1923 fair catalogue, cited in Furlough 1993). These popular fairs became a central means for educating and transmitting information on household affairs that broke with traditional forms of knowledge transfer, from mother to daughter. Yet the appliances presented at this fair were beyond the financial reach of most visitors until after World War II, when spectators finally became customers.[5] At these fairs, technological 'progress' was framed as being the new normal (Leymonerie 2006).

Very quickly, the *Salon* moved beyond appliances to showcase interior design, furniture, and architecture – or a more complete vision of this 'progressive lifestyle'. In 1926, the name changed to *Salon des Arts Ménagers*, or the Art of Living Fair, with appliances more closely tied to notions of beauty, comfort, and style. In the late 1920s, based on the notion that the technological home might seem too audacious for certain clients, the fair began to combine traditional living spaces with the latest modern appliances:

> This was a fruitful juxtaposition because a member of the new middle class (say, the wife of an account executive at Citroen) could promenade through one part of the Salon and invent her past in a Louis XV parlor, then walk through the rest and imagine her future in a rationalized kitchen-as-laboratory. (Frost 1993, p. 127)

As social gatherings and consumption rituals, these salons were effective in that 'Prospective consumers could observe demonstrations, tour model houses, listen to lectures, and taste food prepared in new appliances' (Furlough 1993, p. 504). Other forms of advertising, such as mail-order shopping guides, 'product testing' services, or 'pseudo-informative pamphlets' were also among the techniques aimed at 'urging the housewife to buy new things under the guise of training her in her role as skilled consumer' (Cowan 1976, p. 21).

In the 1930s, in a *Salon* journal series titled *Mesdammes, êtes vous Art-Menagères?* (Ladies, are you art-of-living housewives?), women activists and artists were interviewed about how these appliances contributed to 'practical feminism', or making life better through comfort and convenience. At the 1934 *Salon*, Louise Weiss and other feminists joined together to cook a meal with new appliances (Furlough 1993). Over the years, the Parisian fair grew in size, both in terms of exhibitors and visitors. By 1951, the layout and style of the fair had changed. One area was dedicated to smaller appliances that could be tried out and purchased on location, more accessible to the general public; a second area was dedicated to larger, more expensive appliances set in model kitchens, designed to market not only products but a new lifestyle in a manner that may have seemed elusive and aspirational to many visitors.

The art show was another tool deployed to further promote the American consumer lifestyle in Europe. In the early 1950s, and with support from the United States government, New York's Museum of Modern Art (MoMA) toured across Europe with design shows that included over 500 household objects (Küntzel 2011). In France in 1955, MoMA showcased *50 Years of American Art*, including artworks but also 'architectural models, furniture, tableware, kitchen appliances and tools – shipped into Paris in the same container' (McDonald 2004, p. 398). Model homes designed by Frank Lloyd Wright sat beside Eames chairs, Tupperware products, and toasters, blurring the division between art, design, and household goods. These shows toured western Europe and were 'a vital means of quelling French fears of American cultural homogenization and of building support for the American way of life' (McDonald 2004, p. 398) while also developing a European market for American goods.

A novel form of direct marketing – the traveling salesman – was also deployed, and became a key factor behind the rapid diffusion of certain appliances. In the 1930s and 1940s, brands such as Swedish Electrolux, General Electric's (from the United States) Thor brand, or Canadian Hoover (which all opened UK factories in the early 20th century) hired salesmen to travel door to door, and to set up demonstrations in department stores. Salesmen would offer to test out appliances when visiting a home, offering their primarily female clientele a direct experience with a new appliance, but also creating – in Collins' sense – a type of social event. In a 1954 textbook on salesmanship, the author notes, 'Generally speaking, direct selling is most necessary where sales resistance to a product is high. Where the consumer is asked to pay a large sum of money for a speciality, which will bring him no visible monetary return' (cited in Scott 2008, p. 769). The emotional energy shared at such a meeting may have had something to do with the success of this sales strategy, including a sense of pride in belonging to a group, or an emotion that comes from 'the feeling that one's self fits naturally into the flow of interaction', as Collins suggests (2004, p. 120).

General media also played a role in disseminating key messages around new appliances. In a 1953 issue of *Elle* magazine, a journalist claims that the refrigerator is now an essential household good and sign of 'interior comfort', rather than the grand piano, a former symbol of 'exterior wealth' (cited in Leymonerie 2006). The electric kitchen was a part of the house of the future and promised more leisure time to women. In Figure 7.1, the well-heeled French actress Henriette Ragon, better known as Patachou, sits in her 'modern' designer kitchen, reading a magazine. As a journalist writing for *L'Unité paysanne* (*The Farmer Union*) stated, in reacting to these electric kitchens, '[W]hat I realized upon visiting the Salon 1955 for the first time is all that is sinful and depressing in my own home' (translated from French, cited in Leymonerie 2006, p. 49). The main message was that housewives could do better for their families through these appliances while also 'liberating' themselves from chores. Not to be progressive in this way was almost reprehensible. Feelings of shame, according to Collins (2004), break the social rhythm, if only for a micro-moment, but can have more long-lasting effects, such as creating an impression of exclusion from a social situation.

In her critique of the impact of these appliances on family life, Cowan (1976) draws from historical data to paint a more nuanced vision of the 'liberated housewife' and underlines this sense of shame communicated around household appliances. Cowan describes the proliferation of marketing tools, designed to perpetuate the vision of a happy housewife and to change household practices. She found that two main feelings were communicated through women's magazines in the 1920s: feelings of guilt and embarrassment. As she explains:

Figure 7.1   *'La maison électrique'*, Paris Match *magazine, special issue on the* Salon des Arts Ménagers *(1955)*

In earlier times women were made to feel guilty if they abandoned their children or were too free with their affections. In the years after World War I, American women were made to feel guilty about sending their children to school in scuffed shoes. Between the two kinds of guilt there is a world of difference. (Cowan 1976, p. 22)

As Cowan (1976) tells us, in the context of the United States and after World War I, 'Housework changed: it was no longer a trial and a chore, but something quite different – an emotional "trip." Laundering was not just laundering, but an expression of love; the house-wife who truly loved her family would protect them from the embarrassment of tattletale grey' (p. 16)

If household appliances liberated any time at all it most often went to more or new chores.[6] Yet, the notion of the liberated housewife was a meaning that came to be tied *explicitly* to these appliances. This was reinforced by a strong message, communicated in an *implicit* manner through objects such as appliances, that taking care of the family was – and is – actually more than a just a chore, and that not doing so would be shameful.

A Current Trend: Community-supported Agriculture in Europe

CSA is part of a growing trend around the world, building on Japanese initiatives called 'teikei' in the early 1970s (Dubuisson-Quellier and Lamine 2004). Researchers claim that 100,000 consumers use this service in France, a similar number of families do the same in North America, and up to 16 million people are part of CSA initiatives in Japan (Dubuisson-Quellier and Lamine 2004; Porcher 2011). Switzerland has been a pioneer in this respect, with CSA activities inspiring early initiatives in the United States (Henderson and Van En 2007).

A CSA offer has existed in Geneva since 1978, with *Les Jardins de Cocagne* most likely the first such initiative of its kind in Europe. This CSA was started by politically motivated people who still seek to uphold 'a living alternative to the dominant economic market' (Les Jardins de Cocagne 2014). In this model, customers enter into a contractual engagement as members of the association, paying an annual fee that varies depending on declared income. Weekly vegetable baskets are delivered to residential buildings that act as distribution points, with members under obligation to assist with the farming or delivery of produce three to four times per year. One of the main goals of such efforts was to create a direct link between farmers and consumers, providing farmers with decent salaries and consumers with seasonal and organic food. In the 1980s and 1990s, *Les Jardins de Cocagne* was the only such service available in Geneva and had a waiting list of three years for new members. By the early 2000s, several new organizations offered similar services. In 2008, the *Fédération romande pour l'agriculture contractuelle de proximité* (western Switzerland federation for CSAs, or FRACP) included over 25 member groups. In 2012, *Les Jardins de Cocagne* had 200 members, with other member groups in the 80- to 150-member range. In 2011, the *Les Mangeur* service began offering vegetable baskets and organic apples through partnerships with FRACP members.

Switzerland is a unique context in which to understand the rise in popularity of CSA services. While interest in organic farming grew in the 1960s and 1970s, Belz (2004) argues that Swiss organic producers were considered 'strange and sectarian' at the time and that 'the symbolic image and cultural interpretation hindered further diffusion' (p. 102). The two main food chains, Migros and Coop – which dominate the Swiss retail food market – played an important role in transforming the food-production system. In the 1970s, Migros launched the M-Sano program, setting new standards across its agrofood chains. Rather than promote exclusively organic farming, Migros opted for what was called 'integrated production', a type of farming that would use as few chemicals as possible, setting a new Swiss standard (Belz 2004). Following the 1980s Chernobyl and Sandoz disasters, awareness of environmental issues was heightened; as a result, farmers and consumers launched in 1991 an initiative to support organic agriculture, which was in turn endorsed by the Swiss federal government. Migros reintroduced its Bio label in 1995, which had been originally launched with limited success in the 1960s, offering fruit and vegetables. Today, more than 1000 Migros products bear the Bio label, ranging from chocolate and baby foods, to meat and dairy products. Generally more expensive than similar, non-organic products, the organic produce at Migros is based on the following criteria: excluding artificial or chemical inputs; avoiding genetically modified organisms and transport by plane; and supporting free-range animal rearing and organic feed. As the corporate website states, 'In this way, you can be assured that you are truly eating organic produce, sustainable and close to nature, which allows you to enjoy with peace of mind' (translated from French).[7] Building on earlier fears around environmental disasters, the main message behind promoting organic foods remains safety and confidence, presumably toward one's own health but also toward a broader environment. As integrated production became the new benchmark, organic became accepted as a higher standard in Swiss supermarkets, rather than a novelty, which may explain the rise in CSA offers in recent years, as a way to go above and beyond this standard.

One of the first things that becomes apparent when talking to people about vegetable baskets are the many diverse reasons people first engage with this service and the feelings they have toward it. Many respondents had experienced poor health personally or among family or friends, or began to change their eating habits with the arrival of a baby. Being informed about pesticides and antibiotics also influenced certain people, particularly when it came to the industrialized meat industry. Some people made a link between what would be good for their personal health and what would be good for the earth and general environment, but caring for the planet was generally a secondary reason; important, but perhaps not sufficient in and of itself.

The main emotions tied up with the *Les Mangeurs* offer are that of reassurance and trust – which many state they do not feel toward supermarket products, even if they bear the Bio label. As one young woman put it, '*Les Mangeurs*, we completely trust them and we're right to. There's no question. It's local, it's organic, it's honest.' One reason why people trust this service might be because the founders have direct interaction with the people growing these products. As several people told me, you can ask them questions about how something is grown, how it arrived in the store, or even how it should be stored and prepared, and they will give you exact details. The founders communicate with people at the point of transaction but also over email and through their website. This social interaction seemed important to all those interviewed and can be experienced more generally in the restaurant, a space that carries feelings of warmth, coziness, and conviviality.

Certain people seem frustrated by all the labels on produce in stores, complaining that Migros includes industrially produced goods under its 'local' (*De la region*) designation, using the notion of 'local' in a way that is not respectful of organic principles. Launched in 1999, this local label includes more than 8000 products, or eight times more than the current organic range. People also feel that the Migros Bio label is of a lower standard than what they gain through the *Les Mangeurs* baskets. The lack of trust in these labels was a source of frustration for most of the respondents. People feel uncomfortable talking about their own food consumption patterns that are not aligned with the values associated with eating local and organic food – drinking coffee, for example, that is neither organic nor locally produced, or not wanting to 'seem difficult' when they eat out in restaurants or at friends' houses. During the winter months, when celery and potatoes can appear in the vegetable baskets for weeks on end, some people claim that they get frustrated with the lack of diversity and will purchase out-of-season produce available year-round in the supermarkets. As one person expressed it, 'the occasional avocado, the early strawberry from southern Europe, or "fair trade" bananas'. There are slight feelings of embarrassment or shame associated with these statements, which usually began with the words, 'I must confess . . .' or 'I'm embarrassed to say . . .'.

Taste and quality are also important to people who sign up for these CSA services. The different types of produce offered is a novelty for some members who are not familiar with how to prepare seasonal vegetables such as the Jerusalem artichoke or parsnips. The CSA vegetables also arrive in non-standard shapes and sizes, quite different from the perfectly shaped and colored vegetables that are most present in supermarkets. Yet, most respondents were familiar with these vegetables from their past. They either grew up with their own vegetable garden at their parents' or grandparents' home or remember buying fresh produce from local markets and, in rarer cases, in special arrangements with local farms. These emotions are revived as people encounter these same vegetables again, and tap into memories of their childhood – filled with washing garden salads and dirt-covered potatoes. The dominant trend of buying vegetables year-round in supermarkets is a fairly recent phenomenon, one that has taken hold only over the past one or two generations in Switzerland.

Wasting food evokes negative feelings in people. While larger families generally manage to eat all the vegetables delivered in their CSA baskets, others did tell me that some of the produce was wasted, particularly couples or individuals who may not be eating their meals at home as regularly as families with children. So as not to waste food, some people share vegetables with friends and neighbors, or prepare meals and share them with people in their immediate vicinity.

More positive emotions are evoked through a sense of solidarity with other consumers in the CSA and with the growers. The notion of supporting local agriculture was important to many respondents, or that buying into these vegetable baskets is a way of 'doing your part' to support local farmers. While *Les Mangeurs* plays an important role as a space for social interaction in the neighborhood – what one person described as an island where people share similar values – not all of the CSA services offer this type of meeting space. Other vegetable baskets are distributed at specific points in the neighborhood, where people set up self-service stands and where few social interactions occur. Baskets are picked up, names are crossed off lists, and members do not necessarily meet, other than at general assemblies, or ever have direct contact with the farmers. In some instances, the CSA contract requires some participation in terms of working the land. There is a surprising amount of solidarity in these groups – a sense of belonging to a community and being supportive of the wider collectivity – despite limited in-person interactions among group members. The *idea* of belonging seems as important as actual, physical interactions with other community members.

An interesting source of positive emotions is the element of surprise associated with not knowing what products will come in each week's delivery. Most people appreciate the fact that vegetables arrive according to the season and not based on choices they have made in a supermarket, and that these vegetables will dictate what they will be eating in a given week. People talk about this constraint as something liberating. As one woman put it, 'I like that it's somebody else deciding for me what I should eat. Rather than make decisions about what we should eat this time, we just get it, and we explore, and it's fun.' One would assume that not having a choice is a constraint, but rather people actually experience this constraint as a form of liberation from choice, what psychologist Barry Schwartz (2003) famously termed 'the paradox of choice'. Excessive and complicated choices do not free people up but rather bog them down with an additional responsibility as they seek to balance values related to personal health, environmental concerns, and solidarity with certain groups, among others

– a responsibility they would much rather pass on to the people managing *Les Mangeurs*.

It is important to note here a distinction between explicit and implicit meanings: people will not directly say 'I like to have my choices taken away' as 'freedom of choice' has been constructed in our value system as a normative good. It was only through in-depth discussions that I was able to understand how people feel about having their choices restricted, and generally this was not a negative feeling, so long as the offer is aligned with their values. For example, having choice restricted to solely industrial produce would not be acceptable for this group of people. Trust in the CSA service is also central to positive emotions associated with ceding control of food selection.

The primary means through which people hear about CSAs is word of mouth. The baskets seem to attract people who are already convinced about the value of such a service and who grew up eating these types of vegetables. When speaking to people who do not adhere to CSA services, the perceptions regarding vegetable baskets seemed to be quite consistent: the vegetables are too expensive compared with what can be found in supermarkets, even under the organic label;[8] being part of this service means you have to work the fields, 'like living in a kibbutz' as someone put it; and that it would be inconvenient to receive these vegetables on a weekly or bi-monthly basis. There are few opportunities to experience a lifestyle associated with CSA baskets, in the same way that appliances were tied up with the 'art of living' salons popular across Europe at an earlier point in time. While fairs focusing on Slow Food, organic, or local food production are gaining in popularity, they do not seem to attract the general public in the way that the Salons once did. Opportunities for 'interaction rituals' that involve locally produced and organic agriculture derived from CSAs are thus much more limited.

DISCUSSION AND CONCLUSION

This chapter set out to understand whether a cultural reading of consumption, focused on symbolic meaning and related emotions (Collins 2004; Spaargaren 2013), could bring a new dimension to a social practices approach to sustainable consumption. To do so, I used two food-related European case studies – a historic account of household appliances in the post-World War II period and empirical data from an existing CSA food basket service.

The first conclusion is that the messages surrounding household appliances centered on situating appliances as part of a new and presumably improved lifestyle, as a form of liberation from chores, and as a form of patriotic capitalism associated with productivity and progress. Even if the economic benefits of acquiring appliances were not evident to most consumers, the message was clear: in the post-war period in North America and western Europe, household electric appliances were no longer considered frivolous accessories, but rather had become necessities. This meaning was intended, or indeed crafted, by various interest groups that converged around the theme, from government agencies, to consumer organizations and women's groups, to commercial interests and their marketing and sales agencies, and, not least, the general media. Rather than rely solely on advertisements, pamphlets, and other one-way forms of communication, public and private interest groups organized events to promote household appliances through training sessions by consumer groups, prominent city fairs, and traveling salesmen. All of these strategies translated into social gatherings where cultural meanings were explicitly and consistently communicated, during interactions where emotional energy was transmitted, toward appliances and across different consumption spaces, from the home, to the fair, to the store.

The variety of meanings and emotions associated with CSA products is neither as clear nor as widely discussed as in the case of appliances. The CSA offers often rely on word of mouth and although organic agriculture is subsidized in much of Europe, there is no overt effort by commercial and public interests to replace industrialized agriculture with organic methods. The symbolic meaning of acquiring appliances as part of a new, modern, and liberated lifestyle was much more explicit than the interpretations that might be intended around promoting local and organic foods at different food fairs. Not all CSA offers include an actual social space of exchange as part of their service, which might suggest that feeling virtually connected could be as significant as coming together in social happenings. The range of emotional energy that people experience when they engage with a CSA includes nostalgia for their own past, trust toward CSA providers, and solidarity toward local farmers and other CSA members. People also share a certain peace of mind and reassurance toward personal and family health, as well as coherence with their values, as a type of emotional energy.

Of interest in both cases are the implicit meanings, which are not overtly communicated but operate under the surface of public discourse, and translate into strong emotional energy. In relation to household appliances, women may have been made to feel ashamed of not having these 'modern' accessories, guilty for not being better mothers or housewives, or unpatriotic for not supporting this industry. Here, the meanings tied up with appliances came to change the meaning of housework altogether, from a chore to something more important: 'an emotional trip . . . an expression of love', as Cowan (1976, p. 16) nicely puts it. A new set of values was created out of the practice of preparing food with new appliances, and this set of values was then carried through other practices that had to do with caring for family and home. The cultural meaning associated with objects – in this case household appliances – came to change the meaning of the practice and related practices altogether. The implicit, under-the-surface meanings tied up with CSA services – which are not expressly communicated around vegetable baskets – seem more positive and center on people experiencing feelings of pleasant surprise when they receive their baskets, experiencing them not as a constraint but a form of liberation that stimulates creativity. The dominant discourse, at least in the context of Europe and North America, is that choice is a consumer right, an ultimate freedom. But in practice, people seem to be happier when their choices are constrained, as long as the offer is aligned with their core values and guiding principles. Finally, guilt is also a prominent emotion around CSA services: people feel culpable when their consumption patterns are not aligned with these same values; when they drink imported coffee, eat out-of-season produce, or waste food.

One question remains: whether such emotions are carried through over space and time. In the case of appliances, most likely feelings of women's liberation or patriotic duty are no longer prominently associated with the use of household appliances, at least in the European context. Certain equipment has become the norm in most households, such as the refrigerator and oven. New appliances are no doubt coveted, such as the latest fruit blender or coffee machine, but people may not necessarily feel guilty about not acquiring them. In the case of CSAs, it is harder to say how feelings associated with locally produced, organic vegetables might evolve over time. CSAs are becoming more common but the meanings and emotions associated with these programs may change in different cultural contexts.[9] The case studies presented in this chapter suggest that more interaction rituals in CSAs are necessary to foster a situation where, to borrow from Lave and Wenger ([1991] 2009), people come together as practitioners in a community of practice – learning about the material dimension of consumption, but also sharing stories and emotional energy.

Feelings of trust, solidarity, and duty could be motivating emotions toward more sustainable consumption, and are emotions that would merit further study. Feelings of guilt and shame, communicated in a non-explicit fashion, seem to be quite effective in the recruitment of new practitioners to a practice – as was the case with household appliances. The same feelings, this time *explicitly* communicated, however, make existing CSA practitioners doubt their own discourse and actions. If moralistic messages, delivered directly through certain environmental and social campaigns, for example, may be creating undue stress for those who already adhere to sustainability values in their daily lives, is it effective to continue with these types of communication? By contrast, as we saw in the example of household appliances, *implicit* messages around guilt – that are not overtly stated but rather implied – do seem to be effective. People appear to be attracted by clear messages that convey meanings associated with strong positive emotions, such as leading the 'good life', laced with implicit moralistic messages, such as being a 'bad mother and wife'. This is an approach that marketing agencies have understood quite well, starting in the post-World War II era and continuing through today. This leads me to question whether we, as researchers, would be comfortable delivering moralistic messages around what is right or wrong when it comes to consumption through subliminal means.

What remains to be explored is whether people have to meet and exchange in a social context to share emotional energy, or if meanings can be shared between imagined communities. Benedict Anderson ([1983] 2006) argues that people can feel part of the same geographic space – the 'nation state' in his work – while never actually meeting each other personally. For Anderson, this sense of belonging, what we might call emotional energy and sense of attachment to a community, comes about through language, communication, and learning. For Collins, it is precisely this sense of group solidarity that showcases the positive emotional energy associated with interaction rituals (Kemper 2011). How people come to feel emotionally engaged in more sustainable communities of practice, toward greater solidarity within a group and beyond, would be an interesting avenue for further research. Projecting a 'good life' that is more sustainable would be an important step in this direction. Rather than reinvent the wheel, turning toward existing communities of practice, including CSAs, to understand the sense of belonging, imaginaries, and emotions tied up with 'sustainable living' seems like a good place to start.

NOTES

1. For the many millions of people around the world that live without viable access to these resources, water and energy are replete with social meaning. This argument pertains to the context of the global North, where access to resources has become both expected and normal, for the vast majority of people.
2. Questions of whether household appliances are sustainable or CSA services are unsustainable merit further discussion but these issues are not explored here. My main interest is in understanding how practices change over time and how practitioners might be recruited toward more 'sustainable' consumption practices. I make a general assumption that household appliances, whatever their social and environmental impact, are part of the dominant economic model – where more consumption is generally considered a

good thing and CSA services are positioned as an alternative to the customary market economy.

3. The work of Pierre Bourdieu and Anthony Giddens is discussed elsewhere in this book. Regarding Charles Taylor and Michel Foucault, Reckwitz appreciated their 'praxe-ological' approach to understanding social life. Taylor sought to dispel the notion of a 'disengaged subject', reduced to atomism and mentalism, rooted in concepts from early modernity. He proposed the notion of the 'self-interpreting animal', or a self that is constituted through attempts at 'articulation' that are based on implicit understand-ings and shifting practices (see Taylor 1985). Foucault investigated different theoretical approaches in his career, including structuralism and arriving at a discussion around the relations among body, agency, knowledge, and ethics in his later work (Foucault 1984), particularly in relation to domains, networks, and power relations.

4. For others, anti-American sentiment grew strongly during the early Cold War years. Duhamel (1931) presaged this critique of the American way of life.

5. Prior to the mid-1950s, there were instances in which Parisian working-class groups would band together to share the costs and benefits of new appliances, in a form of col-lective solidarity, for electric water heaters and clothes-washing machines, for example (Leymonerie 2006).

6. In 1929, an American study found that women reported having less leisure time than might be expected with the arrival of new appliances in the home. Hewes (1930) noted that 'it must be admitted that an examination of the actual uses made of time saved is disappointing as compared to the promises of things possible made by the salesmen of electric appliances' (Hewes 1930, p. 241).

7. See Migros website (2014). Les principes de Bio (Organic principles), retrieved 30 March 2014, from http://www.migros.ch/fr/supermarche/bio/principes.html.

8. A television program oriented around the promotion of consumer interests in Switzerland (*A bon Entendeur*) recently evaluated several CSA offers and found them to be providing produce that was less expensive than comparable fruits and vegetables in conventional stores.

9. See Freidberg and Goldstein (2011) for an account of how a CSA service failed in Kenya. According to the authors, the CSA was not necessary in this context, as community markets already existed and promoted locally grown produce as well as solidarity between urban communities and rural areas.

REFERENCES

Anderson, Benedict ([1983] 2006), *Imagined Communities: Reflections on the Origin and Spread of Nationalism*, New York: Verso.

Baudrillard, Jean (1968), *Le Système des Objets [The System of Objects]*, Paris: Gallimard (in French).

Belz, Frank-Martin (2004), 'A transition towards sustainability in the Swiss agri-food chain (1970–2000): using and improving the multi-level perspective', in B. Elzen, F.W. Geels and K. Green (eds), *System Innovation and the Transition to Sustainability: Theory, Evidence and Policy*, Cheltenham and Northampton, MA: Edward Elgar Publishing, pp. 97–113.

Bourdieu, Pierre (1979), *La Distinction: Critique Sociale du Jugement [Distinction: A Social Critique of Judgment]*, Paris: Les Editions de Minuit (in French).

Clarke, Jackie (2012), 'Work, consumption and subjectivity in postwar France: Moulinex and the meanings of domestic appliances 1950s–70s', *Journal of Contemporary History*, **47** (4), 838–859.

Collins, Randall (2004), *Interaction Ritual Chains*, Princeton, NJ: Princeton University Press.

Cooper, Gail (1998), *Air-Conditioning America: Engineers and the Controlled Environment, 1900–1960*, Baltimore, MD: Johns Hopkins University Press.

Cowan, Ruth Schwartz (1976), 'The "Industrial Revolution" in the home: household technology and social change in the 20th century', *Technology and Culture*, **17** (1), 1–23.

de Grazia, Victoria (2005), *Irresistible Empire: America's Advance Through Twentieth-Century Europe*, Cambridge, MA: Harvard University Press.

Douglas, Mary and Baron Isherwood (1979), *The World of Goods: Towards an Anthropology of Consumption*, New York: Basic Books.

Dubuisson-Quellier, Sophie and Claire Lamine (2004), 'Faire le marché autrement: l'abonnement à un panier de fruits et de légumes comme forme d'engagement politique des consommateurs' ('Another way of going to market: community supported agriculture as a form of consumer political engagement'), *Sciences de la Société*, **62**, 144–167 (in French).

Duhamel, Georges (1931), *America the Menace: Scenes from the Life of the Future*, London: Allen & Unwin.

Foucault, Michel (1984), *Histoire de la Sexualité Vol III: Le Souci de Soi (History of Sexuality Volume 3: The Care of the Self)*, Paris: Gallimard (in French).

Freidberg, Susanne and Lissa Goldstein (2011), 'Alternative food in the global South: reflections on a direct marketing initiative in Kenya', *Journal of Rural Studies*, **27** (1), 24–34.

Frost, Robert (1993), 'Machine civilization: home appliances in inter-war France', *French Historical Studies*, **18** (1), 109–130.

Furlough, Ellen (1993), 'Selling the American way in interwar France: "Prix Uniques" and the Salon Des Arts Menagers', *Journal of Social History*, **26** (3), 491–519.

Giddens, Anthony (1984), *The Constitution of Society: Outline of the Theory of Structuration*, Malden, MA: Policy Press.

Goodman, David, Erna Melanie DuPuis, and Michael K. Goodman (2012), *Alternative Food Networks: Knowledge, Practice, and Politics*, New York: Routledge.

Henderson, Elizabeth and Robyn Van En (2007), *Sharing the Harvest: A Citizen's Guide to Community Supported Agriculture*, White River Junction, VT: Chelsea Green Publishing.

Hewes, Amy (1930), 'Electrical appliances in the home', *Social Forces*, **9** (2), 235–242.

Jack, Tullia (2013), 'Nobody was dirty: intervening in inconspicuous consumption of laundry routines', *Journal of Consumer Culture*, **13** (3), 406–421.

Kemper, Theodore (2011), *Status, Power and Ritual Interaction: A Relational Reading of Durkheim, Goffman and Collins*, Farnham, Surrey: Ashgate.

Küntzel, Sabine (2011), 'Museum of modern art: transatlantic taste-maker and promoter of modern architecture and design', *Transatlantic Perspectives*, retrieved 30 March 2014, http://www.transatlanticperspectives.org/entry.php?rec=51.

Lave, Jean and Etienne Wenger ([1991] 2009), *Situated Learning: Legitimate Peripheral Participation*, New York: Cambridge University Press.

Les Jardins de Cocagne (2014), retrieved 30 March 2014, from http://www.cocagne.ch.

Leymonerie, Claire (2006), 'Le Salon des arts ménagers dans les années 1950: théâtre d'une conversion à la consommation de masse' ('The art of living salons in the 1950s: a stage for conversions to mass consumption'), *Vingtième Siècle*, **3** (91), 43–56 (in French).

McDonald, Gay (2004), 'Selling the American Dream: MoMA, industrial design and post-war France', *Journal of Design History*, **17** (4), 397–412.

Pantzar, Mika (2003), 'Tools or toys: inventing the need for domestic appliances in postwar and postmodern Finland', *Journal of Advertising*, **32** (1), 83–93.

Parr, Joy (1997), 'What makes washday less blue? Gender, nation, and technology choice in postwar Canada', *Technology and Culture*, **38** (1), 153–186.

Plessz, Marie, Sophie Dubuisson-Quellier, Séverine Gojard, and Sandrine Barrey (2014), 'How consumption prescriptions affect food practices: assessing the roles of household resources and life-course events', *Journal of Consumer Culture* (in press).

Porcher, Natacha (2011), *L'Agriculture Contractuelle de Proximité en Suisse Romande* (*Community Supported Agriculture in Western Switzerland*), Master's thesis (in French), Institut Agronomique Méditerranéen de Montpellier, Montpellier, France.

Princen, Thomas, Michael Maniates, and Ken Conca (eds) (2002), *Confronting Consumption*, Cambridge, MA: MIT Press.

Pulju, Rebecca (2011), *Women and Mass Consumer Society in Postwar France*, New York: Cambridge University Press.

Reckwitz, Andreas (2002), 'Toward a theory of social practices: a development in culturalist theorizing', *European Journal of Social Theory*, **5** (2), 243–263.

Sahakian, Marlyne (2010), 'Combining life cycle thinking with social theory: case study of compact fluorescent lamps (CFL) in the Philippines', *Sustainability*, **2** (7), 2349–2364.

Sahakian, Marlyne (2014), *Keeping Cool in Southeast Asia: Energy Consumption and Urban Air-Conditioning*, New York: Palgrave Macmillan.

Sahakian, Marlyne and Julia K. Steinberger (2011), 'Energy reduction through a deeper understanding of household consumption: staying cool in metro Manila', *Journal of Industrial Ecology*, **15** (1), 31–48.

Schatzki, Theodore (1996), *Social Practices: A Wittgensteinian Approach to Human Activity and the Social*, New York: Cambridge University Press.

Schwartz, Barry (2003), *The Paradox of Choice: Why More is Less*, New York: HarperCollins.

Scott, Peter (2008), 'Managing door-to-door sales of vacuum cleaners in interwar Britain', *Business History Review*, **82** (4), 761–788.

Shove, Elizabeth (2003), *Comfort, Cleanliness and Convenience: The Social Organization of Normality*, New York: Berg.

Shove, Elizabeth (2012), 'Habits and their creatures: the habits of consumption', *Helsinki Collegium for Advanced Studies*, **12**, 100–112.

Shove, Elizabeth and Alan Warde (1998), 'Inconspicuous consumption: the sociology of consumption and the environment', retrieved 10 September 2009 from http://www.comp.lancs.ac.uk/fass/sociology/papers/shove-warde-inconspicuous-consumption.pdf.

Spaargaren, Gert (2013), 'The cultural dimension of sustainable consumption practices: an exploration in theory and policy', in M.J. Cohen, H.S. Brown, and P.J. Vergragt (eds), *Innovations in Sustainable Consumption: New Economics, Socio-technical Transitions and Social Practices*, Cheltenham and Northampton, MA: Edward Elgar Publishing, pp. 229–251.

Spaargaren, Gert (2014), 'Environmental agency and power in the global network society', paper presented at the XVIII International Sociological Association World Congress of Sociology, Yokohama, Japan, 13–19 July.

Taylor, Charles (1985), *Human Agency and Language: Philosophical Papers 1*, New York: Cambridge University Press.

Wilhite, Harold and Loren Lutzenhiser (1999), 'Social loading and sustainable consumption', *Advances in Consumer Research*, **26**, 281–287.

Wilhite, Harold, Hidetoshi Nakagami, Takashi Masuda, Yukiko Yamaga, and Hiroshi Haneda (1996), 'A cross-cultural analysis of household energy use behaviour in Japan and Norway', *Energy Policy*, **24** (9), 795–803.

Wilk, Richard (2002), 'Consumption, human needs, and global environmental change', *Global Environmental Change*, **12** (1), 5–13.

Yin, Robert K. (2009), *Case Study Research: Design and Methods*, 4th edn, Thousand Oaks, CA: Sage.

PART IV

Sustainable consumption and social innovation

8. Researching transitions to sustainable consumption: a practice theory approach to studying innovations in consumption

Melanie Jaeger-Erben and Jana Rückert-John

INTRODUCTION

Novel or alternative social practices have great potential to shift current unsustainable forms of consumption. They can be introduced through collective means, such as citizen-energy cooperatives, swapping and sharing networks, and do-it-yourself (DIY) workshops. These collective institutions are typically organized on a collaborative basis and oriented toward finding less environmentally and socially damaging ways to produce and consume resources. Further, such initiatives can communicate values of solidarity, communality, and sufficiency. Since they are expected to provide impetus for social change and problem-solving, such efforts are often referred to as 'social innovations' (European Commission 2010, p. 8).

In terms of promoting climate protection and sustainable behavior, many expect that social innovations have the potential to mobilize consumers more effectively than 'top-down' policy interventions (Bergman et al. 2010; Transition Towns Network 2008). This outcome is expected because social innovations are 'grounded in the social relations and experiences of those in need' (Moulaert et al. 2013, p. 1) and typically are diffused through personally relevant social networks. In this way, social innovations are able to obtain high levels of acceptance (McMichael and Shipworth 2013) and – as will be argued further below – have the potential to transcend individualistic approaches to sustainability (see also Chapters 1 and 3). Given their capacity to stimulate sustainable development, social innovations have attracted attention among policy-makers (Barroso 2011; Bureau of European Policy Advisers 2010).

The diversity of initiatives that fall under the category of social innovations makes the concept difficult to define, theorize, and evaluate

(Caulier-Grice et al. 2012; Fifka and Idowu 2013). Although there has been a recent upswing in academic interest regarding social innovations (Caulier-Grice et al. 2012; Howaldt and Schwarz 2010; Moulaert et al. 2013; Mulgan 2006), there is still need for a coherent theoretical framework. Such a conceptual structure should facilitate description of the great varieties and heterogeneities of cases currently found in the field and provide analyses that could account for the dynamic character of social change. As we will reveal in more detail below, much of the academic emphasis on social innovations is connected to a technophilic and economic orientation. From our perspective, more emphasis is needed on the potential for social innovation to change social practices. This is particularly relevant for those practices that – from a normative point of view – can be described as unsustainable.

The concept of social innovation derives from innovation theories where it is assumed that innovation can be a motor of social change through remaking established routines and expectations (Ogburn 1969; Rogers 2003; Zapf 1994). However, to date scientific discourses have had little to do with social innovation, focusing primarily instead on the invention of new products and technologies (Bormann et al. 2012; Howaldt and Schwarz 2010). The term 'social innovation' describes an alternative worldview: social change is a function of social and cultural action and should therefore involve a process-based approach to implementing solutions to societal problems (Caulier-Grice et al. 2012; Moulaert et al. 2013). From our point of view, this contrast between technological and social innovation is problematic as it creates two distinct 'worlds'. The former is dominated by objects or technologies; the latter is governed by social action. As already emphasized by other innovation theorists, we argue that innovation should be understood as a thoroughly social phenomenon embedded in social contexts and seen as an evolutionary process of variation, selection, and stabilization of social practices (Drucker 1985; John 2005; Nelson and Winter 1996; Rammert 2010). According to this definition, new technologies and products are not the core of innovation, but rather elements in a process of changing routines. We argue that a social practice perspective is useful for theorizing social innovation processes. Such an approach should focus on the dissolution of established practices through the development and establishment of alternative social practices or, as Shove et al. (2012, p. 21) describe it, the 'making and breaking' of linkages among elements of social practices.

In this chapter we present and apply an integrated theoretical framework for the study of social innovation. This framework combines the evolutionary perspective of innovation theory with a focus on the transformation of social practices. We aim to contribute to a more thorough understanding of processes of social innovation that enlarges the usual emphasis on specific objects or social benefits by considering their embeddedness in social practices. Furthermore, by highlighting the advantages of integrating assumptions from innovation studies and practice theories we aim to contribute to theoretical discussions on sustainable consumption. We argue that innovation research lacks a thorough grasp of how changes are implemented via practical actions and that an innovation-oriented perspective can enhance analysis of social change by practice theorists. We develop this perspective by providing terms and categories to analyze intended processes of transition while highlighting the role of different types of actors. We first describe our framework that integrates elements from innovation and practice theory. This approach consists of a process-based model of social innovation rooted in three theoretical premises. We next refer to a research project involving application of the model. We show how our theoretical model facilitates the description of different forms of innovation in social practice. Finally, we illustrate how our model enables the identification of distinguishable dimensions of innovation that are relevant to different phases of change.

AN INTEGRATIVE FRAME TO STUDY INNOVATIONS IN SOCIAL PRACTICES

In our conceptual framework we combine elements from innovation theory (Drucker 1985; Nelson and Winter 1996) and theories of social practice (Brand 2014; Reckwitz 2002; Schatzki 1996; Shove et al. 2012). Our definition of and approach to social innovation are based on three premises. The first two premises stem from innovation theory. First, we argue that innovation can be understood in an evolutionary sense as a three-phase process of 1) variation of established structures, 2) selection of alternatives, and 3) stabilization of those alternatives (Drucker 1985; John 2005; Nelson and Winter 1996). Secondly, social innovations are processes that are characterized by intentionality or reflexivity (Schubert 2014). This means that, in contrast to changes in routines that develop over long periods of time (related to the ever-present need for adaptation and assimilation), processes of social innovation become manifest by the presence of identifiable 'change agents'. These individuals and organizations initiate variation and shape processes of selection and stabilization. However, this does not mean that innovation should be understood as a process that can be purposively directed by particular actors. Nevertheless, like Spaargaren and his colleagues, we understand social innovations as 'processes of change with a certain focus, orientation and direction that are all formulated, put forward and defended by designated (groups of) human agents' (Spaargaren et al. 2012, p.9).

The third premise (based on social practice theories) is that this process can be described in terms of the breaking and making of linkages between established and alternative practice elements. At this point, new practices-as-entities are evolving and reproduced continuously in routinized performances (Reckwitz 2002; Shove et al. 2012; Warde 2005). This determination is based on analytical differentiation between 'practices-as-entities' and 'practices-as-performances' (Shove et al. 2012). Social practices can be described as entities which are historically and collectively shaped. They are abstract forms that consist of a meaningful nexus of elements that is temporally and spatially bound. Views among practice theorists vary on what elements of social practices are deemed relevant (see Gram-Hanssen 2010 for an overview), but in the following we consider competencies, social meanings, and material arrangements (compare Shove et al. 2012) as basic practice elements. Since social practices are usually embedded in specific social configurations (Røpke 2009), we follow the definition of Brand (2014) and consider the social setting of the respective practice as a fourth element of practices. Social setting refers to the social or institutional context or the practice field (for example, family, academia, workplace, court) in which the social practice usually takes place. The inclusion of social context also sheds light on the interactions and forms of cooperation that enable practice. However, social practices also need to be considered as performances whereby practices-as-entities are continuously reproduced through practice. This means that social practices are appropriated, carried out, combined, and bundled in everyday life. They are tailored according to available resources (for example, time and social and financial capital) and infrastructures, social and personal demands, and other relevant social practices (Jaeger-Erben and Offenberger 2014).

We view the differentiation between practices-as-entities and practices-as-performances as an important key to understanding processes of change. The complexity of performing practices in different settings, and the need to combine or connect different practices, lead to a volatility or 'convertibility' of social practices and an unpredictability of practice performances (Reckwitz 2003). That means that social practices-as-entities do not entirely structure performance. In fact the human agent, or rather, his or her practical intelligibility – that is, understanding of what actions are appropriate when and in which order (Schatzki 2002) – is continuously prompted to improvise or experiment. Routines, therefore, are never exactly the same and everyday practice adaptations always occur at some scale. In contrast to these implicit variations in routines, we will focus on changes in social practices that are likely to introduce social change. Under these circumstances, alternative practices evolve that compete against established routines on a larger social scale than individual everyday lives. Innovation theory informs an understanding of innovation as a reflexive, evolutionary process. On these grounds we propose the following phase model of innovation in social practice.

Phase 1: Variation of Established Social Practices

Innovation processes are put to work on established practices when conventional solutions to everyday problems no longer seem to be appropriate. These challenges to conventional practices come mostly from dedicated groups or communities and are described as 'agents of change' (Seyfang and Haxeltine 2012). These change agents can be inspired by media reports, social discourses criticizing specific mainstream practices, or significant events such as food crises. From the perspective of social practice theories, the impetus for change can either concern a whole field of social practice (such as mass consumption) or specific social practices like driving or meat consumption. In these cases, change agents question all or most elements of the relevant social practices as well as their linkages (how different practices are interconnected in systems of provision). In other instances, the challenge concerns particular elements of practices, for example material arrangements such as the predominance of environmentally damaging products, or the lack of sustainable products, or the absence of sustainability as a relevant meaning. Efforts to define established practices as problematic often commence with solutions for alternative practices already in mind. Thus the transition from the first to the second phase of variation is subtle and often not clearly distinguishable.

Phase 2: The Formulation of Alternative Practices

The innovation process continues when change agents develop and select alternatives to established practices. This phase entails an ability to perceive challenges (such as dissatisfaction) as opportunities for change (Drucker 1985). The breadth and depth of the challenge shapes the scope of change: from alternative practice elements (for example, more sustainable products or changed meanings) to alternative practices (for example, repairing instead of disposing) to whole bundles of interconnected practices (for example, retail chains for recycled products). From a practice theory perspective, this phase is characterized by experimentation with different, newly introduced, or already existing elements of practices that are linked in novel or alternative ways. The experimentation facilitates and strengthens linkages among prevailing elements. Therefore, the focus on practices-as-performances is particularly relevant in this phase. This process normally takes place in 'niches' shaped by individual or organizational experimentation and initially an innovation affects only a few human agents. These individuals might try out new ways of organizing consumption, such as by swapping unused products instead of prematurely disposing of them, or developing alternative products. Ideally, the alternative elements (like social or material settings) that are established can facilitate alternative ways of consuming. In terms of swapping, this could include the activation of Internet platforms or the patronizing of stores and events that facilitate such exchanges. Furthermore, new or different social meanings come to be attached to the alternatives (for example, communality as an aspect of swapping).

Phase 3: The Stabilization of Social Practices

After an alternative practice has been established, the next obstacle to be overcome is achieving wide-ranging stabilization. Prerequisites for a novel practice to become a successful innovation are its normalization and diffusion beyond the level of an experimental niche. From a practice theoretical perspective, a nexus of interconnected practices (see Shove et al. 2012) must be established that can either compete with the established ones or replace them. If alternative practices fail to interconnect with other practices, their continuity, in terms of continuous reproduction, is endangered. If, for example, virtual swapping platforms do not connect to conventional ways of using the Internet, the extra effort involved in using them would prevent long-term adoption. Furthermore, the alternative practices need to be institutionalized in such a way that they are not threatened by established systems. Car-sharing, for example, can be seen as an alternative practice that has reached the level of institutionalization in many German cities (Loose and Bundesverband CarSharing 2009). Originating out of private initiatives implemented on a local basis, car-sharing was soon adopted by professional stakeholders in the mobility sector who are now able to offer flexible and reliable car-sharing options over a wide area. This example illustrates the types of changes in the locally established practice of car use that are now readily observable (Firnkorn and Müller 2012).

Practice theories, as incorporated into the study of sustainable consumption, tend to use a horizontal perspective that prevents the study of practices on different societal levels. That is, the diffusion and stabilization of innovation are mainly researched in terms of connections among practices and the formation of systems of practices. We argue that a vertical or hierarchical approach – as promoted by the so-called multi-level perspective (MLP) – can be helpful in understanding the stabilization of alternative practices and social innovations. As articulated in the MLP, we argue that alternative social innovations are primarily initiated in niches, but for stabilization to occur it is crucial that they escape their niches to interfere with established practice regimes.

To enhance understanding of this process, we turn to Coburn's (2003) concepts of depth, spread, and shift in reform ownership that she introduced for the study of educational innovations. 'Spread' refers to the quantitative replication of a social phenomenon and 'depth' is focused on the quality of change and the implementation of innovation in social routines. 'Shift in reform ownership' refers to the stage when innovative practices can persist without direct assistance from their former inventors or promoters. Combined, these concepts illustrate how innovations can engage with current regimes of practices. We assume that we can only speak of processes of social innovation if alternative practices have stabilized within wider social frameworks. This can happen through integration of a practice into legal frameworks that are able to protect it from the grasp of mainstream practices. Alternatively, stabilization could occur through the process of becoming embedded in wider social frameworks, whereby a variety of actors adopt pertinent meanings and integrate them into their own systems of relevancy.

Our three-phase model describes an ideal process of innovation and strives to offer a heuristic approach for studying innovations in social practice. The model achieves this by highlighting some foci of attention as well as observation categories that are relevant from our point of view. Nonetheless, the model is not intended to offer an all-encompassing account of how changes in practices occur. Interruptions and disruptions, unintended changes, or unexpected influences are, of course, possible throughout the process.

We describe below a research project where we applied our phase model. Our objective was to use this approach to better understand and describe the processes of change in social practices away from mainstream routines. The aim was to test the applicability of the model for studying empirical cases of social innovation and, at the same time, to enrich it by identifying terms and categories to describe processes of innovation. In addition, we sought to demonstrate how the findings could facilitate attempts to encourage innovations in practices.

BACKGROUND AND METHODOLOGY OF THE RESEARCH PROJECT 'SUSTAINABLE CONSUMPTION THROUGH SOCIAL INNOVATIONS'

The following sections describe the methodological background of a research project initiated on behalf of the German Federal Ministry of Environment and the German Federal Environmental Agency that ran from June 2012 until May 2014. The funding organizations were interested in how policy-makers could better understand and support social innovations for sustainable consumption, particularly in Germany. Our mandate was thus to systematically describe the heterogeneous field of social innovations for sustainable consumption, to comprehend changes in social practices from a consumer perspective, and to apply the attained knowledge to political action. Our working assumption was that policy-makers and other stakeholders (municipal administrations, foundations, and non-governmental organizations) should have access to insights on how to support social innovations for sustainable consumption and the diffusion of sustainable practices. Our contribution here focuses on how to describe processes of change through social innovation and on explaining the types of conclusions that can be advanced by integrating assumptions from social practice theories and innovation theory.

Focusing on sustainable consumption, we related our research to a normative model of societal transformation toward sustainable development. We defined social innovations for sustainable consumption as innovations in unsustainable practices, where alternative meanings, competencies, material arrangements, and social settings are introduced under the premise that they are potentially more ecologically and socially friendly (see below for more detail). We conclude by drawing conclusions on the scope of political intervention and support of social innovations for sustainable consumption offered by our approach.

General Approach

Our study investigated 62 empirical cases of innovative practices related to sustainable consumption. The analysis was marked by a combination of deductive and inductive research strategies described as a 'modified grounded theory approach' (Perry and Jensen 2001, p.4). Accordingly, analysts should derive the main categories for data analysis from theory and complement these through additional categories developed from empirical data. To facilitate the analysis of empirical cases and to increase the comparability of the different case analyses, we developed a theory-based template (see below). The case analysis was marked by the principle of constant comparison as formulated in grounded theory (Strauss and Corbin 1990) as well as the guidelines for empirically grounded development of typologies described by Kluge (2000).

Concurrently, we used the approach of communicative or member validation (Tuckermann and Rüegg-Stürm 2010) to reflect upon our approach and findings with experts from research and practice as well as with representatives of the investigated cases. We organized several consultations (two expert workshops, one conference with experts) and conducted guided interviews with ten people representing different examples of the innovative initiatives to assess the validity of our conclusions. In the following subsections, we describe the case analysis in more detail.

Case Selection and Analytic Framework

To identify relevant cases, we conducted a generic and broad-based collection of innovative sustainable practices. We referred to scientific and popular publications on innovative forms of consumption like swapping, sharing, and DIY. Although we considered innovative initiatives in a range of European countries, we mainly focused on cases in Germany. We consciously adopted a broad perspective in our investigations, and also considered ideas with the potential to become social innovations. We were thus able to capture interesting or promising developments that were not yet in the mainstream.

We identified over 80 examples from the assembled cases covering a wide range of practices, forms of organization, and fields of consumption. We chose to analyze 62 cases more thoroughly based on the following criteria: 1) the cases involved alternative social practices intended to replace or innovate mainstream practices (therefore we did not consider awareness or information campaigns or discourses on sufficiency); 2) the cases mainly considered consumption-relevant practices (rather than new forms of governance like the transition town movement or economic practices like crowdfunding); and 3) the cases had the potential to promote sustainable forms of consumption. To assess the sustainability of practices, we considered the ambitions and claims of the change agents as well as empirical evidence for sustainability improvements (for example, reduction of carbon-dioxide emissions, decrease of waste generation, introduction of equity criteria).

After we identified the cases for analysis, we prepared a portrait of each case by completing theory-based templates, which included: 1) a general description of the case (name, field of consumption, objectives, target group, related social practices and consumption modes, profit orientation); 2) a reconstruction of the case's history oriented by the three phases of innovation (challenge/variation, problem-solving/experimentation, restabilization); and 3) a characterization of the obstacles, challenges, and success factors that were indicative of the history of the case.

We extracted data for the analysis of the 62 selected cases from a variety of documents provided by the innovators or change agents (for example, websites, brochures), popular and scientific publications, and social media publications (for example, blog entries, Internet forums). Further information was retrieved from the consultations described above. We tried to complete the templates as comprehensively as possible until we reached saturation (Sandelowski 1995). Various members of the project team crosschecked each case portrait.

We then compared the case portraits with each other and grouped them accordingly in an iterative process. We sought to identify categories that described the main differences and similarities among cases using the template described above. Our objectives were to gain a systematic description of social innovations for sustainable consumption and to enrich our model of the innovation process. The case portraits were initially analyzed to reveal general characteristics of innovative practices that were developed as alternatives to established practices. We next sought to identify categories that were capable of capturing those differences and similarities in the innovation process relevant to the implementation and stabilization of innovative practices.

CATEGORIES TO DESCRIBE AND ANALYZE INNOVATIONS IN SOCIAL PRACTICES

In the paragraphs that follow we focus on the first step of our analysis where we sought to identify general characteristics of alternative consumption patterns. This step mainly considered the first and second phases of the innovation process: challenging established practices and passage to the selection phase where alternatives become possible. Our discussion concentrates on these phases of innovation to shed light on the emergence of novel practices. As indicated in our phase model, innovation is created in the challenge and experimentation phase. This is when those elements (for example, social meanings, material arrangements, competencies or social settings) and linkages among elements in established practices become increasingly apparent. In this way, we aim at a social practice-oriented definition of innovation. Furthermore, we strive to identify and describe those characteristics of alternative practices that can lead to transformations of current unsustainable consumption patterns.

After presenting the findings of this first analytical step, we turn to the second step of the analysis where the selection of alternatives (Phase 2) and the stabilization (Phase 3) of the innovation process come into focus.

Patterns of Problem and Solution Orientation

As noted above, innovation processes are characterized by a certain amount of reflexivity and intentionality. This is particularly evident in Phase 1. On one hand, human agents advocate changing established practices because they hold perceptions that are different in terms of expectations, attitudes, demands, or needs and are dissatisfied with the range of available opportunities. In addition, these human agents may realize that customary social practices are no longer appropriate for their own everyday lives. For example, among our empirical cases we identified projects where the initiators criticized the 'throwaway mentality' inscribed in established systems of provision. They objected to the general disregard for used (but still usable) products that are treated as garbage. From a practice theoretical perspective, at the core of the challenge were meanings ascribed to materials in different stages of the life cycle (new vs. old or used) and the ways these materials were treated as a result of these meanings.

For the innovation process to start, the critique needed to be complemented by an idea for an alternative. For example, some critics developed 'upcycling' (creation of new products on the basis of recycled material) as an alternative practice or set of practices. They thus sought not only to replace the critical element of the established practice but to create new linkages between an alternative meaning (appreciation of resources) and materials, as well as competencies connected to their treatment. This insight led us to realize that we had to consider two different types of foci in the initial phase of the innovation process. One focus related to the problematization of established practices (or elements of practices) and the other connected to the formulation of an alternative (which starts in the first phase and becomes increasingly tangible and concrete in the second phase). Both foci can be oriented toward different elements of established practices that are at the core of the challenge.

Concerning the first type of focus, we identified two different emphases: 1) an emphasis on the challenge of problematic meanings and values that are inherent in the social practices in question (for example, the association between mass consumption and a tendency to undervalue products and resources); and 2) an emphasis on challenging material arrangements (for example, services, infrastructures, products) that are insufficient to satisfy consumption needs (for example, no or rare possibilities to share or rent products). We found no examples where social settings or competencies were at the core of this process of problematization.

Concerning the second, solution-oriented focus, we observed three directions. Some cases were mainly concerned with alternative social settings for consumption and community-based practices as the solution. Another angle was geared to consumer competencies as an element of social practices and the alternatives evolved around the creation or fostering of skills and know-how. A third orientation was toward creating new material arrangements: alternative practices here concerned the creation of different kinds of products (like upcycled commodities) and services (like opportunities for renting). We found no cases where novel meanings were at the core of the solution.

As Kluge (2000) suggested, the five possible foci in defining problems and solutions were combined in different ways and formed the basic modes of alternative patterns of consumption. These modes could be understood as a kind of central logic behind innovative consumption-related social practices. We developed five different ideal types of modes. Figure 8.1

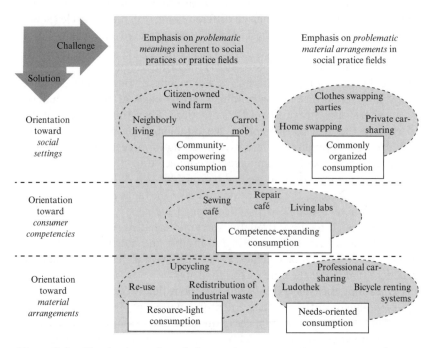

Figure 8.1   Five basic modes of alternative consumption patterns and related empirical cases

provides an overview and identifies some exemplary cases for each type. These cases are described in more detail below:

- *Community-empowering consumption*: In some instances, innovations challenged meanings in established practices and proposed solutions geared toward alternative social settings and community-based practices. Exemplary cases were urban gardening (community gardens mostly on unused public spaces) and community-supported agriculture (CSA) (co-financing of a farm by a group of consumers who receive agricultural products in return). Also included here were more flexible social practices like consumer mobs (for example, carrot mobs).[1] In these examples, the alternative social setting and the formation of a community were not primarily means for organizing consumption differently. Rather, they comprised a crucial element and meaning of a whole network of evolving practices. This could be interpreted as a response to a perceived absence of communality due to lack of cooperation, cohesion, participation, and solidarity in established practices. Because such features of communities are central to the success of this type of innovation, we labeled this mode *community-empowering consumption*. The empowerment is sometimes an outcome of engaging in the particular practice: from their collaborative efforts, practitioners *expected* a higher impact and influence on the practice fields under scrutiny. Cases that incorporated community-empowering consumption generally embraced a whole set of alternative practices or an alternative organization of established and alternative practices. Urban gardening, for example, is not exclusively devoted to growing vegetables in a city setting. Indeed, most initiatives combine agriculture with leisure practices, educational activities, art projects, or political activism. As such, consumption plays a less prominent role in urban gardening than it does in CSAs. While the former might only satisfy a tiny part of consumption needs, the latter aims to create a system of provision that is structured differently from established systems. Regardless, the power of communities to self-organize and to change modes of production and consumption plays a crucial role in both cases.
- *Commonly organized consumption*: Some of our cases were oriented toward establishing alternative social settings for consumption, where the core challenge was a lack of sustainable consumption opportunities. Fairly short-term or ephemeral communities or social networks were developed as a solution to this problem. Exemplary practices included sharing, swapping, and other forms of collaborative consumption, often referred to as the 'sharing economy'. The

social settings for associated practices often built on exchanges involving a small number of participants. We referred to this mode as *commonly organized consumption* with an emphasis on consumption to satisfy needs. Initiators of home-swapping platforms, for example, described a lack of possibilities in the domain of tourism and travel. In this case, mainstream consumables were perceived as standardized, anonymous wares that do little to facilitate learning about the local culture of the vacation destination. This limitation was combined with the need of many travelers to find inexpensive accommodation and the opportunity to offset their travel expenses by renting out their own home. The formation of a network should not only facilitate contacts between households willing to travel but also enlarge the geographical possibilities and create a setting of social control, since participants can evaluate each other and share experiences. Thus, unlike the first mode, where consumption can also be understood as a means to build a community, the advantages of a community here are operationalized as a means to facilitate consumption.

- *Competence-expanding consumption*: The challenge in these cases was fundamentally geared to established systems of provision that were perceived as fostering incompetent and passive consumers. The consumer in these arrangements was bound to buy and use mass-marketed products and to replace them if broken or expired. This challenge draws attention to the meanings attached to the role of consumers and their lack of opportunities to escape indifference and dependency. Alternative practices arose around the formation of competencies for producing and repairing consumer goods. Most cases concerned new social settings or services where skills could be appropriated and formed, and DIY practices could be fostered. Projects like repair cafés or living labs (facilities where consumers can use equipment and get support for producing or repairing products themselves) are not limited to only presenting alternative social and material settings. They are also meant to provide new narratives opposed to established systems of provision, where consumers can become more or less independent and self-reliant producers.

- *Resource-light consumption*: Like competence-expanding consumption, this mode also seeks to create a different narrative from established systems of provision. The focus here, however, is on the characteristics and meanings associated with material arrangements. The challenge to mainstream practice is based on arguments that resources and consumer goods are wasted and not sufficiently valued in conventional production and consumption practices. This solution is oriented toward establishing material settings that can redefine waste as a resource and transform it back into a marketable product. Examples include upcycling and re-use projects that aim to enable *resource-light consumption*. Consumers are sometimes, but not necessarily, themselves involved in these alternative practices. These routines, however, often enlarge consumption possibilities by widening the scope of the types of products on offer. Some of the cases we studied concentrated on production systems that aimed to create networks to redistribute materials among established producers and other actors, such as start-up companies, artists, and educational projects. These resources were treated as waste by the former but were needed as inputs and commodities by the latter.

- *Needs-oriented consumption*: The challenge underlying *needs-oriented consumption* is that there are insufficient opportunities to use products efficiently. This mode mainly addresses the inefficiency of owning products and the solution highlights the advantages of sharing resources. In contrast to commonly organized consumption, needs-oriented consumption does not necessarily include the formation of a community or network. Solutions are oriented toward the creation of alternative material settings – settings that facilitate services that offer products that consumers can rent. The consumers may form a kind of community of clients, but they are not typically connected to each other as is the case for commonly organized consumption. The shared products are owned by the service provider, who also organizes most of the process. Inefficient arrangements, such as owning rarely used products, are avoided because products are in nearly constant use. In comparison with modes like community-empowering consumption, the associated alternative practices or practice networks are less complex and primarily involve renting instead of buying.

The five modes described above share a common problem of typologies, namely they formulate ideal forms of combinations of characteristics that do not entirely fit any of the cases to which they have been assigned. There are cases that fall between two modes or exhibit characteristics of more than one typological category. Some of the cases that are designated as commonly organized consumption, for example, also have a strong emphasis on changing consumption infrastructures. Nevertheless, the modes highlight the focal points around which changes evolve. They show various ways of challenging unsustainability in established practices as well as different forms of sustainable alternatives. In the cases of community-empowering consumption, the solution to unsustainable practices evolves from different approaches to the social organization of consumption. Competence-expanding consumption enhances and formulates new roles for consumer competencies as a pathway to more sustainable practices. Only resource-light and needs-oriented consumption can be connected to conventional-, efficiency-, and technology-oriented sustainability strategies by developing alternative material arrangements. However, resource-light consumption, in particular, stresses changing problematic values such as distrust of or disgust for used products. The goal of initiatives related to resource-light consumption, therefore, is a more profound change of social practices than merely replacing inefficient products or material arrangements.

RELEVANT DIMENSIONS FOR INNOVATION IN SOCIAL PRACTICES

As mentioned above, the five basic modes mainly refer to the first phase of the innovation process (variation/challenge) and the transition to and beginning of the second phase (formulation, implementation, and selection). This part of the process is particularly relevant if we want to observe how established practices dissolve and new practice elements and linkages evolve. Nevertheless, the second and third phases are crucial. As described above, one can only speak of an innovation in social practice if the alternatives and the innovative practices have stabilized. Since it was our goal to enrich the whole phase model of innovation with categories that are relevant to the development of an innovation, we focused our next analytical step on the innovation process that followed the formulation of alternatives and how the modes were put into practice. We describe here the following four central dimensions that help to explain some of the differences and similarities of the innovation journey (van de Ven et al. 2008) of the investigated cases of innovative practices.

Results from the first step of the analysis described above revealed one process-related dimension: we realized that challenges and solution orientations could be more or less comprehensive. That is, the initiative could embrace many or few elements (meanings, materials, competencies, and social settings) of mainstream practices and the proposed solution could strive to replace a discrete number of them or whole sets of established social practices. For example, an effort to establish a CSA could be regarded as a complex set of alternative practices developed to rewrite current practices that span agriculture, economics, and household consumption. Such an initiative requires a new way of thinking about agricultural production, where customers participate in farming activities, and introduces novel purchasing practices, where one pays for food that has not yet been produced (and possibly will never be, in say, the case of a poor harvest). In contrast, professional car-sharing or renting household devices utilizes established practices and the innovation is in restructuring the nature of ownership and does not fundamentally alter how the goods are used. Furthermore, renting and leasing can connect, to a certain degree, to existing systems of provision. The term *degree of innovativeness* aims to capture differences in the extent to which a case challenges established practices and supports alternative practices. In our evaluation, the more the outlined alternative differs from mainstream practice, the higher is the degree of innovativeness with respect to a particular case.

Comparing the modes and their constitutive characteristics also suggests that the *degree of communality* can be an important dimension. Although social practices are always shared, collective ways of doing things, social settings, as well as communality, could play a crucial role in facilitating the performance of practices. As we followed the modes and the associated cases further on their innovation journeys, we found that the cases differed according to their necessity to form socially cohesive groups. As described above, communality furthermore constituted a more or less central meaning of the alternative practices. The degree of communality was mostly prevalent in the second phase of the innovation process where alternative social settings were formed or within which new practices became subject to experimentation. The degree of communality played an important role as either an obstacle or a potential success factor to stabilize the innovation (see below).

Comparing modes and their associated cases with each other further revealed that consumers and their competencies, interactions, and cooperation play a relatively important role in establishing an innovative practice. Going further through the innovation phases, we found that the cases differed significantly in the *degree of personal engagement* they demand from consumers. Community-empowering, commonly organized, and competence-expanding consumption all required more self-organization, acquisition of skills, and readiness to change actors' current allocation of resources (for example, knowledge, time) to support alternative practices than was the case for needs-oriented or resource-light consumption. The expansion or development of consumer competencies is therefore a focal point of these approaches to innovation. We identified the degree of personal engagement as a differentiating dimension prevalent in the second and third phases of the innovation process. A high degree of necessary engagement could also be an obstacle to the stabilization in the third phase, as we will elaborate in the next section.

We describe a fourth dimension that was relevant to the stabilization phase as the *degree of formality* of alternative practices. We found that innovations normally stabilize as either formal organizations (for example, cooperatives, associations, enterprises) or as informal settings (for example, platforms, temporary initiatives). The degree of formality is crucial to the stability of alternative practices since it influences the strength of linkages among elements. In addition, the degree of formality influences the extent to which alternative practices become embedded in wider social frameworks as described in Phase 3 of the innovation process. For example, cases associated with resource-light or needs-oriented consumption generally formulated new material arrangements as a solution. Alternative practices of production or new types of services were developed that had to be linked to existing legal frameworks and systems of provision. Thus the cases associated with resource-light and needs-oriented consumption were more formalized and structurally stable than the examples of commonly organized consumption that depended more on the continuous personal engagement of consumers.

The four dimensions can vary in their relevance to different phases in the innovation process. Moreover, they may also be characteristic of distinct social practices. As a final step, we distinguished among a high, medium or low degree of the four dimensions to more thoroughly map differences across cases. In contrast to labeling the five modes to describe the evolution of innovative practices presented (Figure 8.1), the dimensions innovativeness, communality, personal engagement, and formality are categories that explain differences and similarities in the evolutionary process. Table 8.1 summarizes the main characteristics of these dimensions.

In the research project described above, the five *modes* and the four *dimensions* formed the background to a typology of social innovations in sustainable consumption, complementing some of our previous work (Jaeger-Erben et al. 2015). Our contribution here focuses on the particular modes and dimensions because we would like to provide process-relevant categories to describe innovations in social practices. This served our intention to test and enrich the phase model of innovation. In the following section, we discuss the practical applicability of our findings in terms of defining ways to support social innovations for sustainable consumption.

ENABLING TRANSITIONS TO SUSTAINABLE PRACTICES

As described above, the empirical part of our project comprised a thorough analysis of the history or evolution of a heterogeneous set of examples of social innovations. We identified community-empowering consumption,

Table 8.1 Main characteristics of dimensions to describe innovations in social practices

	Innovativeness	Communality	Personal engagement	Formality
In which innovation phase(s) is the dimension particularly relevant?	Relevant to challenging established practices and selecting alternatives	Relevant to selection and stabilization of alternatives, but in relation to emphases and orientation in challenge phase	Relevant to selection and stabilization of alternatives, but in relation to orientation in challenge phase	Mostly relevant to the stabilization of alternatives
Where does the dimension relate to in the transformation of new practices?	Transformation of elements, linkages, sets of practices in general	Social settings and meanings (like solidarity, cooperation)	Competencies and meanings (like participation, autonomy)	Linkages between practice elements, embedding of practices in wider social framework
Degrees: High	Establishment of sets of interconnected practices (e.g., producer–consumer communities)	Formation of communities, communality as a core meaning (e.g., urban gardening)	High self-organization and allocation of personal resources (e.g., CSA)	Establishment of enterprises, cooperatives, etc. and formal relations (e.g., consumer-initiated energy cooperation)
Medium	Alternative practices or combinations of existing practices (e.g., clothes-swapping parties)	Short-term or target-oriented formation of groups (e.g., home-swapping)	Activity beyond consumption, facilitation by third parties (e.g., carrot mobs)	Partly professional suppliers, weak relations (e.g., platforms for private car-sharing)
Low	Alternative elements within existing settings or practices (e.g., leasing of devices)	Low or no necessity to form groups (e.g., professional car-sharing)	Activity mainly concerns consumption (e.g., use of upcycled products)	Individualized practices, mostly informal settings (e.g., DIY)

commonly organized consumption, competence-expanding consumption, resource-light consumption, and needs-oriented consumption as different approaches to innovative practices that are able to facilitate more sustainable consumption. Since these modes use different tactics to challenge established practices and formulate alternatives, they highlight a range of 'drivers' of change. We identified innovativeness, personal engagement, communality, and formality as dimensions that are able to explain differences in the development and diffusion of innovative practices. We can assume that these dimensions are crucial to the implementation and stabilization of an innovation because we systematically compared 'successful' cases where innovative practices could be established and disseminated with cases where innovative initiatives disappeared again or were still struggling to stabilize. Therefore, strategies seeking social innovation are more systematically developed and applied when integrating these dimensions. In the discussion that follows, we will present some general suggestions for such strategies.

If innovativeness is high, consumers tend to view the alternative practices associated with a particular social innovation as being unusual. The adoption and diffusion of alternative practices can be difficult due to the fact that know-how and competencies still need to be acquired and facilitating structures are generally not yet established. These circumstances may lead to low levels of acceptance of the practices. This is especially pertinent to initiatives based on the principle of competence-expanding consumption. In such cases, measures to establish facilitating structures and to support the acquisition of competencies should be a strategic focus.

Social innovations that require a high degree of personal engagement – as in community-empowering consumption – demand many resources (for example, time, know-how) from change agents and associated consumers. We found that recruitment of members and limitations on the availability of resources are an obstacle to such innovations. In these instances it is important to consider the circumstances that motivate people to adopt innovative practices, and strategies must be devised to diffuse such motivations. The five modes that we describe above provide insights by highlighting different social meanings that are relevant to the innovative practices.

A high degree of communality, for example in cases of community-empowering consumption, can facilitate member recruitment as we found participation in communities to be a strong motivator for the uptake of the innovative practices. At the same time, it is necessary to adopt certain responsibilities and duties, as well as to accept potential social friction. We found that social conflict and tension among members interfere with participation in innovative practices. One strategy to alleviate this problem is to support new communities with offers of free or affordable mediation or social skills training.

Highly formalized organizations, like enterprises and legal associations found in resource-light and needs-oriented consumption, provide a considerable degree of stability and reliability to the consumer. At the same time, they require more thorough preparation and development from initiators and are labor-intensive and may be economically risky in terms of maintenance. Initiators also require organizational and management skills, and such investments often need to be made in advance with full knowledge that there may not be enough demand to enable a financially viable business model. Supportive measures can strive to minimize these risks and facilitate the acquisition of necessary skills.

A strategy that we found to enhance the development of all cases of social innovation is to provide spaces of experimentation to facilitate the process of variation and selection. Providing opportunities to trial ideas involves making resources available in the form of funds, training and consultation possibilities, and prospects for action and networking that facilitate project initiation. A fine line exists between protecting initiatives from overregulation, expectation, and bureaucratic burdens while simultaneously allowing them to develop on their own. This is where particularly innovation-oriented policy-makers need to act as facilitators by connecting different initiatives to each other to enhance the sharing of experiences, mutual learning, and collaboration. Individuals with such inclinations can act as promoters by engaging in lobby work for social innovations in general or specific efforts pertaining to, for example, collaborative consumption. For instance, they can present cases in the frame of educational campaigns to the public or put social innovations on the political agenda in different ministries. Finally, politics can serve a conventional role as a regulatory body and introduce laws and other measures that facilitate the formalization of initiatives; or fulfill a more advanced function that integrates elements like the re-use of waste material or mandatory product characteristics – for instance reparability – into regulatory schemes for industrial processes.

The adoption of roles like facilitator and promoter calls for a change of conventional policy practices. This goes hand in hand with greater attention toward changes in social practices and a practices-oriented approach in politics (Shove et al. 2012; Spaargaren and Oosterveer 2010). This new orientation would shift the focus from individualized consumers and their motives and attitudes toward the making and breaking of linkages among elements within social practices and their accompanying societal processes and settings. It would further expand the focus of technology-oriented sustainability strategies to include a more integrative view of social change. Indeed, such a shift seems to be fundamental. This is because many of the innovations that we observed in social practices followed other strategies in going beyond efficiency. Notable examples included the implementation of alternative meanings associated with resources, the activation of the 'power of communities', and the enhancement of consumer competencies. A participative approach in the development of policy strategies and other measures can facilitate the understanding of such 'drivers' of social innovation. The suggestions that we advance above are put forth to mark a starting point for an alternative political approach that, we contend, should be further developed and evaluated.[2]

CONCLUSION: FACILITATING THE STUDY OF INNOVATIONS IN SOCIAL PRACTICES

Having developed and presented a framework for the analysis of innovations in social practices, we now reflect on possibilities for cross-fertilization between theoretical discourses in practice and innovation theory. As stated above, although the notion of social practices has been broached in innovation theory, it is not yet sufficiently integrated into theoretical concepts. In this respect, our practice-theory-enriched and evolutionary model of social innovation should be regarded as providing a general framework. Furthermore, our research provides some categories that can facilitate description of the evolution of innovative practices. We found that adopting a practice theory facilitated a more thorough investigation of innovation processes in terms of investigating the replacement of established practices by alternative meanings, competencies, social settings, material arrangements, and their linkages. A focus on reconfigurations of practices in terms of their elements and interconnections shows where change happens and helps to distinguish core elements from relatively marginal ones. This perspective helped us to discover five different modes that serve as basic starting points and orientations for social innovation. In addition, the methodology enriched formulation of four process-relevant dimensions which are able to explain differences among various types of innovations in social practices and how they develop and stabilize.

Practice theory approaches can benefit from the vertical perspective that is often applied in innovation theory. The MLP embeds the evolution of novel or alternative social practices in broader processes of social change. The evolutionary model we deployed here distinguishes between the variation and selection phases that happen in a 'niche' – a social space that can be more or less clearly defined in terms of space and personnel – and the stabilization phase – which should be studied under consideration of established systems or regimes of social practices. We therefore argue that the MLP is helpful in understanding the whole process of social innovation. Moreover, a focus on social innovation facilitates efforts to distinguish different kinds of changes in social practices. In particular, our model allows researchers to differentiate between processes of change that have a particular orientation toward development and introduction of social innovations (for example, upcycling as an alternative practice to dumping) and long-term variations in practices (for example, the transformation of eating habits by convenience food).

Nevertheless, the framework needs validation from empirical research. To be established as a general model for social innovation, our conceptual approach needs to be applied in studies with a greater variety of cases, possibly extending the scope beyond German examples and sustainable consumption that we applied here. Likewise, the modes and dimensions that we highlight should be tested with respect to their relevance to other cases and their development and diffusion to, for example, innovative financing practices like crowdfunding and cooperative investment. Further research might explore the extent to which the carriers of social innovations for sustainable consumption act as a prerequisite for their diffusion. That is, are there social groups or milieus that are more inclined to adopt innovative practices and whose adoption is more likely to diffuse the innovation? Further investigation could explore how the modes and dimensions described above relate to the established conduct of everyday life or existing competencies and how these relate to each other in the process of adoption. Generally, more research is needed on processes of social innovation in the global South and developing countries since most current research focuses on developments in the northern hemisphere and industrialized countries.

NOTES

1. In carrot mobs, consumers are mobilized to purchase products within a prescribed timespan and in a specific store (for example, where the owner has committed to spend a certain percentage of the earnings from that action on energy-efficient store equipment).
2. Since we focused in this chapter on presentation of our innovation model and respective findings, the recommendations we put forth here may seem vague and overly generalized. Further details and more precise suggestions can be found in our other work (see, for example, Jaeger-Erben et al. 2015).

REFERENCES

Barroso, José (2011), 'Europe leading social innovation', speech presented at the Social Innovation Europe Initiative, Brussels, 17 March 2011, available at http://europa.eu/rapid/press-release_SPEECH-11-190_en.htm (accessed 23 March 2014).

Bergman, Noam, Nils Markusson, Peter Connor, Lucie Middlemiss, and Miriam Ricci (2010), 'Bottom-up, social innovation for addressing climate change', Sussex Energy Group Conference: ECEEE 2010, Sussex, UK, 25–26 February 2010, available at: http://www.eci.ox.ac.uk/research/energy/downloads/Bergman%20 et%20al%20Social%20Innovation%20WP.pdf (accessed 25 October 2014).

Bormann, Inka, René John, and Jens Aderhold (eds) (2012), *Indikatoren des Neuen: Innovation als Sozialmethodologie oder Sozialtechnologie?* (*Indicators of the New: Innovation as a Social Methodology or Social Technology*), Wiesbaden: VS Verlag (in German).

Brand, Karl-Werner (2014), *Umweltsoziologie: Entwicklungslinien, Basiskonzepte und Erklärungsmodelle* (*Environmental Sociology: Lines of Development, Basic Concepts, and Explanatory Models*), Weinheim: Beltz-Juventa (in German).

Bureau of European Policy Advisers (2010), *Empowering People, Driving Change: Social Innovation in the European Union*, Luxembourg: Publication Office of the European Union.

Caulier-Grice, Julie, Anna Davies, Robert Patrick, and Will Norman (2012), 'Defining social innovation', Part I of *Social Innovation Overview*, Brussels: European Commission, DG Research, available at http://youngfoundation.org/ publications/tepsie-social-innovation-overview-parts-i-ii-iii-iv-andbibliography/ (accessed 23 March 2014).

Coburn, Cynthia (2003), 'Rethinking scale: moving beyond numbers to deep and lasting change', *Educational Researcher*, **32** (6), 3–12.

Drucker, Peter (1985), *Innovation and Entrepreneurship*, New York: Butterworth-Heinemann.

European Commission (2010), *This is European Social Innovation*, Brussels: European Commission, available at: http://ec.europa.eu/enterprise/flipbook/ social_innovation/ (accessed 25 October 2014).

Fifka, Matthias and Samuel Idowu (2013), 'Sustainability and social innovation', in T. Osburg and R. Schmidpeter (eds), *Social Innovation: Solutions for a Sustainable Future*, Heidelberg: Springer, pp. 309–315.

Firnkorn, Jörg and Martin Müller (2012), 'Selling mobility instead of cars: new business strategies of automakers and the impact on private vehicle holding', *Business Strategy and the Environment*, **21** (4), 264–280.

Gram-Hanssen, Kirsten (2010), 'Standby consumption in households analyzed with a practice theory approach', *Journal of Industrial Ecology*, **14** (1), 150–165.

Howaldt, Jürgen and Michael Schwarz (2010), *Social Innovation: Concepts, Research Fields and International Trends: Studies for Innovation in a Modern Working Environment – International Monitoring*, Volume 5, Aachen: Technische Hochschule, available at http://www.internationalmonitoring.com/fileadmin/ Downloads/Trendstudien/Trends_V2/IMO-MAG%20Howaldt_final_mit_cover .pdf (accessed 9 July 2015).

Jaeger-Erben, Melanie and Ursula Offenberger (2014), 'A practice theory approach to sustainable consumption', *GAIA*, **23** (S1), 166–174.

Jaeger-Erben, Melanie, Jana Rückert-John, and Martina Schäfer (2015), 'Sustainable consumption through social innovation: a typology of innovations for sustainable consumption practices', *Journal of Cleaner Production*, published online first: doi:10.1016/j.jclepro.2015.07.042.

John, René (2005), 'Innovationen als irritierende neuheiten: evolutionstheoretische perspektiven' ('Innovations as irritating novelties: evolving theoretical perspectives'), in J. Aderhold and R. John (eds), *Innovation: Sozialwissenschaftliche*

Perspektiven (*Innovation: Perspectives from Social Sciences*), Konstanz: UVK, pp. 49–64 (in German).

Kluge, Susan (2000), 'Empirically grounded construction of types and typologies in qualitative social research', *Forum: Qualitative Social Research*, **1** (1), Art. 14, available at http://nbn-resolving.de/urn:nbn:de:0114-fqs0001145 (accessed 15 September 2014).

Loose, Willi and Bundesverband CarSharing (2009), *The State of European Car-Sharing*, Final Report, Momo Project D 2.4 Work Package 2, available at http://ec.europa.eu/energy/intelligent/projects/sites/iee-projects/files/projects/documents/momo_car-sharing_the_state_of_european_car_sharing_en.pdf (accessed 15 September 2014).

McMichael, Megan and David Shipworth (2013), 'The value of social networks in the diffusion of energy-efficiency innovations in UK households', *Energy Policy*, **53**, 159–168.

Moulaert, Frank, Diane MacCallum, Abid Mehmood, and Abdelillah Hamdouch (2013), 'General introduction: the return of social innovation as a scientific concept and a social practice', in F. Moulaert, D. MacCallum, A. Mehmood, and A. Hamdouch (eds), *The International Handbook on Social Innovation: Collective Action, Social Learning and Transdisciplinary Research*, Cheltenham and Northampton, MA: Edward Elgar Publishing, pp. 1–6.

Mulgan, Geoff (2006), 'The process of social innovation', *Innovations*, **1** (2), 145–162, available at http://farm.tudor.lu/sites/default/files/2006_The_Process_of_SI_Mulgan.pdf (accessed 15 September 2014).

Nelson, Richard and Sidney Winter (1996), *An Evolutionary Theory of Economic Change*, Cambridge, MA: Belknap Press.

Ogburn, William F. (1969), *Kultur und Sozialer Wandel* (*Culture and Social Change*), Ausgewählte Schriften, Neuwied: Luchterhand (in German).

Perry, Chad and Oystein Jensen (2001), 'Approaches to combining induction and deduction in one research study', Australian and New Zealand Marketing Academy Conference, ANZMAC 2001, Auckland, New Zealand, available at http://anzmac.org/conference_archive/2001/anzmac/AUTHORS/pdfs/Perry1.pdf (accessed 15 September 2014).

Rammert, Werner (2010), 'Die innovation der Gesellschaft' ('The innovation of society'), in J. Howaldt and H. Jacobsen (eds), *Soziale Innovation* (*Social Innovation*), Wiesbaden: VS Verlag, pp. 21–51 (in German).

Reckwitz, Andreas (2002), 'Towards a theory of social practice: a development in culturalist theorizing', *European Journal of Social Theory*, **5** (2), 243–263.

Reckwitz, Andreas (2003), 'Grundelemente einer theorie sozialer praktiken: eine sozialtheoretische perspektive' ('Basic elements of a theory of social practices: a social theoretical perspective', *Zeitschrift für Soziologie*, **32** (4), 282–301 (in German).

Rogers, Everett M. (2003), *Diffusion of Innovations*, New York: Free Press.

Røpke, Inge (2009), 'Theories of practice: new inspirations for ecological economic studies', *Ecological Economics*, **68** (10), 2490–2497.

Sandelowski, Margarete (1995), 'Sample size in qualitative research', *Research in Nursing and Health*, **18** (2), 179–183.

Schatzki, Theodore (1996), *Social Practices: A Wittgensteinian Approach to Human Activity and the Social*, New York: Cambridge University Press.

Schatzki, T. (2002), *The Site of the Social: A Philosophical Account of the Constitution of Social Life and Change*, University Park: Penn State University.

Schubert, Cornelius (2014), 'Social innovations: highly reflexive and multi-referential phenomena of today's innovation society? A report on analytical concepts and a social science initiative', Technology Studies Working Papers, TUTS-WP-2-2014, Berlin: Technical University, available at http://www.ts.tu-berlin.de/fileadmin/i62_tstypo3/TUTS_WP_2_2014.pdf (accessed 15 September 2014).

Seyfang, Gill and Alex Haxeltine (2012), 'Growing grassroots innovations: exploring the role of community-based initiatives in governing sustainable energy transitions', *Environment and Planning C: Government and Policy*, **30** (3), 381–400.

Shove, Elizabeth, Mika Pantzar, and Matt Watson (2012), *The Dynamics of Social Practice: Everyday Life and How It Changes*, Thousand Oaks, CA: Sage.

Spaargaren, Gert and Peter Oosterveer (2010), 'Citizen-consumers as agents of change in globalizing modernity: the case of sustainable consumption', *Sustainability*, **2** (7), 1887–1908.

Spaargaren, Gert, Peter Oosterveer, and Anne Loeber (eds) (2012), *Food Practices in Transition: Changing Food Consumption, Retail and Production in the Age of Reflexive Modernity*, New York: Routledge.

Strauss, Anselm and Juliet Corbin (1990), *Basics of Qualitative Research: Grounded Theory Procedures and Techniques*, Newbury Park, CA: Sage.

Transition Towns Network (2008), *Transition Towns Wiki*, available at http://www.transitiontowns.org/ (accessed 15 September 2014).

Tuckermann, Harald and Johannes Rüegg-Stürm (2010), 'Researching practice and practicing research reflexively: conceptualizing the relationship between research partners and researchers in longitudinal studies', *Forum: Qualitative Social Research*, **11** (3), Art. 14, available at http://nbn-resolving.de/urn:nbn:de:0114-fqs1003147 (accessed 15 September 2014).

Van de Ven, Andrew, Douglas Polley, Raghu Garud, and Sankaran Venkataraman (2008), *The Innovation Journey*, New York: Oxford University Press.

Warde, Alan (2005), 'Consumption and theories of practice', *Journal of Consumer Culture*, **5** (2), 131–153.

Zapf, Wolfgang (1994), *Modernisierung, Wohlfahrtsentwicklung und Transformation* (*Modernization, Welfare Development and Transformation*), Berlin: Edition Sigma (in German).

9. How policy frameworks shape environmental practice: three cases of alternative dwelling

Chelsea Schelly

INTRODUCTION

This chapter examines three cases of alternative residential dwelling and explores how policies operate as systems of provision to shape social practices in the home. The analysis is motivated by the fact that the social and technological organization of residential life has profound environmental impacts. Residential dwelling practices contribute significantly to carbon emissions, waste production, and material inefficiencies, which, in turn, compound environmental degradation. Alternative forms of dwelling can reduce the environmental impact of residential life. The chapter analyzes adoption of residential solar electric technology, off-grid living in homes called Earthships, and life in an intentional community to shed light on how policies shape collective practice and to show how people assign symbolic understandings when choosing alternative forms of dwelling. Based on interviews and ethnographic fieldwork, the three case studies demonstrate a range of alternative possibilities in the domain of residential dwelling involving renewable energy technologies, more sustainable forms of organization, and – most importantly – innovative practices with both environmental and social benefits.[1] These outcomes are actualized through practices as routine interactions with evolving technological systems. Dwelling practices that differ from conventional residential forms are facilitated and constrained through policy frameworks that operate as systems of provision to shape and give meaning to social practices.

Work utilizing a social practices approach examines particular domains of routine activity such as food consumption, mobility, energy use, and so forth (Kennedy et al. 2013). Rather than concentrating on individual behaviors, a social practices perspective seeks to understand how activities that take place within these domains are shaped by social context; the analytical lens focuses on practices rather than personal choices or motivations. In this chapter, the domain of interest is residential dwelling, which actually involves a constellation of practices such as the acquisition and utilization of energy, the performance of subsistence and sanitation, and the organization of material comfort. I specifically examine three empirical cases of alternative residential dwelling: adoption of residential solar electric technology, off-grid living in dwellings called Earthships, and life in an intentional community.

Adoption of solar electric technology (also known as photovoltaic or PV) is growing in many countries and reaching a point of cost parity with other energy options (Branker et al. 2011; Zweibel 2010). In the United States, diffusion of residential PV equipment has been incentivized through a federal tax credit (currently of 30 percent of total system cost) and numerous state, municipal, and utility policies that vary greatly from place to place. Comparing residential PV adoption in different states allows for the study of how policies shape specific behaviors and their contextualized meanings among homeowners living with solar electric technology. A more radical form of residential dwelling involves living entirely disconnected from the mainstream 'grid' – the systems that provide electricity, municipal water, and municipal waste removal and treatment in many parts of the developed world.[2] Homes called 'Earthships' are made out of tires and rammed dirt, providing for almost all of the needs of a residential dweller using resources available on site and offering one way to live 'off-the-grid'.[3]

Both residential PV adoption and Earthship living are forms of alternative residential dwelling organized around the practices of a single-family home. In contrast, the third case study focuses on an income-sharing intentional community in rural Virginia in the United States. In this setting, shared practices are shaped by the policies that govern the area as well as both formal and informal policies within the community itself.

While a social practices perspective offers opportunity for fruitful insight regarding how technologies become normalized and stabilized, most practice theoretical scholarship examines 'the reproduction of practices' (Hargreaves et al. 2013, p. 406) and very little work has 'actively considered how technological innovation could lead to more sustainable social practices' (Brown et al. 2013, p. 3). Some researchers have examined how new practices emerge (Gram-Hanssen 2011; Shove and Walker 2010), and others suggest that social practice theory ought to focus on 'transitions in *practice*' (Hargreaves et al. 2013, p. 405, italics in original, citing Shove 2012). This chapter focuses on alternative residential dwelling, where participants have already shifted away from conventional forms of technology and infrastructures (like electricity provided by the grid) and the typical practices corresponding to those material forms. I thus highlight transformations in practices, examining how policies operate as systems of provision to shape dwelling practice and constrain changes in practice even among those who have transitioned to alternative technologies and adopted new practices with lower environmental impact.

A SOCIAL PRACTICES PERSPECTIVE ON ALTERNATIVE DWELLING

Recent scholarship demonstrates the potential of a social practices perspective for deepening understandings of human interaction with the material world as shaped by and made meaningful through social context (Halkier 2013; Hargreaves et al. 2013; Kennedy et al. 2013; Spaargaren 2013). As discussed in Chapter 1 and based on an important lineage of cultural theories eschewing the purported dualisms of agency–structure and thought–action (such as Anthony Giddens, Pierre Bourdieu, and Michel Foucault; see Halkier 2013; Reckwitz 2002; Schatzki 1996), social practice theories move away from individualist interpretations and value-oriented explanations of action. Social practices perspectives focus attention on the routines and habits of social groups. This approach specifically illustrates how action takes place within material, structural, and cultural frameworks that prod, constrain, and shape collective behaviors.

Rather than provide a single unified theory, social practices perspectives offer a set of approaches focused 'on the mutual interactions between technology and ordinary daily human behavior' (Brown et al. 2013, p. 3). Scholars working from this perspective seek to explain how practices emerge and become stabilized (Hand et al. 2005) and challenge the notion that behavior is the result of individual values, calculations, or decisions (Shove 2003). Social practice theories reformulate understandings of consumption to capture how social context influences and gives meaning to what are often considered individual choices regarding how and what to consume (Kennedy and Krogman 2008; Warde 2005). An individualist perspective is 'inappropriate because householders "have to" use the social and material infrastructures set forth by the provisioning systems' (Spaargaren 2013, p. 237). Instead, 'making conceptual room for the co-structuring role of objects, technologies, and infrastructures in the reproduction of social practices makes it possible to analyze the crucial role of technology in environmental change' (Spaargaren 2013, pp. 229–230). Accordingly, practice theories reorient attention to the socially embedded and contextualized nature of behavior (Reckwitz 2002).

Work from social practices perspectives argues that constellations of behaviors are shaped by social context and are often rendered invisible through social normalization (Schatzki 1996; Shove 2003). Researchers suggest 'there is strong path-dependence in the emergence of ordinary social practices' and 'technology and social practices coevolve such that current practices appear normal and inevitable' (Brown et al. 2013, p. 9). A related literature suggests that consumers can become 'locked in' to particular technologies and infrastructures (Sanne 2002; Unruh 2000), but social practices perspectives extend this insight by demonstrating how actual practices are shaped by socio-technical systems.

Spaargaren (2003) specifies that action (practice) takes place and is assigned significance within systems of provision, which operate to facilitate or constrain patterns of consumption. The concept of 'systems of provision' (Spaargaren 2003) provides a tool for understanding how social practices endure. Architectural forms operate as systems of provision because 'certain forms of demand are unavoidably inscribed, for example, in the design and operation of electricity and water infrastructures and in the architecture of the home itself' (Shove 2010, p. 1278). The technological infrastructures that provide electricity and water, transfer waste, and accommodate mobility are systems of provision because they embed users within particular structures and social contexts that are difficult to alter through individual practice (Shwom and Lorenzen 2012).

To argue that policies operate as systems of provision suggests that they function as structures that shape patterns of human practice (Spaargaren et al. 2006). Policies operate to embed and provide contextualized meanings to users who *make use of the possibilities offered to them in the context of specific systems of provision* (Spaargaren 2003, p. 688, emphasis in original). Policies are systems of provision insofar as they mediate and make meaningful the relationship among technology, residential dwellers, and the behaviors in which they engage at home (Shove and Walker 2010). Social practices are organized constellations of 'behavior-*in-circumstances*' (Schatzki 1996, p. 80, emphasis in original), and policies provide a context in which residential dwellers organize their practices.

Technologies and infrastructures thus constitute systems of provision because they operate as structures that make certain practices possible while making alternative forms of practice limited or even invisible; policies do the same by shaping the options available for technological development and the habits that form in connection with technology use. In the case studies presented here, the policies shaping practice are not international treaties, federal regulations, or large-scale governance mechanisms that may come to mind when reading the word 'policy.' Instead, the policies that matter for the cases described below are localized rules in the form of utility regulations, building codes, and zoning laws at the county (sub-state jurisdiction) and municipal level. This inquiry asks how such policies, in conjunction with more or less formalized community govern-ance structures, operate as systems of provision to induce particular forms of practice while limiting or rendering invisible other possible forms of residential dwelling practice. This investigation provides more general insight into how practices may change and may remain solidified depend-ing on how policies facilitate or constrain engagement with new forms of social practice.

ADOPTION OF RESIDENTIAL SOLAR ELECTRIC TECHNOLOGY

PV technology allows homeowners to produce electricity from a renew-able energy source (the Sun) for their own consumption and, in many cases, to sell any excess to a local utility company at a predetermined rate. Technological developments have made it quite simple to install the required equipment while remaining connected to the local electricity grid, eliminating the need for battery storage. In the United States, there are multiple economic incentives for residential installation of PV technology, including a federal tax credit and rebate programs provided by many states, local communities, and utility companies, although these vary widely across jurisdictions and over time.

Comparing the experiences of residential PV adopters in two different states of the United States demonstrates how policy mechanisms operate as systems of provision shaping social practice (Schelly 2014). In 2011 and 2012, a total of 96 homeowners (48 each in Wisconsin and Colorado) participated in a research project involving semi-structured interviews regarding motivations for adopting residential PV equipment and experi-ences installing and using this technology. The findings of this research suggested that local policies shape the practices of adopters in unexpected ways.

The state of Wisconsin is one of the few states to experiment with a feed-in tariff (Rickerson et al. 2007; Schelly and Price 2014; Wiser et al. 2011). Also referred to as a buy-back agreement, this policy mechanism stipulates that residential PV adopters are paid for every kilowatt-hour of electric-ity they produce in excess of what they consume. In Wisconsin, adopters could be compensated between two and two-and-a-half times the retail price of electricity, depending on their utility provider. Thus, PV adopters could eliminate their electricity bills or even receive a monthly check for excess generation.

This policy had consequences in terms of practice. First, it broad-ened the potential motivations for adoption. Less than two-thirds of homeowners in Wisconsin said that they identified as environmentalists or were motivated to install based on environmental values. Almost 40 percent of homeowners in the state were like Jeff and Jolene, who told me, 'We have never been what I would call extremely green, but I think we're also extremely conservative. And I think our conservative approach means that we want to do things efficiently, effectively. We appreciate having more to do more with.' In contrast, the structure of Colorado's incentive program for PV adoption does not allow homeowners to eliminate their entire monthly bill via a solar system or profit on excess generation, and all of respondents in Colorado identified environmental concern as a motivating factor in their decision to adopt PV technology (although not the only motivating factor). The practice of installing solar electric equipment at home was motivated by different factors in these two states, influenced by how policy mechanisms operated as a system of provision to frame and give meaning to individual behavior.

Furthermore, the incentive structures for residential PV adoption in Wisconsin encouraged future energy conservation. The more electricity homeowners produced but did not use, the more money they made through their buy-back agreements. Thus, homeowners were encouraged to adopt conservation practices even after installing solar technology. In interviews, Wisconsin homeowners talked about replacing old appliances, moving to compact florescent lighting, using power strips to easily shut off multiple devices to reduce phantom loads, and changing behaviors in their homes to use less electricity. In Wisconsin, respondents pursued energy conservation even after installing PV technology and even without environmental motivation in response to policies that constructed their social practices.

In contrast, the structure of rebate programs for residential PV in Colorado has prevented homeowners from making money from their installations. Colorado homeowners pay retail rates for electricity but are paid back at wholesale rates for the excess electricity they generate, and respondents talked about intentionally using more electricity just to avoid getting the much lower credit for excess generation. The structure of utility policy incentives actually encouraged homeowners to use more electricity in their homes after they installed their PV systems. Respondents described how they used electricity to offset natural gas or propane usage since they could not get paid back for any extra electricity they generated or use excess generation to cover their other utility costs. Thus they began using electric space heaters or switching their appliances to electric. As Rich put it, since installing his PV system, 'I want to be offsetting something that's worth more, like retail electricity or the cost of propane. So, the fact that I zero it, you have to keep in mind that I'm deliberating using more power.' The policies in Colorado reshaped practice so that homeowners (who all acknowledged being environmentalists or environmentally concerned) actually consumed more electricity after installing their renewable energy systems.

The specifics of policy design to incentivize adoption of residential solar technology in Wisconsin and Colorado shaped the practices of homeowners who installed PV technology. In Wisconsin, respondents engaged in conservation practices even without a preconditioning environmental orientation. By contrast, homeowners in Colorado with self-professed environmental values intentionally used more electricity. Respondents in both states organized their practices in response to the regulatory and incentive structures governing their respective utility rebate programs. These policies provided context for the constellation of practices involved in using electricity and structured practice so that homeowners in each state reported engaging in the same behaviors in response to the state's policy framework.

EARTHSHIPS AND EARTHSHIP BIOTECTURE

The term 'Earthship' refers to a particular kind of off-grid structure, based on design principles developed by architect Michael Reynolds and utilized by his organization Earthship Biotecture. These homes are constructed from discarded tires rammed with dirt and are entirely disconnected from the utility grids that provide electricity, water, and waste removal to most residential homes, meeting almost all of the needs of the dweller with resources available on site. Based on passive solar design, large southern windows (in the northern hemisphere) provide natural day lighting and a source of heat; the homes are partially buried and the tire walls are covered with earthen plaster for thermal regulation. Small-scale solar and wind systems provide electricity, and waste is treated on site using biological methods. Rainwater is collected, filtered, and first used in sinks and showers, then treated using internal plant beds (making some food production possible) before being directed into toilets and then subsequently treated via an external plant bed, maximizing the efficiency of water usage. Earthships offer a radically sustainable way of living within the limits imposed by the natural world (see Reynolds 1989; 1990a; 1990b; 1993; 2001).

Reynolds' company, Earthship Biotecture, is located in New Mexico, and there are three Earthship housing developments in the area surrounding the city of Taos. The firm comprises a for-profit architectural arm, a non-profit development organization, and an educational institute. Earthship Biotecture sells building plans and employees will travel anywhere as a design and construction crew to build a house. The architect and his crew also build Earthships around the world as an activity of the non-profit organization, often focused on disaster relief projects, educational facilities, or training opportunities. Earthship Biotecture runs active educational programs, and people come from around the world to live in, learn about, and participate in building Earthships. My examination of Earthship dwelling is based on ethnographic research conducted between 2011 and 2013 that included in-depth interviews with homeowners and employees, focus groups with interns, countless informal conversations with homeowners, employees, interns, and seminar participants, and participant observation as an intern and seminar participant.

The practices involved in Earthship dwelling are widely divergent from the routines of a conventional residential home. Like other buildings based on passive solar design, Earthships 'encourage more connection with the outdoors' and residents 'note that they spend more time gazing out the windows . . . and enjoying the experience of merging interior and exterior space' (Brown et al. 2013, p. 16). In Earthships, the internal plant beds that line the glassed side of the home are used to treat wastewater, provide a means of food production, and enhance the blending of inside and outside by bringing what is typically outside inside.

Connection to nature affects Earthship dwelling practice in a profound way. Because the homes rely on resources available on site, living in an Earthship requires awareness of natural rhythms and processes and may require attentive conservation, depending on what is available from the proximate biophysical environment. Skylights and window blinds must be actively opened and closed to help maintain thermal comfort. Doing several loads of laundry while watching a movie marathon may not be possible if solar power is the home's sole source of electricity and it is a cloudy day. Dwellers must be attentive to water usage, especially if the local area is experiencing drought conditions. Earthship homes require that dwellers change their dwelling practices to live within the limits of the natural world. Homeowners talked about experiencing a profound connection to the environment because of their interconnection with it. They described in detail how the grey water recycling system and on site waste treatment systems made them more aware of the products used while showering, cleaning, and eating, all of which stayed within the general confines of the home and had to be processed via biological treatment methods. Respondents discussed using different products and interacting with home systems differently by monitoring and maintaining batteries, cleaning filters, and being aware of and living within the local ecological limits.

Earthship residents, and those who work for or volunteer with Earthship Biotecture, do not talk about the changes in practice required to live in an Earthship as imposing constraints or requiring sacrifice. Instead, they reflect on the freedom involved in living in a dwelling that meets almost all of one's basic needs without engendering monthly bills or requiring outside experts for system maintenance. One intern described it this way: 'Centralization creates a false slavery concept. And once that centralization is gone, there's a freedom . . . you're working for yourself and doing your thing, you're catching your water for yourself and making sure you have enough energy for yourself. It's a freedom in a vast sense.' According to those involved with Earthship Biotecture, this liberation from economic dependency comes with a responsibility to modify their dwelling practices.

However, locally enacted policies like building codes and zoning regulations sometimes prohibit building Earthships in their purest form. For example, there are some jurisdictions in the United States where collection of rainwater for home use is prohibited (such as the entire state of Colorado).[4] People wishing to build an Earthship in these places cannot rely on rainwater and must alternatively dig a well (which in many places requires having a specified minimum amount of land) or connect to municipal water utilities. This shifts the practices involved in Earthship dwelling, as homeowners no longer need to be attentive to natural rhythms of water provision and modify their usage to live within environmental limits. Many local building codes prohibit the use of recycled grey water out of sanitary concerns (the water from sinks and showers that is circulated through internal plant beds in an Earthship), eliminating the potential for one important means of efficiency maximization in Earthship design. Other local building codes require the use of a septic tank in areas not connected to municipal waste treatment facilities. A particular obstacle for the first subdivisions of Earthship homes, that were organized as communal land to increase the economic accessibility of Earthship construction by requiring that homeowners purchase only the land under their home and a very small buffer space, were zoning regulations in Taos County that eliminated the legal provision that allowed for this land-sharing agreement. Homeowners must now purchase conventionally sized lots, making the practice of building an Earthship less economically viable for many people.

Policies that restrict Earthship construction limit the potential of these radically alternative structures to reshape dwelling practice. While the structures have been built all over the world, their construction is heavily dependent on the flexibility afforded by local building codes. Rather than operating at the state or federal level, these provisions often vary in the United States by county or municipality and are based on prevailing sensibilities within a geographically delimited area. At the same time, the standardization of building codes has made the restrictions on Earthship construction a global issue. Policies themselves have become normalized, an invisible means of reinforcing dominant dwelling practices and limiting the potential to reshape social practices through alternative dwelling forms.

LIVING IN ALTERNATIVE COMMUNITY

Twin Oaks is one of the oldest secular intentional communities in the United States still in existence, originally inspired by a fictional account of a utopian commune by behaviorist B.F. Skinner (1948). Based on egalitarianism and a shared labor system, approximately 100 adults and their children live in this rural Virginia community, where everyone is expected to work the same minimum number of hours per week and all residents receive the same monthly stipend (42 hours per week and $86 per month at the time of my visit in the autumn of 2011, during which I conducted interviews with community members and ethnographic fieldwork), as well as receiving the same benefits and services from the community including housing, meals, utilities, clothing, use of community vehicles, and access to state-subsidized health care. Life at Twin Oaks involves a wide variety of alternative social practices related to the organization of residential life, family life, and work–life balances as well as practices involving material property, most of which is communally shared.

There are no single-family dwellings at Twin Oaks. Residents live in shared living groups, large dwelling structures with communal kitchens, bathrooms, and living spaces, and individuals have only a bedroom as personal space and for personal belongings. For many modern dwellers, residential homes are spaces to be alone or within one's immediate nuclear family. This is simply not possible at Twin Oaks, where communal dwelling structures reshape practice so that residents are rarely alone or exclusively with nuclear family members.

Practices of work at Twin Oaks also differ markedly from conventional norms. People live where they work and while community members technically log more than full-time hours each week, what counts as work is much more broadly defined. In addition to participation in the community's income-generating businesses (hammock making, tofu production, a seed company, and book indexing) and subsistence needs (gardening, cooking communal meals, preparing wood for use as winter heat fuel, vehicle and building maintenance), residents clean communal living spaces, share in childcare, and attend to sick residents as part of their work.

Many of the practices organizing life at Twin Oaks may seem limiting for those not accustomed to this alternative lifestyle. Members do not have much personal space and do not live in nuclear families. They also do not have personal automobiles and must reserve a communal car if they plan to leave the community for any reason. Even clothing and bicycles are treated less strictly as personal property, both of which are freely provided and may be picked up and used by anyone at any time, within the boundaries of both loosely defined and formalized norms that govern the use of collective goods.

Within the community, there are specific informal and formal policies that help mediate practices. In terms of informal stipulations, there are guidelines that shape how Twin Oaks residents relate to one another. For instance, when crossing paths on a trail, eye contact is not required or necessarily expected. This mode of conduct seems to contradict preconceived notions of life in an intentional community. However, residents say that because they are together almost all the time, this informal policy allows people to be alone with their thoughts if they choose, rather than forcing sociability on members at all times.

Also within the realm of informal policies is the free-for-all clothing consignment shop that is accessible only to community members. However, one member explained that the small size of personal rooms and the fact that each individual is responsible for doing her own laundry (in the freely accessible community laundry room) informally shape practice so that individuals do not hoard or excessively acquire clothing. There are also some exceptions made to the general rule of communal property, such as writing one's name in a favorite jacket or labeling a bicycle for a child's use if only one is available in a specific size and there are no other children that also need a bicycle of the same dimensions.

The community has also developed formal policies that shape practice, especially with respect to work. Almost all forms of labor are treated equally, whereby one hour of work is the same regardless of task. The only exception pertains to childcare, where one hour is treated as a half-hour of work for the purposes of labor reporting. This policy supports the kinds of practices the community seeks to encourage, where families do not remain isolated, instead incentivizing one adult to take care of multiple children (receiving a half-hour of work credit for each child) or take a child to work with them, teaching them skills that they will likely need one day so that they, too, can contribute to the community (children are also expected to log work hours).

Local zoning policies also operate as systems of provision for Twin Oaks. Located in a predominantly agricultural region of a southern American state, the community was established in an area where many families or unrelated farm workers once lived together on the property where they worked. Local zoning in the county still allows multiple unrelated people to live together in a single structure. In many parts of the United States, zoning prevents such arrangements, thus effectively prohibiting shared living of the type that takes place at Twin Oaks. Alternative communities that eschew single-family dwelling can only exist in locales where building codes and land-use regulations allow communal dwelling.

At Twin Oaks, both informal and formal policies operate as systems of provision. These policies are generated from within the community itself and from the local jurisdiction in which the community is located. This case study demonstrates that policies govern systems of provision, which shape the informal and formal rules and structures that operate at multiple scales to shape practices.

POLICIES AS SYSTEMS OF PROVISION

Scholars working from a social practices perspective acknowledge that technologies and their infrastructures work as systems of provision to shape patterns of behavior. For example, 'With technological developments in central heating and cooling . . . came the idea that indoor temperature should be fixed within a particular narrow range. . . . Social practices for dressing and choosing various activities developed around this notion of comfort' (Brown et al. 2013, p. 9; see also Shove 2003). The case studies described in this chapter explore how policies, instituted informally and formally and across multiple scales, operate as systems of provision to shape social practice.

In the case of residential solar technology adoption, local and regional differences in how utility companies incentivized and regulated PV installations influenced how adopters engaged with their solar systems and their electricity usage more broadly. Policies in Wisconsin promoted conservation, while policies in Colorado prompted homeowners to consume more electricity in an attempt to offset other utility usage and to avoid being 'paid back' at a much less lucrative rate for excess generation. The utility incentive structures themselves operated as a system of provision, encouraging users to engage in collective patterns of behavior (Schelly 2014). The policies were more influential in shaping practices than individual values. Coloradans used more electricity even though they all espoused environmental values, while Wisconsinites were more focused on conservation even in the absence of environmental concern.

In the case of Earthships, local building codes and zoning regulations have limited the construction of these alternative residential dwelling structures and other off-grid homes that incorporate similar systems and design components. For the people who live in Earthships, and those who work for or volunteer with Earthship Biotecture, living without utilities provides a profound sense of freedom and is worth the concomitant responsibility to develop lifestyles within the limits of the resources available on site. Yet policies at the county and municipal levels often restrict the sustainability potentials of off-grid homes, prohibiting rainwater catchment, grey water recycling, and the biological treatment of waste. These policies correspondingly shape practices, requiring people to utilize systems and infrastructures that encourage technological and economic dependence and limiting the ability of residents to base their consumption on an interdependent relationship with the natural world.

At Twin Oaks, both informal and formal policies shape social practice. The community itself would not be possible without local zoning regulations that allow multiple unrelated individuals to live together and to spatially integrate residential and commercial life. Within the community, both codified rules and unspoken norms shape how residents interact with one another.

In all three case studies, policies including utility regulations, building codes, and zoning laws at local and regional levels influenced how residents engaged with the technologies and structures around them. Furthermore, residents in each instance made sense of their practices based on the policies that shaped their behavior. PV adopters explained the motivations for their behavior in terms of policy incentives and regulatory structures, not values or strict economic calculations of return on investment. Earthship owners talked about how building codes and zoning laws could limit the potential of these radically sustainable homes to reconstruct practices in terms of environmental efficacy and connection to the natural world. Members of Twin Oaks described their sharing economy as a source of abundance, not sacrifice (Schor 2010). The meaning of abundance that Twin Oaks members assign to their sharing practices is shaped by the various policies that structure these practices. As Spaargaren (2013) writes, 'It is practices that "produce" and co-constitute individuals and their values, knowledge, and capabilities, and not the other way around' (p. 233).

Policy making is often based on an understanding of human behavior that prioritizes economically rational action or value-laden normative action (see Reckwitz 2002; Shove 2010) (see Chapter 1). Social practice theories 'make it clear that education, outreach and incentives will have limited effect on people's behaviors if they are determined by routine patterns of everyday life' (Brown et al. 2013, p. 9). Policies meant to promote environmentally beneficial or sustainable consumption behaviors suffer from the inevitable weaknesses of individualist and value-oriented perspectives (Shove 2010). Attempts at changing practice at the individual, behavioral level based on appeals to beliefs and values are likely to fail if they do not take into account how policies matter in giving rise to practice (Heberlein 2012).

A social practices perspective offers a conceptual stance that more accurately captures how individual behaviors become culturally meaningful habits. The case studies presented here suggest that individualist, value-oriented explanations for adopting alternative forms of dwelling are less salient in terms of their impact on practices than policies. Operating as systems of provision, policies provide context to facilitate or constrain particular social practices. Thus policies can, and arguably should, be evaluated in terms of their effect on practices.

CONCLUSION: FROM GOVERNMENT POLICIES TO GOVERNANCE OF PRACTICES

Understanding human behavior from a social practices perspective can enhance the policy-making process. As Shove and Walker (2010) argue, 'effective innovation (in practice) is likely to be an outcome not (only) of producing, promoting, adopting or aligning technologies, not (only) of cultivating novelties within existing regimes, and not (only) of enlisting users but, crucially, of adding to the repertoire of elements available for integration' (p. 474). Policy design and policy mechanisms can operate as structures that promote or constrain additional repertoires for integration into dwelling practices.

Social practice theories have relevance for evaluating policy in terms of the practices that they encourage or constrain. In the case of residential PV technology, if the intention of incentivizing the adoption of renewable energy technology is to promote the environmental benefits, policies that indirectly inspire increased electricity consumption are far from optimal. Policies like Wisconsin's feed-in tariff, which facilitates continued conservation and broadens the potential motivation for adoption, provide multiple benefits.

In the case of Earthship dwelling, local regulations and restrictions on construction shape the context of possibilities for specific building projects. Constraining rainwater catchment limits how Earthships can align practice with natural processes; restricting grey water treatment places an imposed ceiling on the sustainability of alternative housing designs; requiring septic tanks reduces economic accessibility to and biological integration of Earthships. In the United States, the policies providing context for these practices are formed at highly localized scales, yet at the same time the standardization of building codes means that some restrictions present a challenge throughout the developed world.

At Twin Oaks, informal arrangements, institutional rules, and regulations at the county level all work to shape both practice and the meanings assigned to practice. Community members see sharing as a form of abundance rather than sacrifice. This contextualized understanding of practice is shaped by the informal and formal policies that give meaning to the experiences of everyday life.

The case studies in this chapter focus on how alternative forms of residential dwelling are shaped by policies operating as systems of provision, but the conceptual aim has been to demonstrate that policies provide context and meaning for dwelling practices in all residential settings. In some residential neighborhoods in the United States, homeowner associations prohibit installing solar panels, using clotheslines, or xeriscaping (a form of landscaping that requires very little water to maintain). Local building codes and zoning regulations can prohibit the collection and use of rainwater, grey water recycling, alternative waste treatment systems, and composting toilets. These are very local policies that operate as systems of provision by shaping the kinds of practices that are possible in residential life and inadvertently influencing as well the pathways of human interaction with the natural world and with one another.

Efforts that demonstrate how policies operate to influence social practices raise questions regarding the mechanisms of policy making, specifically arrangements for governance. Spaargaren (2013) suggests that a social practices perspective 'enables routine practices to be seen as new cornerstones with which to build environmental governance arrangements' (p. 229). Interrogating how policies operate to shape social practice can help improve policy making so that they promote social practices with meaningful environmental impacts. This interpretation also suggests that social scientists should carefully interrogate who benefits from current policies and the practices they promote. The case studies presented here also highlight the importance of thinking about policy making in terms of participation, asking who gets to meaningfully affect the underlying processes that ultimately shape practice.

This chapter also devotes particular attention to the role of utility companies in shaping energy policy. These firms arguably stand to lose financially from the promotion of solar electric technology, especially when they are required to incentivize overproduction from residential systems through buy-back agreements. Managers of these companies face inducements that discourage them from supporting policies that promote conservation and enhance user independence.

The other cases bring up similar issues of governance. In the case of Earthship Biotecture, issues of both rights and safety arise. Policies determine who has the right to the water that falls on a privately owned home, whether it is the homeowner (as in New Mexico) or the rancher who owns the water rights (as in Colorado). Decisions regarding whether individual homeowners can catch rainwater, use small-scale wind turbines, or hang clotheslines raise issues regarding individual property rights and the rights of an organized institution (whether a homeowners' association or a state entity) to interfere in such matters. Regarding the relative safety of treating grey water inside or residential waste on site, there are many potential voices to consider – including the homeowner/consumer, the environmental scientist, the municipal waste treatment facility, and the architect/designer/builder. Important questions arise regarding what to do when there is no consensus on issues of safety, rights, or the balance of economic and environmental benefits, particularly when policies are thought of in terms of their impact on practices. Future research from a social practices perspective could usefully examine how both policies and practices in the realm of residential dwelling evolve, asking how new policies emerge to shape practice, interrogating whether practices can change in ways that affect future policies, and considering the outcome of changes in both policy and practice in terms of social and environmental benefits.

Examining residential dwelling from a social practices perspective, specifically focusing on cases of alternative residential dwelling, demonstrates the importance of seeing policy frameworks as systems of provision that shape dwelling practices. We all reside within systems of provision, policies that operate as structures to encourage or constrain particular behaviors and the meanings that are assigned to them. Shifting dwelling practices may require changes in policy, which suggests that we need to devote attention to who benefits from the practices supported by current policies and who participates in the policy-making processes that could induce the emergence of new practices.

NOTES

1. This research was conducted using a practice theoretical framework, whereby participants were asked how they organized their lives based on technology use and interaction with policy frameworks (rather than asking about why) and with explicit attention to the actions (doings) of participants instead of an exclusive focus on the language of motivations. See Schatzki (1996).
2. Earthships provide electricity through small-scale solar and wind systems with battery storage. Water is provided via rainwater catchment, filtered and carefully used throughout the home. Thermal comfort is maintained by taking advantage of the Earth's natural regulatory mechanisms. Systems of sanitation and waste treatment are constructed on site using biological methods. Internal plant beds enable the potential for food production. The only external input in an Earthship is propane gas for cooking. See http://www.earthship.com (accessed 14 August 2014).
3. Off-grid living as a reaction to contemporary residential life has a long history, from the back-to-the-landers of the era of the *Whole Earth Catalog* to the survivalists showcased

in contemporary reality television programs. Earthships are one particular form of off-grid living, based on a specific set of design principles.
4. Rainwater collection is often restricted in response to concerns regarding water access rights, as rainwater becomes groundwater, a limited resource in some areas that is claimed by ranchers and others granted water rights.

REFERENCES

Branker, Kadra, Michael Pathak, and Joshua M. Pearce (2011), 'A review of solar photovoltaic levelized cost of electricity', *Renewable and Sustainable Energy Reviews*, **15** (9), 4470–4482.

Brown, Halina Szejnwald, Philip J. Vergragt, and Maurie J. Cohen (2013), 'Societal innovation in a constrained world: theoretical and empirical perspectives', in M.J. Cohen, H.S. Brown, and P.J. Vergragt (eds), *Innovations in Sustainable Consumption: New Economics, Socio-technical Transitions and Social Practices*, Cheltenham and Northampton, MA: Edward Elgar, pp. 1–30.

Gram-Hanssen, Kirsten (2011), 'Understanding change and continuity in residential energy consumption', *Journal of Consumer Culture*, **11** (1), 61–78.

Halkier, Bente (2013), 'Sustainable lifestyles in a new economy: a practice theoretical perspective on change behavior campaigns and sustainability issues', in M.J. Cohen, H.S. Brown, and P.J. Vergragt (eds), *Innovations in Sustainable Consumption: New Economics, Socio-technical Transitions and Social Practices*, Cheltenham and Northampton, MA: Edward Elgar, pp. 209–228.

Hand, Martin, Elizabeth Shove, and Dale Southerton (2005), 'Explaining showering: a discussion of the material, conventional, and temporal dimensions of practice', *Sociological Research Online*, **10** (2), available at http://www.socresonline.org.uk/10/2/hand.html (accessed 7 July 2015).

Hargreaves, Tom, Noel Longhurst, and Gill Seyfang (2013), 'Up, down, round and round: connecting regimes and practices in innovation for sustainability', *Environmental and Planning A*, **45** (2), 402–420.

Heberlein, Thomas A. (2012), *Navigating Environmental Attitudes*, New York: Oxford University Press.

Kennedy, Emily and Naomi T. Krogman (2008), 'Toward a sociology of consumption', *Journal of International Sustainable Society*, **1** (2), 172–189.

Kennedy, Emily, Harvey Krahn, and Naomi T. Krogman (2013), 'Taking social practice theories on the road: a mixed-methods case study of sustainable transportation', in M.J. Cohen, H.S. Brown, and P.J. Vergragt (eds), *Innovations in Sustainable Consumption: New Economics, Socio-technical Transitions and Social Practices*, Cheltenham and Northampton, MA: Edward Elgar, pp. 252–276.

Reckwitz, Andreas (2002), 'Toward a theory of social practices: a development in culturalist theorizing', *European Journal of Social Theory*, **5** (2), 243–263.

Reynolds, Michael (1989), *A Coming of Wizards: A Manual of Human Potential*, Taos, NM: High Mesa Foundation.

Reynolds, Michael (1990a), *Earthship Volume I: How to Build Your Own*, Taos, NM: Solar Survival Press.

Reynolds, Michael (1990b), *Earthship Volume II: Systems and Components*, Taos, NM: Solar Survival Press.

Reynolds, Michael (1993), *Earthship Volume III: Evolution Beyond Economics*, Taos, NM: Solar Survival Press.

Reynolds, Michael (2001), *Comfort in Any Climate*, Taos, NM: Solar Survival Press.

Rickerson, Wilson H., Janet L. Sawin, and Robert C. Grace (2007), 'If the shoe FITs: using feed-in tariffs to meet U.S. renewable electricity targets', *The Electricity Journal*, **20** (4), 73–86.

Sanne, Christer (2002), 'Willing consumers – or locked-in? Policies for a sustainable consumption', *Ecological Economics*, **42** (1), 273–287.

Schatzki, Theodore (1996), *Social Practices: A Wittgensteinian Approach to Human Activity and the Social*, New York: Cambridge University Press.

Schelly, Chelsea (2014), 'Implementing renewable energy portfolio standards: the good, the bad, and the ugly in a two state comparison', *Energy Policy*, **67**, 543–551.

Schelly, Chelsea and Jessica Price (2014), 'Utilizing GIS to examine the relationship between state renewable portfolio standards and the adoption of renewable energy technologies', *ISPRS International Journal of Geo-Information*, **3** (1), 1–17.

Schor, Juliet (2010), *Plenitude: The New Economics of True Wealth*, New York: Penguin.

Shove, Elizabeth (2003), *Comfort, Cleanliness and Convenience: The Social Organization of Normality*, New York: Berg.

Shove, Elizabeth (2010), 'Beyond the ABC: climate change policy and theories of social change', *Environment and Planning A*, **42** (6), 1273–1285.

Shove, Elizabeth (2012), 'Energy transitions in practice: the case of global indoor climate change', in G. Verbong and D. Loorbach (eds), *Governing the Energy Transition: Reality, Illusion or Necessity?*, New York: Routledge, pp. 51–74.

Shove, Elizabeth and Gordon Walker (2010), 'Governing transitions in the sustainability of everyday life', *Research Policy*, **39** (4), 471–476.

Shwom, Rachael and Janet Lorenzen (2012), 'Changing household consumption to address climate change: social scientific insights and challenges', *WIREs: Climate Change*, **3** (5), 379–395.

Skinner, Burrhus Frederic (1948), *Walden Two*, Indianapolis, IN: Hackett Publishing.

Spaargaren, Gert (2003), 'Sustainable consumption: a theoretical and environmental policy perspective', *Society and Natural Resources*, **16** (8), 687–701.

Spaargaren, Gert (2013), 'The cultural dimension of sustainable consumption practices: an exploration in theory and policy', in M.J. Cohen, H.S. Brown, and P.J. Vergragt (eds), *Innovations in Sustainable Consumption: New Economics, Socio-technical Transitions and Social Practices*, Cheltenham and Northampton, MA: Edward Elgar, pp. 229–251.

Spaargaren, Gert, Susan Martens, and Theo A.M. Beckers (2006), 'Sustainable technologies and everyday life', in P.P. Verbeek and A. Slob (eds), *User Behavior and Technology Development: Shaping Sustainable Relations Between Consumers and Technologies*, Dordrecht: Springer, pp. 107–118.

Unruh, Gregory C. (2000), 'Understanding carbon lock-in', *Energy Policy*, **28** (12), 817–830.

Warde, Alan (2005), 'Consumption and theories of practice', *Journal of Consumer Culture*, **5** (2), 131–153.

Wiser, Ryan, Galen Barbose, and Edward Holt (2011), 'Supporting solar power in renewable portfolio standards: experience from the United States', *Energy Policy*, **39** (7), 3894–3905.

Zweibel, Ken (2010), 'Should solar photovoltaics be deployed sooner because of long operating life at low, predictable cost?', *Energy Policy*, **38** (11), 7519–7530.

10. 'Unleashing Local Capital': scaling cooperative local investing practices

Mike Gismondi, Juanita Marois, and Danica Straith

INTRODUCTION

Without a doubt the excessive power of global finance capital and financial markets contributes to social inequality and ecological unsustainability (Buckland 2012; Intergovernmental Panel on Climate Change 2013; Piketty 2014; Rockström et al. 2009). In response to the financial crisis that commenced in 2008 and the failure of markets to meet the challenges of sustainability, organizations like the New Economics Foundation (2014) propose a new paradigm that 'works for people and the planet'. The 'Move Our Money' movement urges individuals to shift their personal savings from Wall Street-based institutions, and in 2011 and 2012 its followers transferred over US$500 million into credit unions and community banks, which are typically smaller, more democratically governed, one-person one-vote depositories (Flacks 2013; Move Our Money 2014). Peer-to-peer lending and so-called 'impact investing' (deliberate investment to address social, ecological, and economic well-being) are growing and offer a mix of products and metrics across asset classes, sectors, and regions (Best and Harji 2013; Jackson and Harji 2012).

The global finance challenge goes beyond individual action, and is increasingly being addressed at a community level. As single national currencies fail to meet societal needs, community and complementary local currencies are being developed to circulate goods and to strengthen services within a region (Seyfang 2006; Seyfang and Longhurst 2013). In this context, grassroots groups and municipalities are financing sustainability through investment in local food, alternative energy, social care, and community development (Alperovitz 2013; Hewitt 2013; Lewis and Conaty 2012). Two notable recent books, *The Resilience Imperative* (2012) by Lewis and Conaty and *Take Back the Economy* (2013) by Gibson-Graham, Cameron, and Healy, focus attention on cooperative investment for mobilizing capital at community and regional levels to finance sustainability efforts. These new forms of cooperative investing are widening membership and increasing the capital pool, while putting financial democracy, community well-being, the environment, and local business creation ahead of personal gain (Co-operatives UK 2014a; Evergreen Cooperatives 2014).

To imagine and enact an alternative financial ecosystem is no small feat and the scale of this challenge gives the question of how best to spread the impact of local finance options' considerable appeal. In this chapter we introduce the 'Unleashing Local Capital' (ULC) program, a cooperative local investment innovation designed by the Alberta Community and Cooperative Association (ACCA), a community development organization based in the Canadian province of Alberta (a western Canadian province with a population of 4 million and three times the geographic size of Great Britain). The ULC project provides rural communities with a financial tool with which to retain local capital and to invest in community businesses. We describe the ULC team's attempts to scale this cooperative investment model across Alberta and the obstacles that they encountered. These impediments include incumbent financial structures and legislative systems and people's habitual practices with respect to investing and borrowing. Our primary objective is to identify the factors that facilitate or hinder the spread of the innovation and to explore their influence. To analyze our findings we apply a framework that is informed by both social practice theories and the multi-level perspective (MLP) common in the study of socio-technical transitions (Hargreaves et al. 2013; Shove 2003).

Both MLP and social practice perspectives recognize that change at a systemic level is essential to meeting contemporary sustainability challenges, though they differ in sociological focus, or unit of inquiry. The MLP proposes that changes in socio-historical systems result from the interaction of developments at three analytical levels: niches, regimes, and landscapes (Markard et al. 2012). First, the niche level is the organizational or locality setting in which novel or radical innovations typically arise. Second, the regime level represents established or incumbent broad-scale institutions, codes, and conventional systems of provision. Finally, the landscape level includes exogenous influences that rise above national political boundaries such as socio-economic forces. MLP theorists find that landscape pressures exert stress upon regimes and can open 'windows of opportunity' where governments are able to intervene to create safe places for the emergence of novel innovations. Also, pressures from social and political movements at the landscape level enable niche innovations to reconfigure existing regimes (Geels 2011; Geels and Schot 2010). A transition is generally considered to take place when an accumulation of niche innovations triggers a change in the way societal functions are carried out at the regime level (Hargreaves et al. 2013). Early MLP work explored past transitions (for example, the shift in transportation from animal power to fossil fuel-powered machines). More recent research explores MLP dynamics to explain how management of 'niche' innovations such as green energy or local food could challenge current unsustainable systems of provision (Geels and Schot 2010). In our use of MLP, local investment cooperatives are the niche innovation. Conventional financial, securities, and tax systems are incumbent configurations that comprise the regime level while global socio-economic and finance issues exist at the landscape level.

Social practice theorists concerned with transitions to sustainability propose a different view of change. Within a practice approach, transition to a sustainable future requires adjustments in the normal patterns of how people consume objects and resources to accomplish daily routines (Shove and Spurling 2013; Warde 2005). For example Shove (2003) studied the change in practice from bathing weekly to showering daily that has occurred over past decades to demonstrate the link between increased water usage and social practices. Büchs et al. (2011, p. 5) define social practices as 'the recurring "sayings and doings" (Schatzki 1996) that people engage in on a daily basis and that are, simultaneously, embedded within and reproduce "social structures" (Giddens 1984) and material infrastructures (Reckwitz 2002; Shove 2003)'. These range from everyday activities like eating, travelling, and cleaning to more complex ones associated with business, farming, and political practices.

Shove and her colleagues (2012) describe three 'elements' that comprise social practices: 1) *materials* that include technologies and physical things like bike lanes or showerheads; 2) *competencies* that encompass skills, know-how, conventional operations, and ways of doing things; and 3) *meanings* that entail symbolic worth, ideas, and rationalizations. These elements are actively and repeatedly integrated into circuits of reproduction and make up everyday practices. It is *the doing* of biking or showering that brings together the elements of practice. For instance, one might break down the practice of 'biking to work' into the following three elements: the 'materials' of a bike, a bike path, a helmet, bike lights, and a lock; with the competency or 'know-how' of riding on a bike and using hand signals; alongside the meaning or 'image' of sustainability, cost efficiency, and healthiness. This analysis should also be extended to assess the collection of practices that interlink with the practice under consideration. In the instance of 'biking to work' this might include negotiated relations within the household regarding the logistics of grocery shopping or picking the kids up from school or perceptions of cleanliness in the workplace and road safety (Watson 2013). A conflict between any of these elements or practices can be the difference between biking to work and driving to work.

Our analysis of the ULC innovation combines these two different, but to some degree complementary, theoretical perspectives. While distinct practices are embedded at the niche and regime levels, elements of practice can also travel across and between levels (Shove and Walker 2010). From the standpoint of social practice theories, transitions in practices occur as a result of the making or breaking of the links among elements, which can occur at different socio-technical levels (Shove 2010; Shove et al. 2012). Hargreaves et al. (2013) argue that it is productive to examine how and where these practices and systems intersect:

> The MLP allows one to examine the emergence of novelty through the inter-actions of the vertically ordered levels of niche, regime, and landscape, while [social practice theory] focuses attention instead on the horizontal dimensions of practices that cut across multiple regimes as they follow their circuits of reproduction. (p. 407)

Using this dual framework, Hargreaves and his colleagues reexamined the failed scaling up of an organic grocery store where it appeared that sufficient changes in niche and regime structures had been introduced to enable a successful transition. The combined approach allowed for identification of a series of 'critical points of intersection' between systems and practices and consideration of how these 'friction points' worked against the spread. For example, the business failed to anticipate farmer resistance to changes in practices of growing food and consumer resistance to altering shopping practices. In separate work, Watson (2013, p. 118) describes these kinds of intersections between MLP and practices as 'systemic sticking points'. Hargreaves et al. (2013) argue that some of these intersections are 'points of possibility' where actors might guide system changes. We apply both approaches to explore local investing as we establish the connections and crossovers between the regime and social practices to grasp factors that could hinder, facilitate, or accelerate the spread of innovation.

In what follows, we first introduce the research setting, methodology, and a multi-level analysis of mainstream investing and borrowing, followed by a social practices analysis of the practice of local investing and borrowing. The final sections explore intersections and friction points that are barriers to change, and points of possibility where intermediaries might spread niche innovations in local investing.

STUDY SETTING: THE UNLEASHING LOCAL CAPITAL PROJECT

In late 2011, ACCA introduced an Opportunity Development Cooperative (ODC) across Alberta. An ODC is a social innovation in finance through which people invest in local business opportunities using a cooperative business structure. This investment model seeks to keep money in the communities where it is generated, including funds that people held in their personal registered retirement savings plans (RRSPs).[1] To accomplish this objective, ACCA developed the Unleashing Local Capital program that, in March 2012, attracted US$1.26 million in grant support from the Rural Alberta Development Fund. ACCA invited the authors of this chapter to join the project steering committee and to collaborate in a participatory research design (Bergold and Thomas 2012). Three years of participation allowed many opportunities for observation, informal conversations, and reflection to validate research findings.

To recruit participants, ACCA implemented an Alberta-wide media campaign including four webinars to introduce the concept of local cooperative investing. ACCA also offered 'Champion Teams' – informal groups of community leaders – US$60,000 of professional training, legal support, and coaching to incorporate and register their first share offering. Each group was expected to contribute US$10,000 for the training. Nine communities applied, with business proposals ranging from meat shops and an arts center to a convenience store/gas station. The Steering Committee selected Champion Teams from the small rural communities of Smoky River, Bashaw, and Vegreville to serve as pilots for the project. Bashaw withdrew from the project for reasons that we discuss in the section called 'Speed'; the Steering Committee chose the runner-up community of Crowsnest Pass to replace Bashaw. ULC intermediaries worked with these communities to refine an ODC incorporation and share-selling process, and basic training guides for engaging investors and borrowers were put online to make them accessible to geographically diverse communities throughout Alberta.

As 2012 ended, the Champion Teams in Crowsnest and Smoky River had incorporated their ODCs and were poised to make share offerings. Smoky River's plan to build a housing development was later delayed when the ODC could not finalize the purchase of land from the municipality. Vegreville withdrew from the project after expressing misgivings about the cooperative model and experiencing low energy in the leadership group following disagreement on a first investment opportunity. Under pressure to meet requirements from the funder, the ULC Steering Committee decided to launch a second round of pilots during the spring of 2013.

An additional six pilot communities were identified with the intention of supporting the projects to the point of incorporation, but with little expectation that a share offering would occur before project completion on 31 December 2013.[2] At the end of project in December 2014, the ULC had incorporated ODCs in Athabasca, Crowsnest, Drumheller, Three Hills, Smoky River, and Vulcan. Crowsnest completed one public offering that raised US$640,000 (ACCA 2014).

METHODOLOGY

Both the design and implementation stages of ULC required original research. To design the opportunity development cooperative structure we researched the cooperative model (Soots et al. 2007) used by Nova Scotia's Community Economic Development Investment Fund (CEDIF),[3] and interviewed leaders from three existing Alberta cooperative investment projects with over US$5 million of community financing: Battle River Railway New Generation Coop, Westlock Grain Terminals New Generation Coop, and Sangudo Opportunity Development Coop (Barney 2012; Cabaj et al. 2009; Evans 2011; Murray et al. 2010). Comparative studies of legislative, tax, legal, and Security Commission regulations related to local investment in Canada and the United States were also conducted to help ACCA actors decide on elements that could be adapted for use in Alberta (ACCA 2011a; Gismondi and Leon 2012; Leon and Gismondi 2012; Miller Thomson 2013a). In particular, ACCA intermediaries and researchers confirmed legal steps to allow retirement savings to be used to purchase cooperative investment shares and for community members to hold those shares in their tax-deductible RRSP accounts.

As implementation began, the research team conducted 36 semi-structured interviews in 18 communities (including discussions with people who attended information sessions but chose not to participate) and three focus groups. We carried out the interviews in phases: the first ten interviews were completed with community leaders in 2012 to explore barriers to project participation (Marois and Gismondi 2013). Subsequent interviews were conducted with pilot-community leaders, project intermediaries, and professional advisors in 2012 and 2013, and with the same group of individuals after project completion in 2014. Focus groups were conducted in the communities of Vegreville and Smoky River and with the team of ULC intermediaries. We gathered data at various critical points in the project: as communities were withdrawing as pilots, as other communities were incorporating their investment cooperatives, and as some reached the project goal of selling shares in a community investment.

We prepared verbatim transcripts of all interviews and focus-group recordings. We also devised a coding system to identify the major regime actors, such as Alberta's Security Commission and the Canada Revenue Agency, as well as practice elements, such as skills to secure loans and invest savings, associated with local cooperative investing. The approach allowed us to track changes 'in process' across the nine pilot communities (Crivits and Paredis 2013; Hargreaves 2011; Pettigrew 1990).

The MLP framework initially helped us to describe how ACCA intermediaries interacted with regime-level financial systems adapting legislative, tax, legal, and Security Commission regulations to make space for the ULC niche innovation. We then employed Shove and Pantzar's (2005) three elements of practices (images, skills, and materials) to contrast mainstream with alternative local investing and borrowing. In applying the combined framework (Figure 10.1), we identified six friction points: discussing money, transparency, speed, cooperation, risk, and trust. We argue that these critical points of intersection between the MLP and social practices perspectives indicate where local cooperative borrowing and investing are being constrained by the inertia of conventional practices entrenched in regime structures and systems.

A MULTI-LEVEL PERSPECTIVE ON LOCAL INVESTING

The ULC team started from three premises. First, there is a need for local capital retention in rural communities. Secondly, current investment practices include annually setting aside money in RRSPs with encouragement from banks and federal tax incentives. Finally, current investment structures – particularly those designed around retirement – drain capital from rural communities. To elaborate, an ACCA (2011b) report states that 'Each year, Albertans invest over $4.4 billion in RRSPs, the vast majority of which are diverted to investments and profits in businesses outside of Alberta. Diverting even 5% of this outflow of capital would result in over $220 million in local capital investment.'[4]

As an intermediary stimulating a niche innovation, ACCA understood the ways that provincial and federal regime-level structures, rules, and regulations concerning taxation, security/risk, and legal and accounting requirements constrain cooperative investing. In its efforts to reconfigure the existing regime structures, ACCA lobbied ministers and bureaucrats within government responsible for promoting rural development in Alberta. The organization also worked with existing regime-level community economic development actors, such as Community Futures, a federally funded agency,

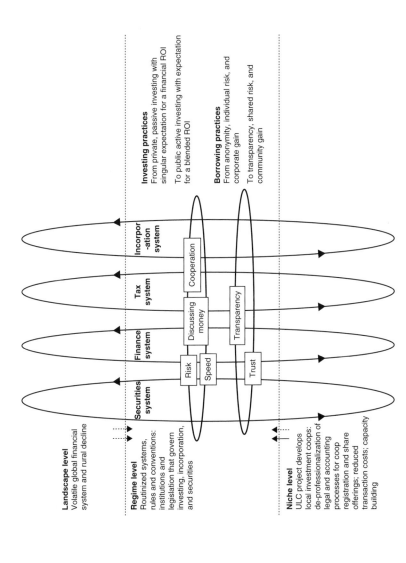

Source: Adapted from Hargreaves et al. (2013).

Figure 10.1 'Unleashing Local Capital' friction points within MLP/SP framework

involving them at various levels (steering committee, pilot-community resources, and animators). Intermediaries used various strategies, including handpicking experienced charismatic local investment cooperative leaders and business entrepreneurs (from Nova Scotia and Alberta) to share their stories of building the cooperative, attracting local investors, and achieving business successes. ULC intermediaries targeted this storytelling at two audiences: communities and regime actors.

Over two years, the ULC legal and accounting experts interacted with representatives from the relevant regulatory bodies to develop and refine a process for cooperative investment. They crafted acceptable legal templates and simplified offering documents that reduced the transaction costs by about 75 percent. Fees to prepare an Offering Memorandum[5] enabling an ODC to legally sell shares were reduced from more than US$100,000 to approximately US$5000–$25,000, with the precise amount depending on the complexity of the project. This fee level was consistent with mainstream investing costs (ACCA 2014).

Despite helping us understand niche tensions with regulatory regimes, the MLP lens left us with an important question: with regime-level adaptations in place, why the slow uptake of the ULC cooperative innovation? Our interviews with ULC intermediaries and community leaders revealed that more was at play. Dan, who founded a successful investment cooperative and advised the ULC team, commented that:

> [T]he legal format ... the legal template, the accounting, ... all that stuff is pretty simple and technical and anybody can do it ... we were able to with the professional help, but that whole people-side in the community ... making some little changes to their beliefs and values and seeing business in a slightly different way. That's a huge step.

Dan's comments point to the need to shift the focus from how the niche innovation engages with the regime structures and systems to what happens when the niche engages with established local investing and borrowing practices. We now apply a social practices perspective to illuminate the challenges involved with changing deeply seated routines, and compare and contrast the mainstream practices of investing and borrowing with local cooperative investing and borrowing practices.

INVESTING PRACTICES

As previously noted, investing practices comprise meanings, skills, and materials (Shove and Pantzar 2005). In the minds of most people, banks are regulated and appear secure, trustworthy, and part of a global system of expertise available in their hometown (Gilbert-Squires 2014). Many people learn the skills to work with financial institutions such as opening a savings account, securing credit, making investments, and saving for retirement. Impressive buildings, computer systems, advertising, and trained personnel with business degrees materially reinforce impressions of investment security. In mainstream investing, individuals generally have little interest in or opportunity to track where their money goes. Reporting back to the investor is limited to information on risk and financial return on investment (ROI).[6] Moreover, the practice of investing does not take place in public; it is a private transaction between individuals and bankers that typically occurs behind closed doors. While each 'performance' of mainstream investing may be unique, as Seth, a ULC intermediary and one of our respondents, described, the images of these performances share much in common:

> People have been putting this money away and they don't know where it's going. When you buy an RRSP, you think there is some expert at a bank, in a nice office, wears a crisp suit and they take care of your money . . . that is going to be your retirement . . . All this money is [earned] in rural communities . . . but we are sending it away . . . to places that are actually counterintuitive to what we want to see in our communities. You know we save all this money to secure our future, but we are not using it for the future of our communities.

Landscape pressures following the 2008 financial crisis have made some people more conscious of their investing practices and more open to novel capital-raising projects such as relational lending, crowdsourcing, social investing, slow money, and other approaches to investing in the future of communities (Gibson-Graham et al. 2013). This pressure creates a window of opportunity in which new innovations like ULC can be nurtured and spread.

The ULC project compels people to rethink the practice of investing and to expand their understanding of ROI to include more than simple monetary gain. The ULC cooperative model of local investment built an expectation of a blended ROI that builds in metrics for new local businesses and services generation, job creation, and enhanced quality of community life alongside profit.[7] Respondents indicated that upon learning how much money was leaving their deteriorating communities, and realizing that the money could be used to provide a blended return, they were prompted to re-evaluate their investing practices. Investors may be satisfied with a lower short-term financial ROI if important long-term social, business, or ecological gains such as employment or energy security are addressed (Lewis and Conaty 2012; Robb et al. 2010; Tasch 2010). John, a community leader from Athabasca, emphasized that 'we can put money where we think it will do the most good'.

The ULC project introduced new tools, skills, and know-how for cooperative investment within communities. While passive involvement is usually all that is required to make an investment with a person's banker or investment counselor, ULC investors are expected to take more active roles. The ODC members review feasibility studies, choose the business investment, and meet entrepreneurs to discuss their ideas and draft investment agreements that simultaneously meet the needs of the entrepreneur and the community. Then they vote (one person, one vote regardless of the amount invested) on which opportunity to pursue. Larry, a Community Futures intermediary and ODC member in Crowsnest Pass, highlights the importance of this active involvement for community development:

> The model is self-sustaining. Once up and running, it should be self-supporting. It's one of those models that can be used for different things . . . you can use the model for anything you can think of for local community development. Your imagination is the limit. It's giving a mechanism for local people to invest locally. If you identify a local need you can use the model.

BORROWING PRACTICES

Local investment cooperatives also confront the practice of borrowing money. Within the mainstream practice of financing a business start-up or expansion, entrepreneurs typically look to personal contacts or a bank. In the minds of borrowers, the bank specializes in commercial loans and has knowledge of the local marketplace; the fees they pay the bank should ensure sound financial advice. Borrowers typically use skills to develop standard business plans and to provide information about their commercial experience, collateral, and personal worth. This information is generally not shared beyond two or three bank employees and the relationship remains formal; terms of loans (security and repayment) are generic and set by the corporate head office, and repayment with interest begins almost immediately.

As Bruce, an ODC member from Didsbury, explained, local investing introduces two new and unfamiliar institutions into the well-established practice outlined above:

> A bank is a business and they're out to make money so they make money by finding an opportunity that they can then leverage . . . to make money off of people with absolutely no risk . . . That's their ideology . . . the capitalist ideology . . . A cooperative has a whole different motivation and a whole different purpose, which is to bring everybody together so we all win. So using community money to fund us all winning means that everybody wins, and not just a bank getting richer . . . To balance that equation, you've also got to

take some risk. So by spreading the risk over a lot of people, the risk becomes smaller, but then we all share the profits. And that is absolutely night-and-day different than a bank.

Bruce sees the community and the ODC as alternative lending institutions (material) that bring with them new images and skills. Entrepreneurs are borrowing from the ODC, which comprises friends and family. Unlike a bank, borrowers and lenders negotiate repayment conditions (know-how) to support the entrepreneurs' success with flexible terms that may not require payments in, say, the first months or year of operation. The cooperative members are often other business people who share their expertise and local knowledge, and who may become clients and promoters. The ODC members benefit through fair dividends and the community profits from enhanced services. Borrowing becomes a public interaction between the entrepreneur and ODC members that will require new legal and accounting skills and ongoing dialogue. Adoption of local investing is unlikely if entrepreneurs do not accept this new system of practices.

BARRIERS TO 'UNLEASHING LOCAL CAPITAL'

Like Hargreaves et al. (2013, p. 416) we were struck by how the problems encountered by ULC when scaling out 'related more to how it connected up with and attempted to reconfigure a range of different everyday practices and systems of practices than to any particular problem . . . as a niche innovation in itself'. In Figure 10.1 we use the combined MLP/social practices framework to indicate six points of intersection that we contend inhibited the diffusion of the ULC innovation.

Discussing Money

Talking with Albertans about money can be challenging. In this oil-rich province, stories of individualism and taking risks to make fortunes are cherished petro-myths, stereotypes of oil kings alongside rugged cowboys. Dominant meanings associated with investing money include maximizing personal financial ROI, reducing costs, investing anywhere in the world where a quick return is likely, avoiding taxes, and constantly seeking to increase profits. Working to counter the value that many Albertans place on individual risk taking and financial reward is strategic to the micro-scale politics of local investing. Asking people to invest money in a social cause is also a point of friction. Although respondents were comfortable donating money to a charity or soliciting their friends and neighbors to donate to a community swimming pool or playground, most of them were more hesitant when asked to invest in a local business of social worth. We found people tended to be calculating regarding risk and profit, beyond expected mainstream incentives for a charitable donation like public recognition and tax deductions.

We found evidence to suggest that the language of conventional banking shaped many commonly held ideas about money. ACCA coaches became more aware of this crucial socialization dynamic as the process evolved. They increased their efforts at educating the community about the merits of keeping their money working locally and accepting a blended ROI (social and financial) on their money. Participants accepted that the cooperative funds would strengthen community assets in contrast to money that they invested globally. The very name 'Opportunity Development Cooperative' emphasized the more involved and democratic role of investors. Nonetheless, shifting people's thinking to support cooperative investment in a business in their community (especially one that adds a social justice or environmental benefit) required new meanings and new vocabulary.[8] The role of the *image* of 'community investment' as a code for a new ideational meaning is as important as *know-how* and *tools* for the adoption of a novel practice.

Transparency

The capitalist financial system celebrates and integrates elements of privacy and confidentiality into its practices – sometimes to a fault. Financial market traders and bankers are often criticized for a lack of transparency that has concealed director bonuses, offshore-tax shelters, and winners and losers when financial crises occur. In contrast, cooperative borrowing and investing are open and accessible processes. An ODC offering will have up to 50 investors, all from the same community. Who invests and how much each invests is treated as public knowledge within the ODC and the wider community, and borrowers need to accept greater expectations of transparency by submitting a feasibility and business plan to the board of directors of the ODC. Unlike a bank, however, the local cooperative board likely comprises people who the entrepreneur knows, perhaps in many contexts – church, parent council, service club, or neighborhood. These connections open their business history to friends and the public. Once the investment is approved, each potential community investor will receive an offering document containing the same information. This transparency means little privacy is left for the entrepreneur. If the application for investment is not approved, there is an additional risk of personal embarrassment in the community. It could mean a loss of reputation (social capital) and good relations among neighbors and friends. While transparency is a point of possibility that may attract people to local investing, privacy and a desire to keep money matters to oneself are cultural conventions that are a constraint for the ULC program.

Speed

The impression of the time required to move an investment in a business project from conception to reality becomes a crucial motivational variable, especially in a crisis situation where closure could mean loss of a major community asset. In Bashaw and Crowsnest Pass, private investors appropriated the initial proposals developed by the cooperative leaders. While some pilot project leaders were satisfied that the business would go forward using a conventional financial investment, others were frustrated that the entrepreneur had not adopted their appeal for the blended benefits of the local investment cooperative. They identified lack of speed in the ULC model as one reason the entrepreneur changed his mind. The imperative of speed is a direct manifestation of the niche-regime tensions presented in the MLP framework. The novel practices of ODC investing must compete in the public mind against the more routinized and expedited tools of financial institutions and security commissions. Paradoxically, neither the Bashaw nor Crowsnest Pass business opportunity proceeded quickly after pursuing private investors. Bashaw Meats & Sausage was closed for almost two years but eventually reopened at a leased building site.

While the *image* of local investing is a positive one, negative perceptions include a sense that the process entails a lengthy time commitment for collective and democratic decision making. People are wary of the meetings and group deliberation involved in alternative cooperative investment processes. ACCA worked to reduce set-up time and complexity by streamlining the incorporation and share-selling processes. In fact, the process from incorporation to share selling and project completion in Crowsnest (the group eventually funded the purchase and renovation of a designated heritage commercial building on main street) took less than one year. But democratic participation in local investing probably will require more resolve from community leaders and investors. Associating local capital investment with slow capital helps turn the speed issue around. Investors may recognize that the high-speed transactions of contemporary money managers and traders contributed to the 2008 financial collapse (Goglio and Alexopoulos 2013; Tily 2010). Slowing capital down could be reframed as a positive feature of the ROI of local investing. Slow capital investments in community assets like bakeries, butcher shops, and local food link cooperative investors to community development instead of 'a casino economy in which speculative behavior prevails' (De Antoni 2013, p. 27; Hewitt 2013).

Cooperation

The practices of cooperative investment, borrowing, and governance are not conventional knowledge. One respondent shared that 'it was the concept of the cooperative or starting up the coops. People consider them but do not do anything because they are not clear on how to get them started.' The cooperative movement started in western Canada as a democratic populist movement during the 1920s. Albertans used cooperatives to provide rural electrification, to ensure farm and fuel supplies, to offset the power of the banks and corporations, and to neutralize 'plutocratic economic parasites of Central Canada' (Epp and Whitson 2001, p. 742). But in the last 30 years, cooperatives have been under pressure from global neoliberal economic reforms. Many have become more corporate in nature; some have changed from cooperatives to privatized companies. In a comparative study, Diamantopoulos (2011) found that familiarity with cooperative governance and cooperative ownership has declined, as has cooperative membership in western Canada; at the same time he reports that cooperatives in Quebec have prospered and grown with provincial support.

The novelty of the cooperative model of investing proved to be problematic in another important way. A handful of respondents thought the ODC only invested in other cooperatives. By using the models of new generation cooperatives in Battle River and Westlock to excite passion about local investment, ULC intermediaries may have contributed to this perception. This mischaracterization was a barrier for some leaders, entrepreneurs, and potential investors interested in supporting a privately owned business. In fact, an ODC *is structured as a cooperative* but can choose to invest in any business model, be it social enterprise, cooperative, municipal, private, or multi-stakeholder enterprise.

Still, at the niche level, the tools remain limited. To develop the necessary materials and tools to engage and educate residents of rural communities and strengthen the know-how component, ACCA developed clear, user-friendly online course materials and Internet discussion boards to increase horizontal learning across communities. But regime actors, structures, and conventions can slow efforts to alter the system (Geels 2014). Local investment cooperatives require a lawyer who is experienced in cooperatives but training in cooperative law is limited in law school. To accelerate administrative processes, ACCA coaches are building community capacities by training citizens to use legal templates and to prepare registries and accounting information to decrease transaction costs. Their efforts to de-professionalize these regime processes can shed light on some of the previously routinized aspects of mainstream legal, security, accounting, and tax systems that shape and constrain local investment. In short, these ACCA templates and teachings act to re-routinize or normalize cooperative models into the day-to-day practices of law, accounting, securities review, and taxation (Spargaaren 1997).

Risk

Risk is a complex friction point in the shift to the practice of local investment. We earlier described the risks to the social capital of entrepreneurs and ODC leaders alongside financial risks. In this section, we focus on risk to the ODCs from business failures and the potential for investment fraud.

Banks use tools like strict conditions and qualifications set by the head office, collateral requirements, and high interest rates to cushion themselves from business failures. The bank on average makes a profit or minimizes losses even when a new business fails. This is important, because studies show that almost 40 percent of small private businesses do not survive more than five years (Industry Canada 2009). Alternatively, ODCs minimize risk with careful consideration of the business plan and investment agreement up front and spread the risk over the cooperative community that also shares in the returns. ODCs often set terms of repayment, timelines, and interest rates that tend to be more patient and support business success. Because investment shares are non-tradable in the marketplace, getting money out can also be perceived as risky. Members of cooperatives cannot sell their stake to a third party; they must be sold back to the cooperative. While the process of withdrawing investments seems cumbersome, risk is reduced because no single large shareholder can sell the cooperative out from under the other members (Groeneveld 2011).

The fear that investment fraud may be higher among local investment cooperatives than private investing is another important obstacle to spreading the model. It is hard to tell from where this apprehension comes. Perhaps all alternatives to the mainstream suffer from similar doubts, because they are unfamiliar. In contrast, revelations from the 2008 financial crisis and bank bailouts indicate that cooperative financial institutions fared better than private businesses (Birchall and International Labour Office 2013; Co-operatives UK 2014b). Awareness of the different patterns of business fraud in private and cooperative investing is something ODC promoters now include in their outreach activities among publics and politicians to unsettle this dominant ideology. At the 2013 ACCA conference, Chris Payne, the manager of Nova Scotia's CEDIF, reported only a 5 percent failure rate for its CEDIF-funded businesses, and no fraud cases. A recent legal report commissioned by ACCA demonstrates that numerous cases of private investment fraud have been reported during the last 20 years in both Canada and the United States, but zero cases of cooperative investment fraud have been reported during the same time period (Miller Thomson 2013b).[9]

Trust

Trust is not simply a measure of the estimated trustworthiness of the trusted; trust is a social fact (Sztompka 1998). It operates as a shared orientation with shared expectations. The success of local investing depends on the reputation (cultural capital) of the cooperative leadership and their capacity to choose a good business proposal and entrepreneur while keeping community interests at the forefront. Paul, a cooperative developer with ACCA, describes this process when he states that:

> A significant point of this is the depth of the leadership. Are these people trusted? Social capital is linked to character lending/character investing that is leading these projects . . . people may like the idea, but they will actually do it because they trust the leadership.

Investors endow their trust in the ODC leadership and together they make a social capital investment along with their financial investment in the entrepreneur. Where there is no trust, there is no local investment. In the states of Wisconsin and Minnesota, investment in cooperatives has been made exempt from securities regulations (Miller Thomson 2013a), and in the UK in 2013 the Treasury Department raised the amount any one investor can invest in a cooperative business without a securities review from US$40,000 to US$200,000 in recognition of their trustworthiness (Co-operatives UK 2014b). The democratic and transparent architecture of the cooperative, its value premise, its operating principles, and its highly visible decision making engender what Sztompka (1998, p. 23) calls a 'culture of trust'.

DISCUSSION

As Steering Committee members and project partners, we experienced many of the implementation challenges and successes of local investing on a first-hand basis. As researchers we tried to distinguish between regular hurdles associated with making changes within systems and making changes that go against the grain of those systems and practices.

Researchers must also be able to sift through and grasp when certain obstacles – the wrong combination of people or a poor judgment call by a leader – are ordinary challenges and when the obstacles are more structural and systemic. We used a framework of social practices and regime-level structures to conceptualize this challenge, noting friction points and codes and conventions.

Like Hargreaves et al. (2013), we found that the friction points at the intersection of practices and socio-technical systems reveal 'points of possibility' where intermediaries and civic actors might strategically intervene to support system change. We found, too, that the interdependent nature of regime scales and practices requires a slightly different employment of the framework. On the one hand, the dual analysis of the dynamic ODC process revealed much about the systems and practices associated with local investing and borrowing; it shed light on the almost invisible and taken-for-granted assumptions and habitual ways of doing things that comprise the status quo. On the other hand, how structures and social practices were intertwined was harder to distinguish. Sometimes details revealed themselves only as the politics of the scaling advanced. In other words, policy issues became clear when a group met with a regulator or public administrator, or asked a specific question about an accounting principle, or first encountered a tax or Securities Commission ruling. For example, ACCA found no appetite among Alberta politicians to offer a tax credit as the Nova Scotia government does for its CEDIF program because Albertans already enjoy a low 10 percent provincial tax rate, and no provincial sales tax. ACCA lost a major incentive and had to focus its efforts on other incentives such as federal RRSP tax deductions.

As the process advanced, each regime presented conventional applications of its rules, readings of regulations, and ways of doing things that acted as obstacles. These challenges had to be overcome or worked around to support the ULC project. ACCA coaches needed not only to navigate the practices and conventions intersecting at the regime level, but also to work to transform the way they welcome and support sustainability innovation. Seen as processes, each encounter is experienced as an intersection point of both resistance and possibility. In the analysis of friction points, we explained how ULC intermediaries and community leaders might turn points of constraint into points of possibility. But can such modest innovations advance system change? Pel (2012) suggests that incremental improvements may in fact be as or more effective at compelling regime changes:

> Novelty, if it is to spread at all, should be acceptable to potential 'adopters', and should not be overly disruptive to existing practices. Initiatives should be radical

enough to constitute transformative potential, but also shallow enough to be acceptable in current institutional constellations: This contradiction between transformation and non-disruption, the 'paradox of acceptable novelty', can be considered a key system innovation challenge. (p. 1)

In the Alberta case, intermediaries connected the popular annual practice of setting aside retirement savings with a local investing innovation. They reconfigured a familiar and trusted financial tool (the RRSP) and used it for community development, allowing people to convert even previously invested retirement funds into current community projects. Watson (2013) describes this as 'systemic symbiosis', when a regime-level system is not replaced but refashioned by the niche innovation.

CONCLUSION

So far the ODC examples in Alberta have focused on strengthening local businesses through democratic investing to enhance rural sustainability. Less attention has been given to issues of ecology and the environment. In Nova Scotia, the CEDIF model has been used to fund community wind energy generation projects, since the provincial government established a community feed-in tariff (COMFIT) in 2011. CEDIF and COMFIT intersect to propel systemic change and to provide clean, low carbon energy. This exciting example of combining two innovations points to further possibilities and indicates a need to build coalitions across the sustainability, cooperative, and local investment movements to deepen synergies.

Morin (2008) suggests that we have arrived *at a new complexity* to conceive living systems and transformation: the autonomy (the niche innovation) cannot be apprehended without its ecology (the dominant regimes and practices). Researchers and practitioners alike must think about how an emergent innovation, such as the ULC initiative, can be generative, supported, alive, and magnetic within its ecology (Seyfang and Longhurst 2013) rather than a stagnant model, process, or policy that must be pushed through a hierarchical system. In the pursuit of a transition to a more sustainable society, it is crucial to identify the intersections of socio-technical systems and social practices so that we can knead out the friction points in ways that spread local financial innovations.

NOTES

1. Popular across Canada, an RRSP is an account for holding savings and investment assets. The plans are registered with the Canada Revenue Agency; contributions are tax deductible and the portfolio grows tax free until withdrawals, typically after retirement.
2. Champion Teams formed in Athabasca, Black Diamond, Didsbury, Drumheller, Three Hills, and Vulcan. All of these rural communities range in population from approximately 3000 to 10,000 residents.
3. The networking and findings from this initial research played into the implementation stage. Leaders from Sangudo and Battle River were later invited to share experiences with pilot community leaders at the ULC workshops in the autumn of 2013. Their testimonials increased trust in the proposed ULC pilot project that we found to be a key element in spreading the innovation (see section on 'Trust').
4. Note that these values are reported in Canadian dollars which were, at the time, on par with US dollars.
5. The Offering Document is what the Agent (Seller) presents to potential investors. The document typically includes the following information: a description of the investment opportunity; who is making the shares available; how much money is being collected; how the funds will be invested; what good/service the business produces or will produce, plus the business' history, financial affairs, and clients; who is eligible to sell the shares; details of risk and disclosure; and share subscription forms.
6. To calculate simple ROI subtract the cost of the investment from the gain of an investment and divide the total by the cost of the investment. The costs are essential for figuring the percentage return on dollar invested, as is the time period involved.
7. Blended ROI is the aggregated financial *as well as* social and environmental benefits created by a business, whether producing products or services for customers.
8. Based on recent success in the UK, ULC leaders are also considering renaming the offering stocks 'community investment shares' to emphasize the value of local money to community development.
9. The researchers were unilingual and noted there may be some cases of cooperative investment fraud in French-speaking Quebec.

REFERENCES

ACCA (2011a), *Accelerating Co-operative Development in Alberta* [White paper], 5 May 2011, available at http://acca.coop/coop/white-paper-accelerating-cooperative-development-in-alberta/ (accessed 31 July 2014).

ACCA (2011b), *Submission to the Rural Alberta Development Fund: Unleashing Local Capital*, October 2011.

ACCA (2014), *Unleashing Local Capital Final Report to RADF*, February 2014.

Alperovitz, Gar (2013), *What Then Must We Do? Straight Talk about the Next American Revolution*, White River Junction, VT: Chelsea Green Publishing.

Barney, Darin (2012), 'That's no way to run a railroad: the Battle River branchline and the politics of technology in rural Alberta', in J.R. Parkins and M.G. Reed (eds), *Social Transformation in Rural Canada: Community, Cultures, and Collective Action*, Vancouver, BC: UBC Press, pp. 309–326.

Bergold, Jarg and Stefan Thomas (2012), 'Participatory research methods: a methodological approach in motion', *Forum: Qualitative Sozialforschung/Forum: Qualitative Social Research*, **13** (1), Art. 30, available at http://www.qualitative-research.net/index.php/fqs/article/view/1801/3334 (accessed 7 August 2014).

Best, Hilary and Karim Harji (2013), *Social Impact Measurement Use Among Canadian Impact Investors: Final Report*, Purpose Capital, available at http://purposecap.com/wp-content/uploads/social-impact-measurement-use-among-canadian-impact-investors-final-report.pdf (accessed 25 April 2014).

Birchall, Johnston and International Labour Office (2013), *Resilience in a Downturn: The Power of Financial Cooperatives*, Geneva: International Labour Office.

Büchs, Milena, Graham Smith, and Rebecca Edwards (2011), 'Low-carbon practices: a third sector research agenda', Third Sector Research Centre: Informing Civil Society Working Paper 59, University of Southampton and University of Birmingham.

Buckland, Jerry (2012), *Hard Choices: Financial Exclusion, Fringe Banks, and Poverty in Urban Canada*, Toronto: University of Toronto Press.

Cabaj, Paul, Mike Gismondi, Richard Stringham, and Darren Wood (2009), *Westlock Grain Terminals: A Case Study*, available at http://auspace.athabascau.ca:8080/bitstream/2149/2956/1/WestlockCaseStudy.pdf (accessed 25 April 2014).

Co-operatives UK (2014a), 'Treasury supports increased investment in co-operative businesses', available at http://www.uk.coop/pressrelease/treasury-supports-increased-investment-co-operative-businesses (accessed 17 August 2014).

Co-operatives UK (2014b), 'The co-operative economy 2014: untold resilience', available at http://www.uk.coop/documents/co-operative-economy-2014 (accessed 4 September 2014).

Crivits, Maarten and Erik Paredis (2013), 'Designing an explanatory practice framework: local food systems as a case', *Journal of Consumer Culture*, **13** (3), 306–336.

De Antoni, Elisabetta (2013), 'Cooperative banking: a Minskyan perspective', in S. Goglio and Y. Alexopoulos (eds), *Financial Cooperatives and Local Development*, London: Routledge, pp. 21–36.

Diamantopoulos, Mitch (2011), 'Cooperative development gap in Québec and Saskatchewan 1980 to 2010: a tale of two movements', *Canadian Journal of Nonprofit and Social Economy Research*, **2** (2), 6–24.

Epp, Roger and Dave Whitson (2001), *Writing Off the Rural West: Globalization, Governments and the Transformation of Rural Communities*, Edmonton, Alberta: Parkland Institute and University of Alberta Press.

Evans, Jordan (2011), *Sangudo Opportunities Development Cooperative: A Case Study*, in partial fulfillment of the requirements of the degree of Masterof Business Administration in Community Economic Development, September, Cape Breton University.

Evergreen Cooperatives (2014), available at evergreencooperatives.com (accessed 3 September 2014).

Flacks, Richard (2013), 'Where is it likely to lead?', *The Sociological Quarterly*, **54** (2), 202–206.

Geels, Frank W. (2011), 'The multi-level perspective on sustainability transitions: responses to seven criticisms', *Environmental Innovation and Societal Transitions*, **1** (1), 24–40.

Geels, Frank W. (2014), 'Regime resistance against low-carbon transitions: introducing politics and power into the multi-level perspective', *Theory, Culture & Society*, **31** (5), 21–40, doi:10.1177/0263276414531627.

Geels, Frank W. and Johan Schot (2010), 'The dynamics of transitions: a socio-technical perspective', in J. Grin, J. Rotmans, and J. Schot (eds), *Transitions* to *Sustainable Development: New Directions in the Study of Long Term Transformative Change*, New York: Routledge, pp. 9–101.

Gibson-Graham, J.K., Jenny Cameron, and Stephen Healy (2013), *Take Back the Economy: An Ethical Guide for Transforming our Communities*, Minneapolis: University of Minnesota Press.

Giddens, Anthony (1984), *The Constitution of Society: Outline of the Theory of Structure*, Berkeley: University of California Press.

Gilbert-Squires, Amber (2014), *Move Your Money? An Exploration of Regimes and Practices in the UK Retail Banking Sector*, MSC School of Environmental Sciences, University of East Anglia.

Gismondi, Mike and Seth Leon (2012), *Community Finance and Investment Options: Local Capital Investment and Finance Options for Rural Alberta Communities*, available at http://auspace.athabascau.ca/bitstream/2149/3206/1/Community%20Investment%20Options%20Section%20Full%20Review%20Version.pdf (accessed 29 August 2014).

Goglio, Silvio and Yiorgos Alexopoulos (eds) (2013), *Financial Cooperatives and Local Development*, New York: Routledge.

Groeneveld, Hans (2011), 'The value of European cooperative banks for the future financial system', available at http://www.helsinki.fi/ruralia/ica2011/presentations/Groeneveld.pdf (accessed 15 August 2014).

Hargreaves, Tom (2011), 'Practice-ing behaviour change: applying social practice theory to pro-environmental behavior change', *Journal of Consumer Culture*, **11** (1), 79–99.

Hargreaves, Tom, Noel Longhurst, and Gill Seyfang (2013), 'Up, down, round and round: connecting regimes and practices in innovation for sustainability', *Environment and Planning A*, **45** (2), 402–420.

Hewitt, Carol Peppe (2013), *Financing Our Foodshed: Growing Local Food with Slow Money*, Gabriola Island, BC: New Society Publishers.

Industry Canada (2009), 'Key small business statistics', available at http://www.ic.gc.ca/eic/site/061.nsf/eng/rd02345.html (accessed 4 September 2014).

Intergovernmental Panel on Climate Change (2013), *Climate Change 2013: The Physical Science Basis. Contribution of Working Group I to the Fifth Assessment Report of the Intergovernmental Panel on Climate Change*, Cambridge, UK and New York, USA: Cambridge University Press, 1535 pp., available at http://www.ipcc.ch/report/ar5/wg1/#.UoK9auIlh20 (accessed 3 September 2014).

Jackson, Edward T. and Karim Harji (2012), *Accelerating Impact: Achievements, Challenges and What's Next in Building the Impact Investment Industry*, Report for The Rockefeller Foundation, New York: E.T. Jackson & Associates Ltd., available at http://iiic.in/wp-content/uploads/2015/02/Accelerating-Impact1.pdf (accessed 24 April 2015).

Leon, Seth and Mike Gismondi (2012), *Raising Capital Through Self-Directed RSPs*, Report for Alberta Rural Development Network.

Lewis, Michael and Pat Conaty (2012), *The Resilience Imperative: Cooperative Transitions to a Steady-State Economy*, Gabriola Island, BC: New Society Publishers.

Markard, Jochen, Rob Raven, and Bernhard Truffer (2012), 'Sustainability transitions: an emerging field of research and its prospects', *Research Policy*, **41** (6), 955–967.

Marois, Juanita and Mike Gismondi (2013), *Barriers to Participation: A Research Report*, available at http://hdl.handle.net/2149/3328 (accessed 31 July 2014).

Miller Thomson (2013a), *Cooperative Securities Exemptions in Wisconsin and Minnesota*, Legal Report for ACCA.

Miller Thomson (2013b), *Securities Fraud in Cooperatives*, Legal Report for ACCA.

Move Our Money (2014), 'Move our Money', available at http://www.moveourmoneyusa.org/about/ (accessed 25 April 2014).

Morin, Edgar (2008), 'Restricted complexity, general complexity', presented at the Colloquium 'Intelligence de la Complexité: Épistémologie et Pragmatique', Cerisy-La-Salle, France, 26 June 2005, translated by Carlos Gershenson, available at http://arxiv.org/pdf/cs/0610049v1.pdf (accessed 7 May 2014).

Murray, Carol, Michele Aasgard, Mike Lewis, Michelle Colussi, and Paul Cabaj (2010), *Exploring Applications of the Nova Scotia Co-op Development System in B.C. and Alberta*, available at http://hdl.handle.net/2149/2808 (accessed 31 July 2014).

New Economics Foundation (2014), 'Economics as if people and the planet mattered', available at www.neweconomics.org (accessed 28 August 2014).

Pel, Bonno (2012), 'Trojan horses in system innovation; a dialectical perspective on the paradox of acceptable novelty', available at http://hdl.handle.net/1765/34795 (accessed 4 September 2014).

Pettigrew, Andrew M. (1990), 'Longitudinal field research on change: theory and practice', *Organization Science*, **1** (3), 267–292.

Piketty, Thomas (2014), *Capital in the Twenty-First Century*, translated by Arthur Goldhammer, Cambridge, MA: Harvard University Press.

Reckwitz, Andreas (2002), 'Toward a theory of social practices: a development in culturalist theorizing', *European Journal of Social Theory*, **5** (2), 243–263.

Robb, Alan, James Smith, and J. Tom Webb (2010), 'Co-operative capital: what it is and why our world needs it', paper presented at the EURICSE conference on Financial Co-operative Approaches to Local Development through Sustainable Innovation, Trento, Italy, 10–11 June.

Rockström, Johan, Will Steffen, Kevin Noone, Åsa Persson, F. Stuart III Chapin, Eric Lambin, . . . and Jonathan Foley (2009), 'Planetary boundaries: exploring the safe operating space for humanity', *Ecology and Society*, **14** (2), Art. 32.

Schatzki, Theodore R. (1996), *Social Practices: A Wittgensteinian Approach to Human Activity and the Social*, Cambridge: Cambridge University Press.

Seyfang, Gill (2006), 'Community currencies: a new tool for sustainable consumption?', CSERGE Working Paper EDM 06-09, Norwich, UK: School of Environmental Sciences, University of East Anglia, available at http://cserge.ac.uk/sites/default/files/edm_2006_09.pdf (accessed 25 April 2015).

Seyfang, Gill and Noel Longhurst (2013), 'Desperately seeking niches: grassroots innovations and niche development in the community currency field', *Global Environmental Change*, **23** (5), 881–891.

Shove, Elizabeth (2003), *Comfort, Cleanliness and Convenience: The Social Organization of Normality*, Oxford: Berg.

Shove, Elizabeth (2010), 'Beyond the ABC: climate change policy and theories of social change', *Environment and Planning A*, **42** (6), 1273–1285.

Shove, Elizabeth and Mika Pantzar (2005), 'Consumers, producers and practices: understanding the invention and reinvention of Nordic walking', *Journal of Consumer Culture*, **5** (1), 43–64.

Shove, Elizabeth and Nicola Spurling (eds) (2013), *Sustainable Practices: Social Theory and Climate Change*, New York: Routledge.

Shove, Elizabeth and Gordon Walker (2010), 'Governing transitions in the sustainability of everyday life', *Research Policy*, **39** (4), 471–476.

Shove, Elizabeth, Mika Pantzar, and Matt Watson (2012), *The Dynamics of Social Practice: Everyday Life and How It Changes*, Los Angeles: Sage.

Soots, Lena K., Stewart Perry, and Jamie Cowan (2007), 'Supporting innovative cooperative development: the case of the Nova Scotia Co-operative Development System', available at http://hdl.handle.net/2149/1112 (accessed 31 July 2014).

Spargaaren, Gert (1997), *The Ecological Modernization of Production and Consumption: Essays in Environmental Sociology*, thesis, Landbouw Universiteit Wageningen, Wageningen.

Sztompka, Piotr (1998), 'Trust, distrust and two paradoxes of democracy', *European Journal of Social Theory*, **1** (1), 19–32.

Tasch, Woody (2010), *Inquiries into the Nature of Slow Money: Investing as if Food, Farms, and Fertility Mattered*, White River Junction, VT: Chelsea Green Publishing.

Tily, Geoff (2010), *Keynes Betrayed: The General Theory, the Rate of Interest and 'Keynesian' Economics*, Basingstoke, Hampshire: Palgrave Macmillan.

Warde, Alan (2005), 'Consumption and theories of practice', *Journal of Consumer Culture*, **5** (2), 131–153.

Watson, Matt (2013), 'Building future systems of velomobility', in E. Shove and N. Spurling (eds), *Sustainable Practices: Social Theory and Climate Change*, London and New York: Routledge, pp. 117–131.

PART V

Concluding remarks

11. Forging further into putting sustainability into practice

Naomi T. Krogman, Maurie J. Cohen, and Emily Huddart Kennedy

Social practice theories allow us to identify the mechanisms of everyday life and to understand both change and stasis as systemic. Such concepts enable researchers to link macro- and micro-scale processes that involve provisioning activities and shifts toward more sustainable consumption behavior. Scholars, policy makers, and advocates are employing social practice concepts to answer questions such as: 'Under what context does change occur?' and 'What are the feedback loops among interacting forces?' Interventions that change the social framework, thereby influencing behavior, show great promise to foster more sustainable consumption.

Various authors have shown that more information about an individual's or group's environmental impact does not necessarily lead to greater systemic change in households, communities, governments, and businesses. New behavioral responses result from a combination of individual, structural (relations among the parts of a complex whole), and cultural (ideas, customs, and norms) mechanisms. The social practices approach allows integration of all of these elements of change, thus providing a nuanced way to assess social change that is appealing to a growing set of interdisciplinary researchers and social change agents.

A key challenge for the future is to more effectively relate research on the social practices of sustainable consumption to policy activities and outcomes. Individuals at the forefront of using social practice theories, such as city planners and applied academic researchers, need to be prepared to explain the utility of the approach, which includes being able to articulate an expanse of issues ranging from how a problem is framed from the standpoint of social practices, to the various methods used to describe or measure social practices, to the policy or practice recommendations that arise from research findings. This book has brought greater clarity to social practice theories related to sustainable consumption and demonstrated that various applications can allow mid-range theories (that is, context-specific theories) to be combined and tested against one another. The work of Debbie Kasper (Chapter 2) is particularly useful in providing an overarching theoretical umbrella for others to situate their work in mid-range social practice theories. Similarly, Chelsea Schelly's (Chapter 9) theoretical approach encourages us not only to look at how social practices should inform policy, but also at how interventions create a set of rules that undergird systems of provision and heavily influence the potential meaning of certain social practices.

Practitioners, social movement activists, and others embedded in governments, communities, and companies are in key positions to identify the interdependent practices that lead to particular outcomes, relating, for instance, to transportation, food provisioning, civic engagement in land-use planning and natural resource management, and so forth. We need more transdisciplinary social practice research to guide effective policy change. In the future, identifying the key practices themselves may require ethnographic and on-the-ground consultation with practitioners of the social practices, particularly in new areas of increasing scholarly and practical interest, like ethical investing (Chapter 10).

There are opportunities to bridge the social practices approach with complementary work that emphasizes the role of age, gender, ethnicity, income, education, and other features of social location that interplay with the social practices themselves. For example, in Chapter 6 Julia Backhaus, Harald Wieser, and René Kemp illustrate the power of combining quantitative and qualitative data that identify country-specific food cultures and personal contextual factors that influence food consumption. Their chapter follows in the vein of Karl-Werner Brand's (2010) and Karl Brunner et al.'s (2006) work that examines organic food consumption in Germany to understand macro-scale trends in the production and distribution chains alongside other prompts that change patterns of consumption, such as a child's departure from home, change in partnerships, pregnancy and birth of children, relocation, illness, retirement, and so forth (what social scientists refer to as the 'life course').

Fertile ground also exists for stronger links with social movement theories, where the actual behind-the-scenes social practices around communication, social media, task sharing, time use, and choice of venues for interacting are recognized as influences on the outcomes arising from social mobilization. For example, in Chapter 3 Emily Kennedy and Tyler Bateman demonstrate how the cultivation of shared norms can strengthen the link between private practices and collective political engagement. Other scholars (for example, Maniates 2001; McClintock 2014) have also exposed the tensions between individual actions and political orientation to support infrastructure and policies that make it easier for people to 'do the right (that is, low environmental impact) thing'. We find this kind of scholarship particularly promising because it moves micro-level movements into a larger public debate for structural and systemic change.

There are many opportunities to offer more extensive instruction in higher educational institutions on social practice theories and related empirical methods and to design continuing education and other professional training for policy researchers and analysts who could apply these approaches to specific problems. Researchers are now using social practice theories to understand an array of provisioning activities, ranging from healthy food consumption in the home (Braun 2013) to forest governance (Arts et al. 2013). As mentioned in Chapter 1, there are professional associations and research councils that now directly address the intricacies of shifts in sustainable consumption, such as the Sustainable Consumption Research and Action Initiative (SCORAI) and the project Dynamics of Energy, Mobility and Demand (DEMAND). We have found that practices that lead to more sustainable outcomes (including lowered environmental impacts and improved health and wellness) are increasingly of interest to scholars across the fields of sociology, civil and environmental engineering, behavioral economics, psychology, consumer studies, and interdisciplinary programs that address social-ecological change, often under the umbrella of 'sustainability science' (see Kueffer et al. 2012; Lang et al. 2012; Miller et al. 2014; Wiek et al. 2012).

We envisage opportunities for greater cross-fertilization with the sustainability sciences (problem-based interdisciplinary research that focuses on sustainable systems) and sustainable design (participatory and biomimicry approaches to design technology, infrastructure, housing, and so forth). Research that examines the relationships among art, theatre, music, storytelling, and experiences in nature and other settings with the potential to influence sustainable social practices deserves more attention than it has received to date. Marlyne Sahakian's contribution to this book (Chapter 7) creatively addresses the role of emotional energy as tied to ideals of modernity, freedom, nostalgia, and community belonging to stimulate greater public interest and commitment to sustainable lifestyle choices. Mike Gismondi, Juanita Marois, and Danica Straith (Chapter 10) point to the need for a new and eventually normalized vocabulary to push the practice of sustainable investment further, beyond policies that open up what are currently understood to be appropriate opportunities. Concepts in this book such as 'environmental civic practices', offered by Kennedy and Bateman (Chapter 3), illustrate the importance of context for cultivating or discouraging the speech acts and community organizing that facilitate citizen engagement. Likewise, in Chapter 8, Jaeger-Erben and Rückert-John demonstrated that sustainable consumption innovations themselves are also context dependent. By categorizing innovations from the rare (for example, carrot mobs) to the increasingly ubiquitous (for example, car shares), the authors allow readers to understand how innovations develop in practice.

In fact, approaches grounded in an understanding of social practices may already have a very broad audience. The popularity of a spate of recently published books suggests growing interest in how people effect change to overcome problematic behaviors that are contingent on norms and other social influences. These books also address how new norms can emerge by breaking routines of fallaciously patterned thinking and the rules of rigid settings. While Thaler and Sunstein's (2008) volume on nudging largely adheres to the rational decision-making model, it has opened the door for other researchers to devote attention to the contextual basis for action. For example, psychologist Daniel Kahneman (2011) in *Thinking, Fast and Slow* emphasizes the role of heuristics, social influence, and various behavioral biases that foster particular pathways of decision making and behavior. More recently, Sendhil Mullainathan and Eldar Shafir (2013), in their book entitled *Scarcity: Why Having So Little Means So Much*, invoke the term 'bandwidth' to describe how shortage of time, attentional capacity (in cases where there are many demands for our attention), money, and other features of our lives limit our ability to make careful, deliberate decisions and exert self-control. We now regularly hear in meetings with academics and government personnel comments such as, 'I do not have the bandwidth to take on that additional task now', realizing that the flow of their day and limits to where they place their attention will not permit them to add another project to their workload. We are at the same time cognizant of how 'busyness' has become a status signifier so we face a situation with powerful and reinforcing feedback loops.

Other contributions on this theme include the recent book by cognitive psychologist Daniel Levitin (2014) entitled *The Organized Mind: Thinking Straight in the Age of Information Overload*. The volume highlights how cues in our environment develop default pathways to the behaviors we have as individuals and as organizations. Finally, journalist Brigid Schulte's (2014) book, *Overwhelmed: Work, Love and Play When No One Has the Time*, describes how the norms of work and motherhood in North America limit deliberate investment in lifestyle practices that deepen ethical goals, such as a sense of 'living right', calmness, connectedness, and belonging to the place and the people around you. We mention these popular books as evidence of apparent public consciousness that the structure of our lives and our cognitive limitations have enormous influence on our behavior, particularly our consumption and its ties to quality of life and the environment. These books and others (for example, Crawford 2015; Kondo 2014) combine self-help advice with accumulated knowledge about the forces that shape routine behaviors.

If we want to create a more sustainable world, these structural, routinized pathways of working, provisioning, householding, commuting, recreating, investing, and so forth deserve an even closer lens than the authors of these books have deployed to engage these topics. Social practices research in sustainable consumption can offer that more exacting view and highlight the contextual mechanisms that allow more deliberate and sustainable lifestyles. The contributors to this volume have paid close attention to patterns of living and have pointed to changes in practices that show a generative social order despite the apparent durability of current arrangements. These chapters show how resource consumption is not a deliberate attempt on the part of individuals to adversely affect the environment, but rather how, in cultural sociologist Ann Swidler's words (2001, p. 91), people 'act strategically in a world that presumes . . . rules'. That is, practices are shaped by myriad elements from symbols and discourse, to how people learn from others, are inspired by others, will take risks with others, and conform to others when new pathways of choice and behavior are readily available to them. As Francesca Forno, Cristina Grasseni, and Silvana Signori (Chapter 4) show, people may carry out the same social practice for different reasons: the goals and motivations behind the adoption and rejection of social practices are diverse, even in their case of solidarity purchasing groups. Julia Backhaus, Harald Wieser, and René Kemp's term 'webs of entangled elements' (Chapter 6) supports the claim that practices can unify disparate values. The authors point to the relationship among practices, their carriers, and production–consumption systems by focusing on how resultant configurations shape certain pathways of behavior.

The contents of this book serve as a bridge between the foundational work in social practice theorizing and more recent efforts to draw upon interdisciplinary and transdisciplinary approaches to solving social and environmental problems. Many of the contributors to this book make use of Giddens' (1984) concept of 'discursive consciousness', or awareness of the rules, resources, and systems that shape daily life (see Chapter 1), and how that awareness is part of a set of recursive loops that reinforce new sustainable practices. Recent intellectual interest in sustainability transitions (see the Great Transition Initiative of the Tellus Institute in Boston, Massachusetts[1]), social innovation (Geels and Schot 2010), and foresight intelligence (Millennium Alliance for Humanity and the Biosphere at Stanford University[2]) is prompting new research into the practical and discursive consciousness that undergirds human choice and behavior. The social practices perspective used in this volume makes use of the role of norms, discourses, symbols, physical structures, and time–space dynamics to better understand social change as it relates to sustainable and unsustainable practices. While households are logical foci of social practices, we find it encouraging to see this approach being applied as well to studies of sustainability in the workplace (Hargreaves 2011) and commercial settings (Seyfang 2009).

This volume also contributes to the chorus of scholars calling for greater policy-related research on the social practices of key actors in various organizational networks who influence actions related to climate change or disaster responses. For example, Ungar (2012) tried to bring the role of routine daily actions into how schools, communities, and governments respond to adversity and learn to develop protective institutional processes to foster resilience when their organizations are under stress. Particularly challenging for social scientists to date has been the study of specific social practices that elucidate the role of power in the daily lives of people who are trying to create change (Holland et al. 1998). Some promise for studies such as these may lie in institutional ethnographies that focus on the social relations that structure people's everyday lives and can speak to the recursive relationship between engaged practices and the ability of an individual or group to change power relations. As Stewart Barr (Chapter 5) points out, social practice research is best informed by the historical and cultural context, so that we take into account how practices are learned over time and avoid short-term, individualistic, and incrementalist recommendations for changing the social system. Gismondi, Marois, and Straith (Chapter 10) insightfully describe the various levels at which social practices and their meanings must change to foster a sustainable finance approach that uses local capital. Their chapter demonstrates how a set of practices may change at one level while other important and complementary practices at higher or lower levels remain fixed, thus making the resultant change uneven, poorly coordinated, or weakly adopted. Scholars of socio-technical transitions more generally make a similar point and assert that systems only change when there is alignment among niche, regime, and landscape levels (Geels and Schot 2010). Connecting these insights more effectively to the theory and practice of policy making is crucial to the pursuit of sustainability.

In conclusion, we contend that the social practices approach has great potential to enhance greater understanding of how to put sustainability into practice. Shifts in organizational capacity to deepen and embolden what sustainable consumption entails, beyond household behaviors, will require more extensive work to identify appropriate social practices and influential carriers of those practices. In the future, researchers and practitioners will need to work more closely to delineate the many contextual influences that lead to social change and to expand their capacity to conduct experiments and pilot projects to inform social change. The desired and unexpected ways in which social practices evolve require learning from existing initiatives, and the contributors of this book point to some fruitful lessons for a more sustainable future.

NOTES

1. http://www.greattransition.org (accessed 29 April 2015).
2. http://mahb.stanford.edu (accessed 29 April 2015).

REFERENCES

Arts, Bas, Jelle Behagel, Séverine van Bommel, Jessica de Koning, and Esther Turnhout (2013), *Forest and Nature Governance: A Practice Based Approach*, Dordrecht: Springer.

Brand, Karl-Werner (2010), 'Social practices and sustainable consumption: benefits and limitations of a new theoretical approach', in M. Gross and H. Heinrichs (eds), *Environmental Sociology: European Perspectives and Interdisciplinary Challenges*, London: Springer, pp. 217–235.

Braun, Jennifer (2013), *Pickles, Beets and Bread: Examining Traditional Food Knowledge in a Rural Albertan Community*, MSc in Environmental Sociology, Department of Resource Economics and Environmental Sociology, Edmonton: University of Alberta.

Brunner, Karl-Michael, Cordula Kropp, and Walter Sehrer (2006), 'Wege zu nachhaltigen Ernährungsmustern. Zur Bedeutung von biographischen Umbruchsituationen und Lebensmittelskandalen für den Bio-Konsum' ('Towards sustainable food patterns. The importance of biographical transitional situations and food crises for the consumption of organic product'), in Karl-Werner Brand (ed.), *Die neue Dynamik des Bio-Markts: Folgen der Agrarwende im Bereich Landwirtschaft, Handel, Konsum und Ernährungskommunikation* (*The New Dynamics of the Organic Market: Effects of Agricultural Change on Agriculture, Trade, Consumption and Nutrition Communication*), Munich: Oekom-Verlag, pp. 145–196.

Crawford, Matthew (2015), *The World Beyond Your Head: On Becoming an Individual in An Age of Distraction*, New York: Penguin.

Geels, Frank and Johan Schot (2010), 'The dynamics of transitions: a sociotechnical perspective', in John Grin, Jan Rotmans, and Johan Schot (eds), *Transitions to Sustainable Development: New Directions in the Study of Long Term Transformative Change*, New York: Routledge, pp. 11–104.

Giddens, Anthony (1984), *The Constitution of Society: Outline of the Theory of Structuration*, Oakland, CA: University of California Press.

Hargreaves, Tom (2011), 'Practice-ing behavior change: applying social practice theory to pro-environmental behavior change', *Journal of Consumer Culture*, **11** (1), 79–99.

Holland, Dorothy, William Lachicotte, Jr., Debra Skinner, and Carole Cain (1998), *Identity and Agency in Cultural Worlds*, Cambridge, MA: Harvard University Press.

Kahneman, Daniel (2011), *Thinking, Fast and Slow*, New York: Doubleday.

Kondo, Marie (2014), *The Life-Changing Magic of Tidying Up: The Japanese Art of Decluttering and Organizing*, Berkeley, CA: Ten Speed Press.

Kueffer, Christoph, Evelyn Underwood, Gertrude Hirsch Hadorn, Rolf Holderegger, Michael Lehning, Christian Pohl, Mario Schirmer, René Schwarzenbach, Michael Stauffacher, Gabriela Wuesler, and Peter Edwards (2012), 'Enabling effective problem-oriented research for sustainable development', *Ecology and Society*, **17** (4), 197–212.

Lang, Daniel J., Arnim Wiek, Matthias Bergmann, Michael Stauffacher, Pim Martens, Peter Moll, Mark Swilling, and Christopher J. Thomas (2012), 'Transdisciplinary research in sustainability science: practice, principles, and challenges', *Sustainability Science*, **7** (1), 25–43.

Levitin, Daniel J. (2014), *The Organized Mind: Thinking Straight in the Age of Information Overload*, New York: Penguin.

Maniates, Michael F. (2001), 'Individualization: plant a tree, buy a bike, save the world?', *Global Environmental Politics*, **1** (3), 31–52.

McClintock, Nathan (2014), 'Radical, reformist, and garden-variety neoliberal: coming to terms with urban agriculture's contradictions', *Local Environment*, **19** (2), 147–171.

Miller, Thaddeus R., Arnim Wiek, Daniel Sarewitz, John Robinson, Lennart Olsson, David Kriebel, and Derk Loorbach (2014), 'The future of sustainability science: a solutions-oriented research agenda', *Sustainability Science*, **9**, 239–246.

Mullainathan, Sendhil and Eldar Shafir (2013), *Scarcity: Why Having So Little Means So Much*, New York: Times Books.

Schulte, Brigid (2014), *Overwhelmed: Work, Love, and Play When No One Has the Time*, New York: HarperCollins.

Seyfang, Gill (2009), *The New Economics of Sustainable Consumption: Seeds of Change*, New York: Palgrave Macmillan.

Swidler, Ann (2001), 'What anchors cultural practices?', in T.R. Schatzki, K. Knorr Cetina, and E. von Savigny (eds), *The Practice Turn in Contemporary Theory*, London: Routledge, pp. 83–101.

Thaler, Richard H. and Cass R. Sunstein (2008), *Nudge: Improving Decisions about Health, Wealth, and Happiness*, New Haven, CT: Yale University Press.

Ungar, Michael (ed.) (2012), *The Social Ecology of Resilience: A Handbook of Theory and Practice*, Dordrecht: Springer.

Wiek, Arnim, Barry Ness, Petra Schweizer-Ries, Fridolin S. Brand, and Francesca Farioli (2012), 'From complex systems analysis to transformational change: a comparative appraisal of sustainability science projects', *Sustainability Science*, **7** (1), 5–24.

Index